AF656024

WOMEN EMPOWERMENT: MYTH AND REALITY

WOMEN EMPOWERMENT
Myth and Reality

Edited By
Dr. S.C. Joshi
M.A., Ph.D.

AKANSHA PUBLISHING HOUSE
NEW DELHI • GUWAHATI • VISAKHAPATNAM

AKANSHA PUBLISHING HOUSE
4649-B/21, Ansari Road
Darya Ganj, New Delhi - 110 002
Ph.: 23263193 / 9811582579 / 09435116718
Fax: 011-23263193
Email: ektabooks@yahoo.com
www.akanshapublishinghouse.com

Women Empowerment: Myth and Reality

© Editor

First Published 2004
Reprint 2013
ISBN 81-87606-60-6

All rights reserved. No part of this publication may be reproduced or transmitted, in any form or by any means, without prior permission of the author. Any person who does any unauthorized act in relation to this publication may be liable to criminal prosecution and civil claims for damages.

[The responsibility for the facts stated, conclusions reached etc., is entirely that of the author. The publisher is not responsible for them, whatsoever.]

PRINTED IN INDIA

Published by Akansha Publishing House, New Delhi and Printed at Harmain Offset, Delhi.

Contents

Contents

Preface

"The position of women in a society is an accurate index of the development of that society."

—Gustav Geiger

As is well known women constitute nearly half of the world population. Though many societies may boast that position of women in their respective societies has been respectable, dignified or high. Yet bitter truth is this that women suffer from one kind of discrimination or other everywhere and everytime.

It is true that the progress of a country can be gauged to a great extent by the advancement in the status of its womenfolk, as they form the vital part of the society. To understand the spirit of a civilization and to appreciate its excellences and realise its limitations is to study the history of the position and status of women. Women's role and function in society was largely dependent on that of men in relativistic terms in majority of cultures. It is the sum of differences between status of men and of women which gives one an idea that women have a distinctive position in society. Social changes are common to every society and a change in its women's status and vice-versa.

Social legislations and social reforms found in unwritten or written forms or the customary laws influence the women's actual role in society at various levels, such as caste, local group, region, state or family. Actual treatment, legal status, opportunity for participation and decision-making, nature and extent of work etc., determine the status of women in a society. The position of women represents a coherent structure in which all the elements are integrated—role in the family, society, economic role, sphere of activity etc. There is a strong correlation between low status of women and low culture levels of society.

A sort of awakening, though aggressive in nature, started in the West some decades ago, namely 'feminism' which spread to all over the globe in one form or the other. Despite this no substantial could be achieved in practice excepting ideological consciousness. In true spirit of the term 'emancipation', women's emancipation can be achieved when they are given enough opportunities for gainful employment in all walks of life. Economically strengthened women can have a final say in decision-making.

Here in the present book, we have chosen the theme of working women, their status, problems faced by them at home, work place, statutory provisions etc. which may be instrumental in their way of emancipation. A few case studies are also included to highlight the actual picture. The entire information is based on secondary sources i.e. books, abstracts, article/papers in various journals and magazines and individual research findings of many learned scholars in the field. I am deeply beholden to all those whose painstaking research findings are literally borrowed. The total credit goes to them all. I am also grateful to all editors, publishers and copyright holders.

I am thankful to my friends, family members, colleagues and superiors for their moral support and constant inspiration to carry out my professional endeavours. Finally I owe a deep sense of gratitude to my publishers for materialising my effort by way of the publishing the same.

—**SCJ**

1

Women at the Global Level

Although throughout history and in many societies women have been sharing similar experiences, in developing countries, the problems of women, particularly those pertaining to their integration in the development process, are different from the problems women face in industrialized countries and are often a matter of survival (United Nations, 1986a, para. 104).

A global analysis which is insensitive to these differences between industrialized and developing countries is of little value for the formulation and implementation of strategies to provide all women with the resources essential for survival, for economic independence and self-reliance. Differences between developing and industrialized countries are reflected in the quantity and quality of data. Fewer data of lower quality are available from developing than from industrialized countries. The data analyzed here reflect these differences. Data from industrialized countries, particularly the market economies, frequently reflect part-time economic activity and a disproportionate proportion of women in unemployment. Those from developing countries frequently reflect high levels of female underemployment, female economic activity in seasonal work and, for many countries, particularly in North Africa, middle and western South Asia and Latin America and the Caribbean, the underenumeration of the economic contributions of women.

To the degree that these general limitations continue to be reflected in data available from national sources, these data identify changes in female participation in economic activity. They document increasing disparities between developing and industrialized countries in the prospects for equality between women and men in opportunities for such participation. This chapter provides an introduction to the statistical concepts and methods used in this analysis in the discussion of economic activity by age. Here, variations in activity by age assessed for females and males. Then begins the analysis for the period between 1950 and 2000, which is duplicated for all regions in the following chapters: the analysis of overall economic activity, gross economically active life expectancies and economic activity by sector.

Economic Activity by Age (1950-2000)

An introduction to statistical information is essential to an understanding of variations in economic activity between females and males and for comparisons for females in the regions. Graphs are presented for Africa (developing countries), excluding northern Africa; northern Africa; East Asia (developing countries); middle South Asia; Latin America and the Caribbean; industrialized market economies; North America; and the USSR. Each of these graphs contains two sets of lines, a set of four lines for females and a set of three lines for males. Each line documents for one time-period the variation in economic activity by age group ranging from 10-14 years to 65 years and over. Each point on the line represents the percentage of the population in that particular age group which is classified as economically active. The space under each line represents that portion of the female or male population which is economically active. The space above the line is the portion considered inactive. Sets of three lines for females and males are presented to document changes in activity by age between 1950 and 1985 and, assuming the continuation of present trends, between 1985 and 2000. The fourth line for females represents the proportion of females in each age group which will be economically active by 2000 if women and men are to have equal access to economic activity by 2025.

An examination of these graphs suggests little variation for male when compared to female economic activity. While the meaning of economic activity varies widely among males—representing high levels of part-time work or underemployment in many of the developing countries in contrast to full-time employment in the industrialized economies—the height and shape of the lines for males are similar by region. Between 1950 and 2000, the major change in economic activity for males is an increase in the proportion of older males who are no longer active, in particular the male population above 60 years. In 1950 a major portion of the male population over 60 was economically active in all regions. By 1985 this portion had declined and is projected to decline further by 2000 (Alternative I).

A comparison of these same graphs shows wide variation in female economic activity. This variation is reflected is reflected in both the height and shape of the lines in the graphs. Variation in height is indicative of differences in the proportion of the female population which is economically active, i.e., higher lines represent higher rates of economic activity. Lines representing female economic activity in northern Africa, middle South Asia and Latin America and the Caribbean, for example, are much lower than are those for East Asia and the USSR.

A closer examination of individual lines provides information about changes in economic activity by age. The lines for Latin America and the Caribbean, for example, suggest increases in female participation in economic activity. In 1950 approximately 20 per cent of females in the age groups between 20 and 59 years were active. In 1985 over 30 per cent were active. Projections assuming the continuation of these trends, Alternative I, suggest further increase during the next 15 years. The lines for middle South Asia, however, suggest opposite trends. In 1950 approximately 40 per cent of the females in the age groups between 20 and 59 years were economically active. By 1985 only 30 per cent were so classified. Alternative I projections suggest further declines between 1985 and 2000.

Lines for Alternative II projections for the year 2000 suggest how much the economic activity of females will have to increase during the next 15 years and, correspondingly, how many opportunities will have to be created if females and males are to have equal opportunity for economic activity within each age group by 2025.

Equality between females and males is possible only if females and males within the same age group have equal access to economic activity. These projections assume that this equality is possible by 2025 and, thus, provide estimates of progress necessary by the year 2000. An examination of the lines for Africa (excluding northern Africa) and for Latin America and the Caribbean serve to illustrate the meaning of these projections. The lines for 1950 and 1985 suggest declines in female economic activity in sub-Saharan Africa during this 35-year period. In 1950, between 60 and 70 per cent of females between the ages of 15 and 64 were economically active. By 1985, these figures had declined and a further decline is projected for 2000 when projections are based on the continuation of past trends. The line for the projections for Alternative II, however, is higher than that for 1950 suggesting the possibility of reversing this negative trend. Obviously, such a reversal with require an enormous effort, the magnitude of which will be discussed later in the analysis. Rather than suggesting a reversal, the line for Latin America and the Caribbean suggests not only a continuation but an acceleration of current trends.

An example of variations in the shape of the lines illustrates different patterns of economic activity for females and males by age groups. The lines for the USSR, for example, suggest that for 1950 the patterns for females and males were quite different. By 1985, however, the patterns were similar and are projected to remain so. The shape of the lines in Africa (excluding northern Africa) is also quite similar for females and males. The major difference is in the height of the lines, which indicates that fewer females than males in this region are economically active or classified as such. The overall shape for females and males, however, suggests little fluctuation in economic activity by age. A comparison of the lines for males and females in 1950 and 1985 for East Asia also suggests an increasing similarity in the pattern of male and female economic activity, which is projected to continue. Graphs for northern Africa, Latin America and the Caribbean, the industrialized market economic and North America suggest that males and females in these countries have a different pattern of economic activity by age. For 1950, the lines suggest a pattern of economic activity for females whereby they become economically active at an early age, and then cease activity for a varying period of time, after which major portions of them resume economic activity. By 1985, the shape of these lines suggests less fluctuation and, in fact, a closer approximation among these regions and, hence, between females and males. This change suggests that increasingly females in all regions are remaining economically active, i.e. engage in economic activity on at least a part-time basis, or they are leaving for shorter periods before resuming activity.

Similarity in the shape of lines suggests that, globally, child care and family responsibilities are playing decreasing role in influencing whether females are economically active. Alternative I projections for 2000 suggest a continuation of this general trend. Alternative II projections assume an acceleration of it. The space under each line represents the proportion of the total female or male population which is classified as economically active. In graphic terms, this rate represents the proportion of the female or male population of all ages which is represented by the total space under the line (the economically active portion of the female or male population) divided by the total population of females or males represented by the entire graph (the combination of the economically active and inactive populations in all age groups).

When used as a basis of analyses over time, 'global' activity rates are influenced by changes in the age structure of the population. Of particular are changes in the younger and older populations. Note the changes in the shape of the lines for the over 64 age group and variations among regions in the first point on the lines for the very young population.

Refined activity rates control for variations in these two age segments of the population. Graphically, a refined rate refers to that portion of the female or male population which is below a line between the points for the 15-19 and the 60-64 age groups divided by the populations of females, or males, represented in the entire graph with these age limits, i.e. the combination of economically active and inactive persons between the ages of 15 and 64 years.

Economic Activity (1950-2000)

Over 1,000 million females, or nearly a third of the third of the world's female population, are projected to be economically active in the year 2000. Over 700 million of them will be active in developing countries. The proportion of the total female population which will be economically active is projected to be lower in developing than in industrialized countries. A 30 cent crude activity rate is projected for developing countries in contrast to a 38 per cent rate for industrialized countries. Refined rates also reflect this differential. In the year 2000, nearly 60 per cent of the women between the ages of 15 and 64 will be economically active in the industrialized countries, in contrast to less than 50 per cent in the developing countries.

While part of this differential is attributable to a greater underenumeration of economic activity in developing than in industrialized countries, it is none the less true that historical trends have contributed to a widening of the many gaps between developing and industrialized countries which, in turn, is reflected in an increased differential in female activity rates between 1950 and 2000. In 1950, the crude activity rates were the same for both developing and industrialized countries. During the next 25 years, the rate declined from 33 to 30 per cent in the developing countries and increased from 33 to 36 per cent in the industrialized countries. During the United Nations Decade for Women (1976-85), an increasing proportion of the world's female population became economically active. This increase, however, was greater in the industrialized than in the developing countries. In the developing countries, the crude activity rate increased from 30 to 31 per cent, while in the industrialized countries it increased from 36 to 38 per cent.

The information for refined rates, even more dramatically illustrates this increasing differential. A larger portion of women—females between the ages of 15 and 64 years of age—in developing than in industrialized countries were estimated to be economically active in 1950: the refined rate of economic activity was 50 per cent in developing and 47 per cent in industrialized countries. During the next 25 years this relationship was reversed as rates in the industrialized countries increased from 47 to 55 per cent, while rates in the developing countries declined from 50 to 49 per cent. During the first half of the Untied Nations Decade for Women, the rate increased from 55 to 58 per cent in the industrialized countries, while it remained stagnant at 49 per cent in the developing countries. During the second half of the Decade, the rate in both remained unchanged. ILO projections for the year 2000 assume the continuation of these divergent trends and, thus, project the continuation of this increasing differential. An increase in the refined rate, from 58 to 59 per cent, is projected for the industrialized countries while a decrease, from 49 to 47 per cent, is projected for the developing countries.

These data suggest that a dramatic change in economic activity for women, which threatens to influence prospects for the advancement of women during the next 15 years, occurred between 1950 and 1985. The distribution of economic activity by sex during this 35-year period. Information for the female share shows that in 1950 females in industrialized countries made up 36.7 per cent of the economically active population. During the next 25 years, 53 per cent of the 5.3 million annual increase of the total were females. This resulted in a growth in the female share from 36.7 to 40.6 per cent. During the first half of the United Nations Decade for Women, females secured 54 per cent of the increase which, in turn, increased their share to 41.4 per cent. During the second half, they secured only 36 per cent of the increase. As a consequence, the female share of the economically active population declined from 41.4 to 41.1 per cent. During the 15 years between 1985 and 2000 in these countries, it is expected that women will secure 40 per cent of the 4 million annual increase in the economically active population. The result will be a stagnation in the female share of the economically active population along with a stagnation of the crude rate. The refined rate will increase only slightly from 58 to 59 per cent.

Between 1950 and 1975, the economically active population grew by 17.7 million per year. Females secured only 37 per cent of this growth, producing a slight increase in the female share of the economically active population during these 25 years from 33.6 to 34.6 per cent. During the first half of the United Nations Decade, 38 per cent of the growth was female, producing another slight increase in the female share, from 34.6 to 35.0 per cent. This gain was lost during the second half of the Decade as women secured only 33 per cent of the annual growth of the active population. Therefore, their share declined from 35.0 to 34.7 per cent. Females in developing countries are projected to receive an even smaller share of the 35.2 million annual increase of the economically active population during the next 15 years producing a further decline in the female share (i.e. 33.7 per cent). If this occurs, women in developing countries will have experienced practically no progress during this 50-year period.

With greater efforts to create more economic opportunities for women than those suggested by the projections during the next 15 years, major progress is possible in advancing women relative to men in both developing and industrialized countries. Only with these intensified efforts can the trend towards an increasing differential be averted. The progress, however, requires a doubling of efforts to create gainful activities for women.

The creation, in developing countries, of 53.5 rather than 35.2 million economic opportunities annually (see Alternative II) would increase the female share of the economically active population from 34.7 to 41.4 per cent, rather than the projected decline to 33.7 per cent. Intensified efforts would produce an increase in the crude activity rate from 31 to 43 per cent and in the refined rate from 49 to 64 per cent. This improvement requires that females annually receive an additional 18.3 million new opportunities, bringing therefore the total annual new opportunities for females to 29.1 million.

Alternative II projections show that 322 million females will be economically active in the year 2000 in industrialized countries. The effort would require the annual creation of 7.4 rather than 4 million opportunities. This increase would bring up the female share to 45.2 per cent by 2000. The crude activity rate would increase from 38 per cent in 1985 to 45 per cent in 2000 and the refined rate from 58 to 69 per cent.

Gross Years of Working Life (1950-2000)

Changes in economic activity for women correspond to changes in the number of years women can expect to be economically active. The consequences of changes in economic activity. The gross years of working life for women in the developing countries (DCs) declined between 1950 and 1985, while it increased in the industrialized countries, in contrast to declines for males in both regions. In 1950, a woman in a developing country could, on average, expect to be economically active for 27 years. By 1985, she could expect to have a working life of only 25 years. The reverse trend is characteristic of industrialized countries. In 1950, a woman could expect to be economically active for 25 years and by 1985 this had increased to 29 years.

The two alternatives for the year 2000 are dramatically different. If present trends continue, the number of years of working life that a woman can expect in the year 2000 will continue to decline to 23 years in developing countries, wand will stagnate at 29 years in the industrialized countries. If efforts to create gainful activities for women are intensified according to Alternative II projections, women can expect to be economically active on average for 34 years in developing and 35 years in industrialized countries. Such efforts would reduce the gap between the gross years of working life of females and males.

Unemployment, Underemployment and Underutilization

It is important that these new opportunities provide women with the resources to be economically independent and self-reliant. As pointed out earlier, the economically active population encompasses both the employed and unemployed populations. The United Nations Decade for Women (1976-85), females in many countries made up a greater share of the unemployed than of the economically active population. As regards developing countries, the share of females in unemployment in 1975 was higher than in the economically active population for 11 out of 22 countries for which official statistics were available. By 1985 this figure had increased to 14.

Data are available for 27 of the industrialized countries. The female share of unemployment was higher than the corresponding share in economically active population in 18 of the 27 countries. In 1985, this figure had increased to 21. It should be noted that in several of these 18 countries the female share of unemployment increased rather than decreased during the Decade for Women (1976-85). While unemployment is considered economic activity, it contributes little, if anything, to progress towards economic independence and self-reliance for women. Such progress requires that women be given opportunities for employment, not an increasing share of the unemployed population.

It is also important to note that major portions of the world's women are underemployed and/or underutilized. The underemployed are those who would like additional work, who work for low incomes or whose skills are underutilized (ILO, 1976). Underemployment is most characteristic of developing countries where large numbers of people are engaged in involuntary part-time work, seasonal activity or full-time work at low pay. Further investigations of the informal sector, as well as of rural employment, will probably reveal high levels of underemployment. "A study of rural Java found 48 per cent of economically active females and 30 per cent of economically active males underemployed 'by reason of low earnings when compared to a standard minimum economic need'" (International Centre for Research on Women, 1980, p. 32, as cited in Dixon-Mueller, 1985, p. 112). Increasing evidence documents growing underemployment in response to unemployment in the industrialized countries. For example, "part-time working has not only been more common in the United Kingdom than in most other European countries but has increased substantial as unemployment has risen" (Standing, 1986, p. 6). Most new jobs created during the 1983-85 period in the United Kingdom were part time and in the services sector where women predominate.

In many parts of the world women's labour is underutilized; of a particular concern are those who are not looking for work because there is no work suitable for them or who have become discouraged because they are victims of prejudice (ILO, 1976). "In rural areas, the discouraged worker effect may be especially strong for women when male unemployment is high, unless the wage labour market is so segregated that women have a good chance of working even if men do not" (Dixon-Mueller, 1985, p. 107). In many countries those whose skills are underutilized constitute an important segment of the economically inactive population. Excluding the women whose economic activity is not accurately counted, a major portion of economically inactive females are appropriately categorized as underutilized. Available data, however, provide only for the assessment of the economically active population. Of particular importance is activity by sector of the economy.

Economic Activity by Major Sector, 1950-2000

Developing Countries

Projections for the year 2000 suggest that 57 per cent of females, but only 51 per cent of males, will be economically active in the agricultural sector of these countries. Conversely, 43 per cent of females and 49 per cent of males will be economically active in the non-agricultural sectors of industry and services. These projections assume the continuation of past trends (FAO, 1986). In 1950, 87 per cent of economically active women were in the agricultural sector along with 78 per cent of men. By 1980 these figures had declined to 71 per cent and 63 per cent respectively. In 1980, 21 per cent of men were in services and 16 per cent were in industry, while 17 per cent of women were in services and 12 per cent in industry. In the year 2000, 64 per cent of all agricultural workers are projected to be male and the remaining 36 per cent female. This projection represents no change in the female share over the 1950 level of 36 per cent, but a decline from the 1980-85 estimates of 38 per cent.

Female economic activity in the sectors of industry and services are less likely to be underenumerated. Even so, much economic of this type takes place in the informal sector of developing countries, and it is quite likely that a good deal of it is not counted. The data which do exist, however, suggested the need for intensified efforts to expand opportunities for women in both of these sectors. In 1950, women made up approximately a quarter of both the industrial and services sectors of the developing countries. Thirty years later they comprised 28 per cent of those in industry and 31 per cent in services. If present trends continue, females will make up 31 per cent of the non-agricultural sector at the beginning of the twenty-first century.

The above trends show that an increased effort should be made in all sectors of developing countries to expand opportunities of work for women so that their share be more equal to the share of men in each in each of the three sectors concerned.

Industrialized countries

In 1950, 53 per cent of females and 65 per cent of males were in the non-agricultural sectors. Approximately one-third of both females and males were in the services sector. A greater proportion of the males were in industry (35 per cent) than were females (20 per cent). At the same time, females were more concentrated than males in the agricultural sector, 47 as compared to 35 per cent. During the next 30 years, agriculture declined significantly for both males and females. At the end of the first half of the United Nations Decade for Women (1976-85), only 16 per cent of females and 13 per cent of males were active in the agricultural sector, while more than 80 per cent of them were in the non-agricultural sectors. As opportunities in agriculture declined, females shifted their participation to the services sector and, to a lesser extent, to industry. During this 30-year period, the proportion of economically active females in services increased from 33 to 58 per cent. Their participation in industry increased from 20 to 26 per cent. Rather than being concentrated, men are evenly distributed between services and industry, 44 and 43 per cent respectively. In the year 2000, 92 per cent of the female economically active population will be in the non-agricultural sectors and 8 per cent in the agricultural sectors. For males the proportions are 94 per cent and 6 per cent respectively.

In the year 1950, 44 per cent of those active in agriculture were female during the 30-year period between 1950 and 1980, the female share of the agricultural sector increased to 45 per cent and is expected to increase to 47 per cent by the end of the century. In the non-agricultural sector the shares of women in 1950 were respectively 24 per cent in industry and 39 per cent in services. During the next 30 years these percentages increased to 30 per cent and 48 per cent, respectively. The projections to the end of the century, available only for both sectors together, show a share proportionally unchanged as compared to 1980.

In conclusion, in the industrial countries the share of females is more or less equal to that of males in two out of the three sectors, namely agriculture and services. Therefore, a greater effort should be made to create additional jobs for women in the industrial sector.

2

Women Employment: Problems and Causes

Women enter into employment due to various causes which are as complex as those influencing other choices that affect their way of life. It is generally believed that socio-cultural changes play a very important role in creating a situation in which women would like to seek employment. While one would not deny the importance of socio-cultural changes, there are several other factors which lead one to take individual decision to work or not to work. It might be that in a particular cultural context, one was in a position to get employment but her desire might not be translated into action, if she was not in a position to go out of home. It is possible that one may have one's own reasons but scrutiny of data collected is likely to show some pattern which might throw light on these underlying considerations. It is, therefore, appropriate to know those factors which pull and push women to enter the working force. The analysis of individual's decision to work give insight about the processes inducing women to take to employment. Such an analysis also helps in making prediction abut the future impact of the employment of women. This is why the study of the factors inducing women to join the working force deserves serious consideration. Here we deal with the factors that explain as to why women go to work.

In one of the ILO studies dealing with women's employment it was presumed that motives differed with marital status both objectively and subjectively. Not only the economic needs but the motivational reasons also vary with marital status. They broadly mentioned two reasons: (a) Women's economic need, and (b) national necessity for increased production. Some other studies have brought to light the fact that loneliness is a powerful motive for women to seek employment outside their homes. The Ministry of Labour, Government of India has pointed out that whatsoever the stage of economic or social development of a country, four factors prevail which lead women to join working force. They are: (a) the inadequate income of the principal earner which forces a women to work and supplement the income; (b) mishaps, such as incapacity of the bread winner; (c) death of the bread-winner; and (d) a women's desire for economic independence or for securing higher standard of living. There is also the desire on the part of the women to give expression to their own talents and skills.

In view of these observations the per cent distribution of the sample of working women accounting to the motives and the board classification of responses are given in Table 1.

TABLE 1

Main Reasons for Employment

	Main Reasons for Work		*Per cent*
1. Non-Financial Reasons			
(a)	Personality traits		15.8
(b)	To utilise time		03.7
(c)	Traditional occupation		03.0
		Sub-Total	22.5
2. Financial Reasons			
(a)	Economic Pressures		58.5
(b)	Other economic needs		14.8
(c)	Higher Standard of living		04.2
		Sub-Total	77.5
	Grand Total		**100.0**

The percentage distribution of responses given by the employed women stating reasons of employment shows that women, essentially worked for financial motives. Like Klein's study, where she found that seventy-three per cent women worked for money, more than three-fourths of the working women (77.5%) of this study mentioned financial reasons while less than one-fourth of them (22.5%) reported non-financial reasons. Delhi and Bombay studies also mentioned that a large proportion of working women worked for economic reasons (sixty-nine per cent and sixty-five per cent respectively).

Financial Reasons

Among financial reasons, three sub-categories are noted: (a) economic pressures which pertain to the fulfilment of basic minimum needs of life, (b) other economic needs—money required to help relatives, (c) higher standard of living some of the women reported that they worked for financial reasons. They desired to have better education of children and a supply of objects of comfort. On the basis of the criteria used to identify financial reasons, it was found that economic pressures accounted for 58.5%. Of these, some women were working so as to satisfy the basic minimum (27.8%), to support dependents (25.7%) because of the death of the principal bread-winner in the family, and 4.5% of them reported that rapid increase in the cost of living had brought the family income to a difficult situation and it was imperative for them to work to provide for the family requirements. Two of them (0.5%) reported that they were working to repay the debts incurred due to necessities such as prolonged illness in the family and marriage of sons and daughters.

Apart from economic pressures, they mentioned other economic needs. 14.3% of them said that they worked to support their relative while 0.5% worked to bear the expenses of medicines that they required to keep them fit.

Higher standard of living was mentioned by a very small number of women. Only 1.5% of working women reported that they wanted to make provisions for higher education of their children as well as for their own education and 2.7% of them maintained that they worked to live decently.

Non-Financial Reasons

The non-financial reasons for working have been classified into three categories.

(a) To Occupy Time: 3.7% of working women reported that they felt boredom with the continuous routine of household tasks and felt lonely and isolated in the home. They want an escape into the work day world to utilise time meaningfully.

(b) Personality Traits: There are several personality factors which are involved in the motivation for employment. For instance, in this study 10.8% working women who had deliberately chosen careers reported that they wanted to fill a need for accomplishment and 1.8% of them said that they worked because they wanted to attain recognition by proving themselves able to compete successfully with men in activities for which they were once debarred. Some (1.8%) considered it as a national duty, 1.2% of them worked for personal independence and only one women said that she was working because of the uncertainty of the future. On the whole, 15.8% of working women have mentioned one or the other type of personality traits to be the factor inducting them to work.

(c) Traditional Occupation: Three per cent of working women reported that they worked because of the tradition of the family in a specific occupation. It also helped them to earn their living.

The financial reasons, thus, seem to be the most important reasons for women's seeking employment. However, it is possible that reasons for work differ among women themselves. Possibly, easily measurable demographic characteristics such as age, education etc. might be useful to explain the variations. To understand this, we shall compare these demographic variables to reasons for work.

Age

The percentage distribution of the response indicates that irrespective of their age, the working women reported that financial reasons were more important for them than the non-financial reasons.

Though the percentage of working women seemed to be increasing with the increase in age, it was found that there were no significant differences in the percentage accounted for by financial reasons. The old as well as the middle and the young working women were pressed almost equally by financial factors. But within the broad group of financial reasons, there were significant differences in the number of those working on account of one particular financial reason. Thus, more than three-fourths of the old aged working women (78.2%), more than three-fifths of the middle aged working women (63.8% and even less than one-half of the young working women (48.8%) worked due to economic pressures. There was, however, a decrease in the percentage of the working women accounting for other economic needs with increase in age. The young and the middle aged were almost equally distributed (15.9% and 15.2% respectively) while the working women of old age in this category were only 4.4%. Young working women's percentage accounting for standard of living is much higher than that of middle aged working women.

TABLE 2

Employment by Age

(in %t)

	Financial				Non-Financial				
Age Groups	*Economic pressures*	*Other economic needs*	*Higher standard of living*	*Total*	*Personality traits*	*To utilise time*	*Traditional occupation*	*Total*	*Grand Total*
Young (170)	48.8	15.9	07.0	71.7	20.6	05.3	02.4	28.3	100.0
Middle (205)	63.8	15.2	02.5	81.5	13.2	02.3	03.0	18.5	100.0
Old (23)	78.2	04.4	—	82.6	04.3	04.3	08.0	17.4	100.0
Age not specified (2)	100.0	—	—	100.0	—	—	—	—	100.0

Of those who worked because of personality traits or to avoid domestic responsibilities the number of young working women was more than that of the women of other age groups. Old working women 8.8%) who stated non-financial reasons as factors in their employment held to traditional occupations.

Briefly, it may be inferred that though economic pressures accounted for a sizable number of young working women, they were less than even one-half of all the working women of young age group. Some of them would like to live a life which gave them some compensation. For middle and old aged working women, and especially for the latter economic pressures were the most dominant factors.

Therefore, Economic pressures, were the dominating factors with the working women irrespective of age. They became much pressing as the age increased. The old working women were continuing largely in the working force not to rise their standard of living or to occupy their surplus time, or for some self-compensation. They worked to provide for the necessities of life. The middle aged working women were working on account of economic pressures. Though young working women also worked largely on account of economic pressures yet some of them were motivated by self-expression and actualisation. Therefore, with the increase in age, the continuance in the working force was mainly determined by economic considerations and self-expression as determinant lost its significance. Standard of living was not found to be a motivating factor in this study.

Caste

In Table 3 details regarding caste status and main reasons of work have been discussed.

It is evident from the table that with the rise in the status of the caste, the number of those working women reporting financial reasons declined whereas the number of those reporting non financial reasons increased. It is to be noted that economic pressures accounted for the largest number of lower and Scheduled Castes/Tribes. Three-fourths of them reported this whereas only one-half of the working women of middle castes and less than half of the upper caste women stated that they worked because of economic pressures. Though the number of working women reporting other reasons was small, there was a reverse trend with the rise in the status of caste. There was a decline in the number of working women reporting other economic needs, higher standard of living or personality traits. Only a very negligible section of working women of lower and Scheduled Castes/Tribes mentioned standard of living and personality trait as reason for employment. The number of upper caste working women was higher than that of lower and Scheduled Castes/Tribes and middle castes.

TABLE 3

Main Reasons for Employment by Caste (400)

(in Per Cent)

Reason for Work

	Financial				*Non-Financial*				
Age Groups	*Economic pressures*	*Other economic needs*	*Higher standard of living*	*Total*	*Personality traits*	*To occupy time*	*Traditional occupation*	*Total*	*Grand Total*
Upper (63)	41.3	17.4	09.5	67.2	27.0	04.8	—	31.8	100.00
Middle (104)	51.9	14.5	05.8	72.2	20.2	06.7	00.9	27.8	100.0
Lower and Scheduled Castes and Tribes (173)	76.9	12.7	01.1	90.7	04.6	01.7	03.0	09.3	100.0
Others (60)	35.0	18.3	05.0	58.3	28.3	03.4	10.0	41.7	100.0

Economic pressure was the compelling reason for employment irrespective of caste differentiation. But it is also evident that it was comparatively more dominant among lower and Scheduled Castes/ Tribes. Standard of living and personality traits were not dominant. However, motive of actualisation accounted for more than one-fourth of the upper caste working women and some of them had also the desire for higher standard of living. Somewhat more than one-fourth of other-castes-working women also reported personality traits as factor in their employment.

Marital Status

Table 4 presents the distribution of the sample in terms of the marital status and cause of work.

The data with respect to marital status and reasons of employment indicate that a substantially large number of the working women irrespective of their marital status were in employment due to financial reasons. But a difference in response was perceptible among those reporting economic pressures. Only one-third of the unmarried working women (33.3%) reported that they were in working force because of economic pressures and almost the same number of them (34.6%) asserted that they worked because they wanted to attain recognition in the community. Only a small percentage of them (11.1%) talked of higher standard of living, but their percentage was higher than that of other respondents in this study. Contrary to this findings, Ferdinand Zweig who has made a study into the attitudes and habits of Lancashire working women, estimates that "among married wives no more than about one in three goes out to work under economic pressure...". In this study slightly more than half of the married working women worked due to economic pressures. It is the widowed and the separated women whose largest number, slightly more than nine-tenths of them (92.6%), reported their being in labour force because of economic pressures. It is in conformity with the findings of a study by the Women's Bureau, U.S.A. Of 8,300 women workers in 100 Trade Union Locals which showed that ninety-eight per cent of those without husbands (widowed, separated and divorced) were working to support themselves and others. None of them has said that they worked to raise standard of living and only 2.1% of them attributed this working to personality traits.

It can be inferred that though the economic pressures was dominant as a factor of employment of the women, it was not much dominant among the unmarried. Their main consideration was to live a life which might give them compensation. Standard of living was not a motivating factors. Was perceptible only in some of the unmarried working women (11.1%). Among married women its percentage was negligible (3.6%). Almost all the widowed and the separated women were working because of economic pressures. It was clear then that marital status played an important role in creating difference in the responses related to reasons for work.

Nuclear and Joint Family Norms

The working women lived in various types of families. The composition of the family in which a working woman lived helped or hindered her entrance into employment.

As indicatesd the financial reasons seemed to be equally important to all the working women irrespective of the nature of their families. However, it may be seen that the percentage of working women with joint families is the highest (80.3%) when compared to the working women belonging to a single member family or nuclear family. But the differences are not much. Economic pressures have been most important for 72.2% of the single member family and 60.1% to the joint family working women as against 56.0% of the nuclear family working women. Other economic needs were mentioned by 15.6% of working women of the joint families, 14.8% of nuclear and only 5.6% of single member families. Higher standard of living was mentioned by working women of joint and nuclear families (4.6% and 4.3% respectively). The working women of nuclear and joint families went to work to occupy their time. Their percentage distribution is 4.8% and 2.9% respectively.

Cause of Work and Size of Family

A large number of the working women irrespective of the size of their families mentioned that they worked for financial reason. The percentage of those with larger families is the highest and of those with small-size families is the lowest. Single member family working women worked for economic pressures whereas the number of those belonging to large families, where others are to support is the lowest in this respect. The percentage of working women with large families mentioning other economic needs and higher standards of living was more than that of others. Some (8.1%) of the working women with small families mentioned that they worked to while away time and 16.4% of large family women reported that they worked to carry on the traditional occupation. As many as 16.7% single member of 16.1% small families' women mentioned personality traits as cause for their taking to work. The distribution of detailed responses can be seen in Table 4.

TABLE 4

Main Reasons for Employment by Size of Family

(in Per Cent)

Reason for Work

Size of Family	*Financial*				*Non-Financial*				
	Economic pressures	*Other economic needs*	*Higher standard of living*	*Total*	*Personality traits*	*To occupy time*	*Traditional occupation*	*Total*	*Grand Total*
Single Member (18)	72.4	05.6	—	77.8	16.7	—	05.5	22.2	100.0
Small (62)	59.7	12.9	03.2	75.8	16.1	08.1	—	24.2	100.0
Intermediate (179)	62.0	13.4	04.0	79.4	15.1	02.2	03.3	20.6	100.0
Large (141)	52.5	18.4	05.7	76.6	03.5	03.5	16.4	23.4	100.0

Number of Children

A very large number of working women, irrespective of the number of children worked because of financial reasons; the highest being the percentage of working women with medium number of children. Though the percentage of working women who worked to occupy time was very small yet of those working women who had no children (9.8%) worked to avoid boredom. Their percentage was three times more than that of working women with small and medium number of children giving boredom as reason for their employment.

Number of Dependents

The data show that those working women on whom depended larger number of persons, were more likely to work because of financial reasons than those who had no dependents or small or medium number of dependents.

Earners

With the increase in the number of earners in the working women's families, the percentage of those who mentioned financial reasons decreased; the highest being only when one was earning i.e.

working woman herself. A reverse trend was noted among those who mentioned non-financial reasons. The percentage was also decreasing with increase in number of earners in the category of those who worked under economic pressures. There was only one working woman with more than six earning members and she said that she worked to avoid boredom.

It is also seen that with the increase in number of earners upto six, there was an increase in the percentage of working women who were in employment because of personality traits or of those who wanted to carry on their family occupation.

Educational

The distribution of Responses of working women reporting the reasons impelling them to join labour force in terms of education is given in Table 5.

An analysis of the cause of employment by the educational standard of the employed women brings out the fact that with the increase in the level of education, the number of the working women reporting financial reasons was declining and increasing where non-financial reasons were in operation. More than three-fourths of the unlettered working women and slightly more than a half of low educated and also a little more than one-third of the highly educated working women reported that they worked due to economic pressures. Contrary to this, the number of working women who reported higher standard of living or non-financial reasons increased with the increase in education. It may be noted that more than three-fourths of non-lettered working women (78.0%) mentioned economic pressures whereas only one of them reported higher standard of living, and only two mentioned personality traits to be the cause of their going to work. Contrary to this only slightly more than one-third of highly educated working women reported economic pressures, one-third of them reported personality traits and eight per cent mentioned higher standard of living. In short, non-lettered women worked mainly because of economic pressures. Among highly educated, slightly more than one-third worked on account of economic pressures and one-third worked because they preferred attainment and recognition.

TABLE 5

Main Reasons for Employment by Education (400)

(in Per Cent)

Reason for Work

Education	*Financial*				*Non-Financial*				
	Economic pressures	*Other economic needs*	*Higher standard of living*	*Total*	*Personality traits*	*To occupy time*	*Traditional occupation*	*Total*	*Grand Total*
Non-lettered (192)	78.0	13.6	00.5	92.1	01.1	02.1	04.7	07.9	100.0
Low Educated (42)	54.7	14.3	04.8	73.8	14.3	04.8	07.1	26.2	100.0
Highly educated (166)	36.8	16.3	08.4	61.5	33.1	05.4	—	38.5	100.0

Occupation

A very large section of the working women employed in unskilled occupations described their work to financial reasons. Their percentage was the highest (94.2%) compared to that of the working women employed in various occupations. The lowest was the percentage in this category of the working women engaged in professions (29.6%). Similarly, the percentage of unskilled working women mentioning economic pressures as cause was the highest. They formed 82.8% of all the unskilled working women closely followed by those employed in petty trades. In this response category, the lowest percentage was again of the professionals (7.0%). Those who mention other economic needs, the percentage of working women engaged in semi-skilled occupations is the highest (30.8%) compared to women employed elsewhere; the lowest being that of the professionals (3.7%) . The higher standard of living accounted for 18.5% of the professionals which was the highest percentage of the other categories of working women; the lowest being that of the unskilled.

The percentage of the professionals is the highest (11.1%) who take to work to occupy time. The semi-skilled workers (20.5%) banked upon traditional occupation. Only one working women was engaged in N.C.C. and she considered it as a national duty. Like her,

59.3% of the professionals and fifty per cent of the skilled workers reported personality trait as cause of employment.

The occupationwise distribution shows that economic pressures were dominant among unskilled and petty-traders, whereas among those employed in N.C.C., professionals and skilled workers, personality traits seemed to be dominating. It was apparent then that the occupation of working women distinguished the factors making for employment. It may, thus, be inferred that working women of prestigious occupations were not working because of economic pressures but mostly because of the desire of attainment and recongition; and those in non-prestigeous occupations worked because of economic pressures.

Family Income

The number of working women reporting financial reasons went on declining with the increase in the average income of their family whereas a reverse trend was perceptible among those mentioning non-financial reasons. Three-fourths of the working women of the Family of the lower income group, less than half of the working women of lower middle income family and even less than one-fifth of the upper middle income family relied on economic pressure compelling them to work. None of the upper-income family working women considered economic pressures as imperative for employment. However, one-third of the working women of the family of the upper income group said that they worked to raise their standard of living. The working women of the lower income families did not consider personality trait as any major cause of their employment. Slightly less than half of the working women of the families of the upper-middle and upper income group considered that they worked because of personality traits.

It is apparent that the family income and the reasons of employment were very significantly related to each other. As the family income increased the percentage of the women working because of economic pressures declined to the extent that no working women belonging to the family of the upper income groups reported that she worked because of economic pressures. Instead, one-third of them reported higher standard of living, approximately one half of them and also slightly less than half of the upper-middle income group families mentioned personality traits, attainment and recognition as cause of employment.

Husband's Income

After this, in order to make things a little more concrete, the analysis was further made to show the income of husband and ratio of working wife in terms of the responses given as reason of their employment (Table 6).

TABLE 6

Main Reasons for Employment by Income of Husbands (225)*

(in Per Cent)

Reason for Work

	Financial				*Non-Financial*				
Age Groups	*Economic pressures*	*Other economic needs*	*Higher standard of living*	*Total*	*Personality traits*	*To occupy time*	*Traditional occupation*	*Total*	*Grand Total*
No Income	(21)	71.4	19.0	—	90.4	04.8	04.8	—	09.6
100.0									
Lower (84)		70.2	16.7	01.2	88.1	01.2	04.8	05.9	11.9
100.0									
Lower middle	(92)	43. 5	23.9	03.3	70.7	19.6	04.3	05.4	29.3
100.0									
Upper Middle	(18)	27.8		22.2	05.6		55.6	44.4	
—	—	44.4		100.0					
Upper	(10)	—		10.0	30.0		40.0	50.0	
10.0	—	60.0		100.0					

*Out of 400 working women, only 225 are living with their husbands.

From the responses one could note that with the increase in the income of husbands there was likelihood of substantial decrease in the number of working women who worked because of economic pressures. However, they would work for recognition and higher standard of living. This is also the finding of a study conducted by

Kapoor of Delhi educated working women. Similar results were obtained by Durand also.

Conclusions

In this Chapter we emphasised the importance of studying the factors involved in women's decision to work. The flow of women into the labour market can be considered as directly related to their general economic conditions. Financial reasons, especially the economic pressures, were the major factors to draw women into the working force. This was more than evident from the responses given by approximately three-fifths of them. There were others who did not work just to keep the wolf away from the door but because of the desire for achievement and self-compensation. Some of these were professionally trained and considered it a duty to utilise their capacities in the interest of the community. A few of them felt social isolation because they had nothing to do in their homes and therefore, they went to work to avoid the boredom. It may, however, be kept in view that the number of women who stated non-financial reasons was small, less than one-fourth of all the working women.

It has been found that with the increase in the age of working women, there was an increase in the percentage of those stating financial reasons and there was a corresponding decrease among those stating non-financial reasons. With the increase in age the continuity in employment seemed to be determined by economic pressures and considerations such as actualisation and self-expression lost their significance. Higher standard of living was not an important motivational force. Irrespective of caste status, financial reasons were stated as the most important; but with the increase in the status of caste there was a decline in the percentage of those stating these reasons. The working women of lower, Scheduled Castes and Tribes worked mostly because of economic pressures whereas it was not so with the majority of upper caste working women. Practically all the widowed and the separated women worked on account of financial reasons, under economic pressures; married working women took to work for the same reasons. A larger section of unmarried working women worked on account of personality traits. Economic pressures had been the main reasons for employment irrespective of the nature of the family. The working women with single member family were mostly in employment because of economic pressures.

The working women with medium number of children, a large number of dependents and less number of earners were mostly working on account of dire economic needs economic pressure was most felt by non-lettered working women. A sizable section of highly educated women worked to eke out their personality traits. Unskilled working women closely followed by petty traders joined the working force due to economic pressures, but a large majority of the professionals worked to give out personality traits. It was observed that the larger the income of the family, the lesser was the chance of women joining the labour force on account of financial reasons and economic pressures, so much so that not a single working woman of upper income group was found in the working force because of economic pressures. Approximately one-half of them worked because of personality traits and one-third of them took to work for higher standard of living. There existed an inverse relation between the percentage of wives in employment and the income of their husbands. The working women whose husbands had no earnings of their own or had low earnings, worked mainly on account of economic pressures whereas a small percentage of working women whose husband's income was higher, worked because of this reason.

REFERENCES

1. ILO, An International Survey of the Conditions of Working Women with Home and Family Responsibilities, as quoted in Myrdal, Alva and Viola Klein, *Women's Two Roles,* London, Routledge and Kegan Paul, 1962, p. 82.
2. Zweig, F., *Women's Life and Labour,* London: Victor Gallanz, 1952, p. 74.
3. Government of India, "International Trends," *Women in Employment,* Labour Bureau, Ministry of Labour and Employment, 1964, pp. 58-59.
4. Klein, Viola, *Britain's Married Women Workers,* London, Routledge and Kegan Paul, 1965, pp. 36-37.

5. Ranade and Ramchandran, p. 18.
7. Leaflet, 11, "Why Do Women Work?" 1951, as quoted in Ray E. Barber *Marriage and the Family* New York, McGraw Hill, 1953, p. 348.
8. Kapoor, Promilla, *Marriage and the Working Woman In India,* Delhi: Vikas Publications, 1970. p. 395.

3

Economic Independence and Attitudinal Change

In primitive human societies, when food was procured by gathering or hunting, there was full equality between men and women. The societies were frequently characterised by a kind of matriarchy in which the dominant chief was a woman, who carried out the function of dividing up the tribal land for cultivation. There is evidence for such matriarchal societies in India. With the increasing development of the productive forces and the intensification of class-exploitation male dominance was established and solidified. There were two main reasons for this: First men monopolised the plough. Second males came to monopolise the means of violence and warfare, possibly because they were the first to react to nature in a violent form. Thus the period of the rise of early class society and the triumph of patriarchy nearly coincided, and women became an oppressed sex. Now the oppressed began to organize collectively and consciously. The newly formed working class began to fight, first for economic survival but with an increasing awareness that they had the power in their hands to change society and end exploitation itself.

A United Nation's study shows that women provide two-third of the world's labour, earn one tenth of the world's income and own only one hundredth of the world's property. This economic vulnerability leads ultimately to social inequality and long term exploitation.

Women are often their own worst victims. The psychological attitudes that women pass down to each other, specifically that female are to be meek, docile and tolerant as against the courageous, aggressive nature of men is in actuality a subtle brain-washing. As women continue to play their cards the situation gradually deepens and bring into existence the 'super ego' in men and 'inferior ego' in women. In its worst expression the super ego extends to the male psychology that she can be bought along with its side repercussions of dowry, rape, prostitution, adultery and pornography. Psychologists asset that these negative social elements are the basic desire to insult and wound a women, i.e., the desire to exert one up manship or superiority over women. What is worse still is women's complacency or indifference results in a complete break-down in society. Instead of contributing to a healthier, stronger society, she establishes disparity, social friction and inequality.

Economic Independence

Most women are still unaware of the subtle brain washing and deprivation to their own sex. When husbands become member of clubs, it does not occur to her that membership should be on both names. When the name plate is put on the door, she will not realize that her name should be added. When a couple prospers as a husband and wife team, she will not care to point out that property, car, etc. should be on joint names. In several cases she has a costly price to pay for her oversight. If any break or friction arises in the marriage she finds herself out on the road penniless, often unable even to claim rights to her children. When a marriage breaks, the convenient remark of the husband is 'get out of my house'. Is the house his own on the first place?

In underdeveloped countries and among weaker sections of society the monetary repercussions are manifold and male domination almost complete. Fathers and husbands to perpetuate this exploitation ensure that their daughters are left completely uneducated. This gives her no choice and forces her to subserviency. Gradually even mothers come to believe in male might and ensure that their daughters are taught to believe in male superiority. Humanists and psychologists refer to this as one of the worst types of mental cruelty. The woman is deprived of her self-confidence, assertiveness, individuality and self-sufficiency. Ultimately, the whole of society feels the impact. A house divided against itself can't stand. There is a lowering of over-all efficiency and material standards with its resultant effect on morality and culture. Either advertently or inadvertently, the law is more oriented to safeguard the interest of men. Whilst it makes certain provisions for women it does not allow to her the same status, dignity and self-respect as that given to men.

Views of Prominent Personalities on Women

While inaugurating the ministerial conference of the non-aligned and other developing countries, Prime Minister Rajiv Gandhi reiterated that role of women in developing countries was very crucial to the rate at which a country developed and in many ways was the indicator as to how well the country was developing. "We have now to fight the historical, the social and cultural backwardness that has been thrust upon women and male superiority which has become in a way a vested interest. Like all vested interests, it is damaging the society, these vested interests have to be removed from our political, administrative, legal and social establishment".

Speaking during her official visit to the United Nations office at Vienna in April last year Ms Briceno said, "Women need to acquire management skills. Women must learn that having children is not a handicap to their careers but a responsibility. Men too have to learn these new attitudes. Efficiency and productivity are related to commitment, not to traditional roles and values". *[Ms Pulido Briceno (U.N. Coordinator).*

Minister for Social and Women's Welfare and chairman of the conference of non-aligned and developing countries for the role of women in development, while inaugurating the conference for the 'Role of Women in Development' Ms Chandrasekhar said, "I feel that one of the most important tasks before us is to inculcate the spirit of confidence and the desire amongst women to achieve their own potential. it is really tragic that women subjected to an unequal status for generations have come to accept this as their fate. Unless women take up their cause seriously and with a full realization of their responsibilities, society is not likely to be helpful to them. *[Ms Maragathan Chandrasekhar].*

Discussing the status of women Justice Manohar says, "If women have to bring about improvement in their social status, they have to become more aware of their rights and become more vigilant in preventing violation of their rights. Only then can they preserve their existing rights and improve upon them". *[Justice Sujata Manohar].*

Talking about discriminatory laws Justice Manohar stated that it was only in 1955 that the Hindu Marriage Act was enacted prohibiting bigamy, permitting divorce and radically transforming marital rights of Hindu women. For the first time Hindu women were granted the same marital rights as men. It was only after the enactment of the Hindu Succession Act, 1956 that a widow and daughter could inherit property in the same manner and in the same proportion as a son.

Though world leaders lay great emphasis on apartheid, racism and other discriminations, very seldom are the atrocities committed on women given equal limelight.

The United Nations Decade for the Advancament of Women has laid out some of the more important changes to be made in social as well as national strategies.

1. That men and women were jointly responsible for rearing and raising a family. Any breach of this rule was tantamount to discrimination and exploitation.
2. That house work be considered a valuable contribution to society and the gross national product and that the monetary figures be accordingly reflected in official statistical data. That monetary value of house work and rearing children be recognized, and due and appropriate compensation be made to women working in the home without dignity and monetary remuneration was tantamount to slavery.
3. Women like men have a constitutional and moral right to employment and economic freedom. Any breach of this

right, goes against the constitutional rights of women to work and earn a basic livelihood.

4. Measures were to be taken to allow women equal opportunities for study and training, special programmes were to be undertaken to correct past imbalances in this field.
5. To mobilise women, particularly poor women in rural and urban areas.
6. Rigid punishment to be implemented in all aspects of degradation and humiliation to womanhood in the forms of rape, prostitution, dowry and obscenity.
7. The programme asserted that government should explicitly state their firm commitment to rectify legislative and customary discriminations against women held for centuries in the vested interests of men. Special emphasis was laid on right to work and earning a livelihood. All legislative provisions in the social, economic and political sphere and in the penal civil codes were to be examined and regulations discriminating against women were to be repeated.
8. To ensure full participation of women in government and other agencies. And to take steps to ensure that women take active part in the decision making process.
9. Legislation for maternity leave was to be examined and appropriately implemented.

Shekar Kapoor (Actor) said that the root cause of this is economic factor. In past a man had to physically protect his family. The man was the stronger force. Now that has gone. A woman can be as equal a financial protector as a man, it is just that in the past few hundred years it has not happened, but it is bound to happen. Once a woman is as capable of earning the same kind of money and giving financial protection to the family. Then the women's status will become equal. But mother-hood is one aspect that can never be changed whether father-hood can become as warm, close and biologically necessary as motherhood. What do you do about motherhood? Baby's biological need of suckling? There is a whole gamut of touch and feel and this the father will never be able to provide. The term 'egalitarianism' refers in respect of the position of women in the society as well as in the family. It is easier to assess her position in the society from the availability of opportunities of participation in the social and productive activities as also a gainful employment. But her position in the family presents many difficulties in regard to such an assessment.

It is evidently a grave mistake to speak of women as a homogenous social class. It is undeniable that like men, all women can hardly be treated as having the same social and intellectual status. Further, the disabilities to which women have been exposed in the past, have not affected all women in the same way and to the same extent; nor did all inequalities apply to all women. For example, the lack of employment opportunities to women applied only to the middle class women, as the peasant's women were occupied in the agricultural activity along with the menfolk and the women of the higher classes had hardly any wish or necessity to take up employment. It is also an admitted fact that the tradition restricted the women to home and this is enough to describe the women's former role in the pre-industrial society. This state of affairs has been rightly described by Voila Klein as under: "daughters were brought up to be decarous, modest and chaste and they were closely guarded and chaperoned so as not to stray from the path of virtue. Knowledge and initiative, intelligence and experience were discouraged. The education of ladies was aimed at producing accomplishments—a smattering of music, art and needle work as well as social manners".

In the first decade after independence when India was seeking to re-establish an identity, every aspect of its life needed to be explored, considered and recognized. Some of the images that had been formed while it was a colony had to be effaced and more authentic one offered.

Status if seen as a derivative, the result of a pattern of relationships between men and women—a pattern composed of images they have of themselves and each other—certainty can not be evaluated by quantifiable measures either. Status for one set of women may be in relation to what other women have—now or in the past; to others what men have thought men would respect. Status really lies in the eyes of beholder. There is bound to be great deal of difference of opinion between societies, between generations as well as probably within them in what is preferred group of characteristics a woman should aspire for. It is doubtful whether the difference in this area can ever be finally resolved. It is a question of morals rather than facts. Imitating men is an unsatisfactory goal for women and such a tendency must be a reaction to a situation where women feel-ill-treated by men.

With a few notable exceptions, Indian sociologists have not devoted much serious attention to the systematic study of the position of women in their own society. There is no dearth of discussion on what may be called the women's question in India. But in the absence of systematic studies, there often leads to opposite conclusions.

This is the situation that the large masses of Hindu women in particular and Indian women from other societies in general face today. Though there are regional variations in the norms governing women's work, a tradition upper class norm that of excluding women from labour outside the family—still remains a status symbol and is often emulated by many who want to enhance their social status.

The forces which have most affected adversely the role of women in the Indian economy are: the general decline of handicrafts; increasing pressure of population on agriculture; increase of poverty in the rural sector resulting in migration; development of modern industry with its increasing technological advance; the spread of education; and the increasing cost of living, particularly in urban areas. Technological changes have similarly affected the employment of women in industries like cotton, textiles, plantation and mines. At the same time the decay of village industries has thrown more and more women on agriculture for their livelihood, increasing their numbers and percentage but reducing their levels of employment. On the other hand, the rising cost of living, education and social changes in the urban areas have led to the withdrawal of taboos that earlier affected women of the upper classes and have enabled some of them to enter new professions/occupations in the tertiary sector which were closed to them earlier.

Because of this differential impact of development, a macro-analysis of women's economic participation purely in quantitative terms is not enough. Thus any appraisal to women's economic roles has to be separated for specific segments differentiated by socio-economic and locational characteristics as well as by their degree of adjustment to the economic process. "The greatest difficulty in understanding the problems of women's participation", says the ICSSR report of the National Committee on Women, "has been caused by looking at women workers as a homogeneous group". This assumption has influenced the collection of data the laws, and the policies adopted to improve conditions of women workers and also the popularly held notions about women's participation in the economy.

The ratio of female to male workers has declined in all categories in the rural and most categories in the urban areas. The participation rates of men and women differ widely in all age-groups except the youngest (one to fourteen), the difference in urban areas being much higher than in rural areas. The distribution of women workers in the nine industrial categories adopted by the census shows their increasing dependence on agriculture and a decline in both the industrial and service sector.

Having found the census report not very useful, the National Committee on the Status of Women in India has for an accurate and more comprehensive assessment classified the whole lot of women workers in two broad categories according to the degree of organization and nature of problems of their sector of employment, the unorganized and organized sectors.

The difference between those two is not functional, as between agriculture, industry and services, because the functions may be found in both sectors. The real difference between them lies in the organization of productive relations, the degree of penetration of public control and regulation, and recognition by data collecting agencies and scientific investigators.

The status of women workers in India is, therefore, very unhealthy from the fact that 94 per cent of them are found in the unorganized sector, leaving only 6 per cent of them are found in the unorganized sector, leaving only 6 per cent in the organized sector. But for the sake of convenience we shall deal with the roles, rights and opportunities of that category of women's participation in the organized economy, which comprises only 6 per cent of working women.

The number of women employed in this sector increased from 1.37 million in 1962 to 2.14 million in 1973, an increase of 56.2 per cent. While this increase was faster than the total increase of employment in this sector, women's proportion in total employment remained practically constant at 11 per cent in this period. As we noted earlier, in spite of the fact that this sector has been steadily growing the women employment in it formed only 6 per cent of the total workers in 1971, 2.7 per cent being industry and 3.3 per cent in the services and professions.

Undoubtedly the number of women employed in the public sector increased by 110.4 per cent, but in the private sector the increase was only 29.9 per cent. The proportion of women in the public sector increased from 35 per cent to 47 per cent while their share in the private sector declined from 65 per cent to 52.8 per cent in this period. Public sector employment is mainly provided by state governments, local bodies and public undertakings. Their position in the Central Government is not very satisfactory.

A study (action plan), besides finding solutions to the problems affecting participation of women, will have to actively promote participation of women as as to bring about improvement in their economic and social status and a positive change in attitudes towards working women. In this context analysis of the existing situation at the national level through an examination of published data indicates that the following guidelines will be meaningful: Increased participation of women in occupations where they can be more or less productive than men. Productive both in terms of jobs/skill requirement and of ability to manage a job along with household chores and fulfill her child-rearing responsibilities. The occupations indicated are largely those requiring either certain levels of professional vocational/technical training and skills requiring manual dexterity in handling the work or no formal education. The major occupations in which women are employed in significant numbers are nursing, medical and health technology, teaching, stenography, typing and punching, maids, sweepers and such other service workers; plantation forestry and mining labour, spinning, weaving, tobacco production. Some of these are occupations where women are perceived as more equally productive as some employment is a result of economic incidence.

Although total employment in factories has been increasing since 1947 steadily. Women's employment in this sector has decreased since 1964, their share being reduced from 11.43 per cent in 1951 to 9.1 per cent in 1971. The number of women employed in mines declined from 109,000 to 75,000 between 1951 and 1971. Whereas total employment increased from 549,000 to 630,000. The women's share of employment of declined from 21.1 per cent to 11.9 per cent a decline of 47.4 per cent the heaviest decline was in coalmins from 55,000 to 2,000. There was, however, a general decline in the employment of women in all categories in 1963. This was more marked among administrative, executive and managerial workers (from 5,000 to 1,000), and professional, technical and related workers (from 55,000 to 31,000). Some new professions like advertising, market research, hotel management and cottage industries employ women in management cadres. Best traditional industries have not yet accepted women at this level. While it is generally difficult to give an all correct profile of women in service and professions, a review of the available data indicates a change in the occupational pattern and two trends are clearly visible; concentration of women in teaching and medicine and recognition of certain low prestige jobs in the clerical services as particularly suited to women.

In 1967-68 the medical work force of 120,000 doctors included 1,2000 women, the new profession of social work has emerged since

Independence, but in 1947, the year noticed the existence of two such schools, the Tata Institute of Social Sciences, Bombay, and the Delhi School of Social Work. There are now more than 20 such institutions. According to a study in 1968 there were 3,153 social work graduates whose number is estimated to have increased to 6,000 by 1971.

The sectorwise examination of women's employment trends indicates that major forces affecting women's employment stem from structural changes within the economy as a whole (from a traditional to a modern market economy, from a laissez faire to deliberate planned development, from unorganized to organized production, from unregulated to regulated relations of production or from labour to capital intensive technology, and from intensification of socio-economic inequalities.

In succeeding pages now we discuss the empirical findings and the views expressed by the sample respondents. On the basis of our empirical findings, we have also tried to make some generalizations.

In regard to economic independence and their contribution to the family, we put several questions to the sample working women and wanted to know to what extent they are economically independent and what contribution they have a made for the development of their families. The first question we put to the sample working women was that "what financial contribution you make to your family per month?" In reply to our this question the reply of the 200 sample respondents are presented below.

It has been observed that 40% contribute less than Rs. 500 to their families. 30% contribute between Rs. 500 to Rs. 10,000; 15% contribute between Rs. 1000 to Rs. 1500 a month. It is worth mentioning that these respondents apart from their salaried job are engaged in some other activities to generate additional finances. Remaining 15% contribute 3/4 of their income every month to their family. Another issue closely connected to that we wanted to check up as to what amount they use to spent on themselves their response in regard to the personal expenditure varied between Rs. 100 to maximum Rs. 500. Two explanations can be given to this. First either they were evasive in their reply or they are really too involved in establishing the fact that they were too much concerned about all-round development of their families. Personal expenditure also varies with the position held by the women. Even though the difference is not very significant as woman's personal expenditure is still not very high. She is more concerned about the welfare of her family members rather spending more money on herself.

Another aspect that as to what amount of their salary they spend on development and education of their children? The response to this issue reflected their admission that either they live in joint family or under the total guardianship of their husband, in such a situation the question of spending on the development of education to their children hardly arise. It was further confirmed by them that it is the duty of the head of the family or the husband to look after the maintenance and educational facilities of the children. However, they admitted that sometimes they use to give pocket money to their children. They also admitted that they are consulted about the right place for the child's education and even at times their decision is respected.

Sense of insecurity about the future is apparently visible among the women whether they are traditional or modernised. The sense of insecurity compel the women to think in terms of saving more in comparison to their male counterparts. Keeping this fact in view were put question before the sample working women as to what saving they make every month out of their earning?

Fifty per cent respondents told that they save between Rs. 100 to Rs. 200. 30% admitted that they save between Rs. 200 to Rs. 500 per month. But some over-enthusiastic (20%) respondents said that they save more than Rs. 500.

However, from the foregoing analysis it can be said that sense of economic independence has developed among the working women. They are alive to their family responsibilities and future apprehension of bad-days. This is reflected from the fact that either they contribute to their family income or they try to give better education to their children or save something for the future.

In regard to economic independence and their attitudinal change, we wanted to know that given the preference what type of job they would like to have. It is interested to note that as high as 85% of them stated that given the preference they would like to join teaching profession either in government schools or in colleges. Alternatively they would like to have some administrative job in government and in public undertaking according to their qualification. A negligible percentage of 15% preferred for the job of typist or a clerk. While making a deeper probe, we wanted to know as to why they will prefer teaching or administrative job. Giving explanation to our this query they said that in teaching profession there is little supervision in and greater independence as also little danger to their chastity and more job satisfaction. Similarly in administrative jobs there are enough facilities, little inconvenience and higher status. In regard to their low preference for typist or clerk's job, they had to state that their jobs are like double-edged sword. Moreover, it is a tangible job and there is no job-satisfaction or less job-satisfaction. They also find these jobs monotonous. In long term it leads to health hazard as either she will be always loaded with heap of files over her head or she has to sit throughout the day on her typewriter. Again it is interesting to note that a negligible percentage of sample respondents preferred for a job in private concern. It is because of the fact that sense of insecurity is always attached with private job. Even if an employee is employed on permanent basis, he or she can't feel secure for the job. This is more alarming in the case of female worker as she has always to dance at the tunes of her master. If she refuses to do so she can be discharged any moment. These are the reasons that the sample respondents preferred to enter into teaching or administrative jobs. Sense of job security in the government service may be the most vital reason for that.

It has often been reported by the researchers and working women themselves that sometimes they find it difficult to make adjustment between their household work and office work. As such as we wanted to know from the sample respondents as to whether they have faced such adjustment problems. The reply of our sample respondents is presented in Table 1.

The table 3 shows that as high as 88 per cent of sample respondents reported that they were quite comfortable with their both the responsibilities and the problem of adjustment hardly arise before them. Only negligible percentage reported that it was very difficult for them to discharge their both the responsibilities of a housewife and a working woman. They said that it becomes so difficult sometime for them that they are compelled to think in terms of quitting the job. But it was reported in a very small case as such it can be said that a comparatively high majority of sample respondents have brought changes in their attitude and tried to adjust in two environment i.e., environment of the house and environment of the office.

TABLE 1

Are You Feeling Comfortable with the Job and Household Work?

Reply	*No. of respondents*	*Percentage*
Comfortable	176	88
Uncomfortable	24	12
Total	**200**	**100**

Now we analyse some of the social characteristics of the sample working women, which may be responsible for the change in their attitude regarding economic independence and other factors.

In a large number of studies social characteristics such as age, marital status, occupation, income, employer-employee relation, motivation and social background have been found to have significant influence on the economic structure of the society. Here we discuss some of the basic social characteristics of the working women which are considered to be the related factors.

Education

As our sample includes the educated elite section of women in

Delhi, we have noted that the level of education is high among them as shown in Table 2.

TABLE 2

Level of Education

Level of Education	*No. of respondents*	*Percentage*
Undergraduates	6	3
Graduates	62	31
Post-graduates	91	45.5
Professionals	41	20.5
Total	**200**	**100.0**

If we combine post-graduates and professionals, we find that 66% of the sample women are highly educated and are engaged in professions like teaching and administrative jobs. Now if we look into the occupation table we note that education and occupation have the direct impact on the attitudinal change of the working women as shown in Table 4.

As shown in Table 3 the occupation distribution verifies that most highly educated women even prefer teaching profession.

TABLE 3

Occupational Distribution of Working Women

Occupation	*No. of respondents*	*Percentage*
Teachers	87	43.5
Lecturers	21	10.5
Clerks—Typist, Steno	48	24.0
Executives	34	17.0
Air-hostess	1	.5
Architects	2	1.0
Research Assistants	7	3.5
Total	**200**	**100.0**

Marital Status

To determine the marital status of working women, we attempted to find out the number of those who were unmarried, married, widowed as per the following Table 6.

TABLE 4

Marital Status

Status	*No. of respondents*	*Percentage*
Married	157	78.5
Unmarried	43	21.5
Total	**200**	**100.0**

It is found that more than two-third of the working women are married (78.5%) i.e., almost 80% of the sample working women. Only 21.5% of the working women are unmarried. It is merely a chance that no widow or separated woman is there in the sample. This distribution is similar to the one given in a survey report of Government of India.

Family Status

Data show almost half of the sample working women belong to the joint family and half to the nuclear family as shown in Table 5.

TABLE 5

Family Status

Status	*No. of respondents*	*Percentage*
Joint	100	50
Nuclear	100	50
Total	**200**	**100**

Number of Dependents

The number of dependents in a working woman's family ranged from 0 to 9. 40.5 per cent working women did not have any dependent. This also includes 21.5% of those unmarried women who are just working to pass their time and to make their career. The table further shows 20% of married women did not have any dependent and they live in nuclear family too. 34% of the working women have more than two dependents to support and 23.5 per cent have two to five and only 2 per cent have more than five dependents to support.

TABLE 6

Number of Dependents

No. of Dependents	*No. of respondents*	*Percentage*
None	81	40.5
Two to three	68	34.0
Two to five	47	23.5
More than five	4	2.0
Total	**200**	**100.0**

Size of the Family

After analysing the data it is evident that size of the family is decreasing. As Table 7 shows that only 2 per cent reported to have more than 2 issues.

TABLE 7

Size of Family

No. of Issues	*No. of respondents*	*Percentage*
None	56	28.0
One	37	18.5
Two	103	51.5
More than two	4	2.0
Total	**200**	**100.0**

The 28 per cent reported having no issue, this also includes the 21.5% of the unmarried sample working women. 18.5 per cent have only one child. This reveals that working women are more concerned about the size of the family as out of the percentage of 80 married women, 78% had one or two children.

Occupational Mobility

As regards the nature of employment as many as 82% of sample women reported that they were permanent and only 18% said that they were temporary. Data did not include part time employees. The data represented in Table 8 regarding the length of service indicate a wide variation among the working women.

TABLE 8

Length of Service

Length of Service	*No. of respondents*	*Percentage*
Less than 2 years	36	18.0
2 years to 5 years	49	24.5
5 years to 10 years	41	20.5
10 years to 20 years	46	23.0
More than 20 years	28	14.0
Total	**200**	**100.0**

From the above table we find that those working for more than 5 years are about 42.5 per cent which clearly indicates that working women have less mobility. It was revealed that during the course of interview most of them are concerned about having an office close to their residence, lesser transfer, lesser change of job and more time for attending their children. It was concluded that majority of them had taken up the job as a source of additional financial support rather than as a profession.

When respondents were asked about their change in occupation, 75.5% reported no change and only 24.5% reported that they had changed their job. These 24.5% when asked to explain this mobility gave several reasons for example some changed their job due to their marriage as they came in Delhi from outside. Some reported that (specially teachers) precious school was very far off. So they changed to their new one. Only a negligible percentage of women reported that after getting more education they competed for higher status jobs and got it. This shows that women still are not very keen on changing their occupation unless they are forced to do so because their job being subsidiary to their husband's job and also not that much concerned for career because of transfer hazards etc. and for responsibilities of family and children. It can be inferred that they could not get any other status jobs because they have choosen the jobs of their choice, i.e. teachers, lecturers and administrators. Besides women did not want to go elsewhere leaving their family and children.

After analysing the social characteristics of the working women in this chapter, our main objective is to correlate the following factors:

1. Has education brought any change in the attitude of the women?
2. Do they feel that their occupation is rightly suited to their education? i.e. the relation between education and occupation.
3. Are they struggling for more prestigious job suited to their education?
4. Is there are any relation between marital status and occupation?
5. Has any attitudinal change of working women visible in the up-bringing of their children.
6. To make an assessment of the impact of job on their family life beside their economic independence.
7. Psychological factor effecting their inter-personal relations.

It has been suggested earlier that as a consequence of their employment, working women may develop a somewhat different outlook in life as compared to the non-working women. As our sample does not include the data of non-working, this is just depending on open data available in other reports. Our objective is to find out how significant are these attitudinal changes. Here are some of the correlation highlighting these changes.

This shows that 66% of the sample are post-graduate and professionally qualified and 71% of the sample are as teachers, lecturers and executives which are their choice as they themselves have mentioned. It is inferred that they could not get any other better status job because they have chosen the job of their choice, teaching and administration. The level of education in case of teaching profession and executive cadre is quite high.

Keeping occupation as a stable variable we have analysed the relation between occupation and marital status. It is evident that teaching and clerical jobs have been the major areas of employment, there is no definite correlation between the occupation and marital status except that unmarried ladies continued working even after marriage in teaching profession and executive cadre. During the personal interview also it was confirmed when unmarried respondents were asked "whether they continue working after marriage?" Most of them who were in teaching profession, executive cadre replied in affirmative.

Attitudinal Change

The view that working ladies in teaching profession, research work did not find any difficulty to adjust their life-style after marriage as they were able to find sufficient time to attend their new requirements. Even though the data shows that the high cadre job ladies are also comfortable but they have also shown their more involvement in the job and their jobs are more demanding. So they face more problems due to their personality rather than office. This is again confirmed when we analyse the fact of adjustability after marriage.

As regard their occupation particularly in teaching profession, we also perceive higher degree of adjustment certain in comparison to other profession in their life-style specially after marriage. In order to confirm the findings, question was asked whether their profession come in the way of their adjustment towards their family after marriage? The ladies in teaching and executive cadre find less difficulty in adjustment. As in teaching they have more time available to them for their family. In executive cadre maturity of mind and high salary both pay to this adjustment. Overall analyses shows the high degree of adjustability after marriage among working women.

The sample survey indicates that 62% of the sample working women are satisfied with their occupations and 29% of them are getting sufficient encouragement from their life-partners. Occupational satisfaction is restricted to the self whereas encouragement by other family members is something else. It can be inferred that only about 30% of working ladies are feeling that they are getting encouragement to work from the elders of their families. As 88% of the sample shows that they all are feeling comfortable though they are in different professions. Even the profession-wise analysis indicates that 85 to 90% of the sample respondents are finding it comfortable. Whether they are encouraged or condemned by their husbands, today's women pursue their career to better their personality or make both ends meet. This was made clear by the sample women in course of informal talk. But is it a positive or a negative sign? Looking at the positive side that husbands are broadminded to recognize that money is vital and also that the burden of managing the house when shared equally, reduces the responsibility of only one person. They appreciate independence, recognize their wive's individuality and allow them to develop their creative talents. But its negative aspect is that women have to play two roles. Most men show their resentment when their wive's job interfers with their housework.

In conclusion, we find that economic independence has brought marked attitudinal change in the working women. However, the degree of change depends on the level of education, the profession they hold and the attitude of the family members towards them.

REFERENCES

Karanjia, T., "Women today what needs changing", *Flair*, Vol. 3, No. 1, January 1986, pp. 48.51.

Gupta, A.R., *Women in Hindu Society,* Jyotsana Prakashan, Delhi, 1982, pp. 153-248.

Jain, Devaki, (ed.), *Indian Women*, Publication Division, Govt. of India, 1975, pp. xi-xxii.

Beteille, Andre, *Position of Women in India Society*, Publication Division, Government of India, 1975, pp. 61-68.

D'Souza, Alfred, ed., *Women in Contemporary India: Traditional Images and Changing Roles,* New Delhi, Manohar Book Service, 1975.

Murali Manohar, K., Ed., *Women's Status and Development in India,* ed. by Gail Omvedt; *Draft Statement on Women's Liberation* Published by SOWSTUD and IIPA Local Branch, Warangal, pp. 222-244.

Devendra, Kiran, *Status and Position of Women in India,* Vikas Publishing House Pvt. Ltd., 1985, pp. 31-p5.

Government of India, *Economic and Social Status of Women Workers in India,* Labour Bureau, Ministry of Labour, Publication No. 15.

4

Women Workers: Past Trends and Future Prospects

Asia is best understood as a region of subregions rather than as a simple entity. Fifty-five per cent of the world's population live in Asia (excluding Japan and including developing countries of Oceania): 13 per cent in East Asia (excluding Japan), 22 per cent in middle South Asia and the remaining 10 per cent in the combined subregions of eastern South Asia (and developing countries of Oceania) and western South Asia (excluding non-Arab countries). The reliability of data for female activity in Asia varies. "In Asian countries with large Muslim populations...women's agricultural contribution remains largely invisible... 'Invisible crop activities'...occupy almost as much of their time as 'visible ones'" (United Nations, 1986b, pp. 39-40).

In many countries of middle and western South Asia, which includes the Middle East or Arab countries, much of the work women do is "invisible" and, therefore, not reflected in statistics from government sources which provide the basis for these data. For these countries, the level of female economic activity is higher than the data indicate. Since governments are generally consistent over time in the degree to which they evaluate the work women do, these data provide for an assessment of trends in female participation—which is the central focus of this analysis. They demonstrate stagnation in eastern South Asia and Oceania, declines in middle South Asia, and increase in East Asia and Western South Asia.

Economic Activity, 1950-2000

Eastern South Asia and Oceania

Eighty-six million females or 33 per cent of the female population are projected to be economically active in the year 2000. Eighty-two million are women between the ages of 15 and 64. The remaining 4 million comprise the active population outside this age range, predominantly girls below the age of 15. This 82 million figure represents 49 per cent of women between the ages of 15 and 64 in eastern South Asia and Oceania. In 1950, 33 per cent of the female population and 52 per cent of women between the ages of 15 and 64 were estimated to be economically active. Over the next 25 years, these rates declined to 31 and 51 per cent respectively. During the Decade for Women, the crude activity rate increased slightly whereas the refined rate remained at 51 per cent, representing stagnation in the advancement of women during this period. Alternative I shows for the year 2000 a slight increase of the crude activity rates from the level reached in 1985 and a further decline in the refined activity rate, i.e. 49 per cent of the women aged 15-64 years.

In 1950, the women of this region represented 36 per cent of the total economically active population. During the next 25 years, they secured 41 per cent of the growth in economic activity. The result was an increase in the female share of the economically active population from 36 to 38 per cent. During the Decade, women benefited insufficiently from the growth to increase their share in the economically active population. Despite their 38 per cent share in 1985, they are projected to benefit from only 33 per cent of the growth during the next 15 years. The result is a projected decline in the female share of the economically active population from 38 to 36 per cent during the next 15 years. This decline assumes the annual creation of 4.3 million opportunities during the 1985-2000 period. Since only 2 million opportunities were created annually in eastern South Asia and Oceania during the 25 years preceding the United Nations Decade for Women, this projected decline represents a doubling of annual efforts to create gainful activities.

Almost a tripling of efforts is necessary if women and men are to have equal access to economic activity in 2025, as suggested by Alternative II projections. To meet this goal, 6.3 million opportunities need to be created annually, of which 54 per cent or 3.4 million should be made available to women. These intensive efforts would result in an increase in the female share of the economically active population from 38 per cent in 1985 to 43 per cent in the year 2000, resulting in 66 per cent or 111 million women being economically active.

Middle South Asia

According to Alternative I, 112 million females or 17 per cent of the female population are projected to be economically active in the year 2000. Of these, 105 million will be women between the ages of 15 and 64. These active women comprise one-quarter of the female working-age population. The remaining 7 million will be predominantly girls below the age of 15 years.

In 1950, 58 million females were estimated to be economically active, representing one-quarter of the female population. Fifty million of these were women between the ages of 15 and 64. During the 25 years preceding the United Nations Decade for Women (1976-85), the proportion of economically active women declined from 38 to 31 per cent. During the first half of the Decade their participation declined to 29 per cent and during the second half to 28 per cent. It is the continuation of this trend which accounts for the continued decline to 25 per cent during the next 15 years.

In 1950, women made up 28 per cent of the total economically active population. During the next 25 years, females secured only 19 per cent of the increase in economically active population, and therefore their share in the total declined to 25 per cent. A further decline of the share to 23 per cent was registered at the end of the Decade for Women. Alternative I assumes a continuation of this trend, and therefore the share of females will drop to 22 per cent at the end of the century.

Intensified efforts are essential to reverse this downward spiral. A doubling of efforts to create economic opportunities during the next 15 years must be combined with a commitment to create opportunities for gainful activity for the women of middle South Asia. A departure from past trends embodied in Alternative II projections necessitates the annual creation of 17.4 rather than 9.3 million economic opportunities, along with a commitment to allocate 56 per cent of this growth to women. The result of these efforts would increase the female share to 36 per cent by the year 2000.

Western South Asia

About 1 per cent of the world's population lives in western South Asia. A major share of the female population in this region is classified as economically inactive, a fact which is the subject of criticism (United Nations, 1986b, p. 32). Data from national sources provide the basis for the estimates and projections which are available for our analysis. Alternative I projections for the year 2000 estimate that 4.9 million females, or 11 per cent of the female population, will be economically active. Most of them will be women between the ages of 15 and 64, 19 per cent of whom are projected to be economically active. This participation represents a small but steady and increasing trend in female economic activity. In 1950, 5 per cent of all women were economically active. By 1975 their participation had increased to 11 per cent and by the end of the United Nations Decade for Women it had increased to 15 per cent. If present trends continue, 19 per cent of women and 11 per cent of all females are projected to be economically active in 2000.

In 1950, women made up 6 per cent of the economically active population. During the next 25-year period women secured an even greater share of the growth in economic activity—17 per cent. As a consequence, the female share of the economically active population increased to 11 per cent. This trend held during the United Nations Decade, the result of which was an increase to 14 per cent. If this slow but steady increase continues to 2000, women will benefit from 23 per cent of the growth in new opportunities, the result of which will be an increase in the female share of the economically active population to 18 per cent in 2000.

Extensive efforts in western South Asia are essential if women in this region are to have the resources necessary for economic independence and self-reliance. Alternative II projections suggest the necessity of a doubling of current efforts. In particular, in order for women and men to have an equal opportunity for economic activity by 2025, 1.2 million economic opportunities need to be created annually, 50 per cent of which should be made available to women. These efforts require the active participation of 10.5 million women or 43 per cent of the female population between the ages of 15 and 64 years.

East Asia

According to Alternative I, over 347 million females are projected to be economically active in the year 2000 in East Asia (excluding Japan), a figure which represents 53 per cent of the female population and over three-quarters of working-age women. These figures reflect a trend of increasing economic activity based on an initial high level of participation in 1950, when 46 per cent of all females, or 130 million, were economically active. The proportion of the total female population which was economically active had declined to 45 per cent by 1975. This decline was a result of an increase in the dependent or non-active part of the female population, particularly among the young. In fact, during the same period, the participation of women aged 15-64 increased from 68 to 72 per cent. An increase of both crude and refined activity rates has been reported during the United Nations Decade for Women.

In 1950, women made up 39 per cent of the economically active population. During the 1950-75 period, they benefited from a greater share of the growth in economic activity (48 per cent), which produced an increase in the female share of the economically active population to 42 per cent. The female share increased to 43 per cent during the first half of the Decade, but stagnated during the second half when women registered equivalent share of growth—43 per cent; and this share is likely to remain stable until the year 2000.

Alternative II projections produce a 45 per cent female share of the economically active population. This set of projections suggests the possibility of nearly 375 million economically active females in East Asia by the year 2000, a figure representing 57 per cent of the total female population. For Alternative II to become a reality, and for women in East Asia to have equal opportunities with men for access to economic activity by 2025, the creation of new economic opportunities must be accelerated during the next 15 years. Instead of 10.3 million per year, 12.2 million, and of these opportunities 53 per cent, should be for women.

Gross Years of Working Life, 1950-2000

The consequences of these varying levels and trends in economic activity in terms of increases and declines in the number of years women can expect to be economically active during the 1950-2000 period. The data also illustrate variations in gross years of working life for males and females, which reflect variations at the regional level and trends in male and female economic activity. As the figures for male working life show, there is comparatively little variation among the regions in the economic activity of the male population. Men have high levels of economic activity which are reflected in gross years of working the ranging from 53 to 57 years in 1950 to 48 to 51 years in 1985, and projections of 46 to 49 years for the year 2000. The trends in all regions are characterised by declines resulting from a variety of changes in the economic lives of men, in particular longer education, earlier retirement and increased coverage of workers in pension schemes. Patterns of working life for the female population vary uniformly with changes in economic activity during the 1950-2000 period. Declines are projected for middle south and eastern South Asia. Along with stability for Eastern Asia and Oceania and increases for western South Asia.

If present trends continue to 2000, the gross years of working life of women in eastern South Asia and Oceania will decline from

30 years in 1950 to 27 years in 1985 and to 26 years in 2000. In middle South Asia it will also continue its downward trend from 22 years in 1950 to 15 years in 1985 and to 14 years in 2000. In western South Asia it will increase, while in East Asia it will remain stable. Women were active for an average of three years in western South Asia in 1950 and for an average of eight years in 1985. In 2000, they are projected to be active for ten years. The corresponding figures for East Asia are 35, 35 and 35 years.

If greater efforts are to be made to advance women towards economic independence and self-reliance by providing them with the increased opportunities suggested by the Alternative II projections, some of these trends would be accelerated while others would be reversed. Instead of being economically active for 26 years, women in eastern and South Asia and Oceania could expect to be active for 36 years. Women in middle South Asia would experience an increase in economically active life from 14 to 29 years. Correspondingly, women in western South Asia would increase their economically active life from ten to 23 years. In East Asia, women could expect to be economically active for 40 years.

Economic Activity by Major Sector, 1950-2000

Eastern South Asia and Oceania (Developing Countries)

Projections for the beginning of the twenty-first century show that the majority of economically active males as well as females will be in the non-agricultural sectors of eastern South Asia: 53 per cent and 58 per cent, respectively. The trends which explain these projections. In 1950, 79 per cent of women and 78 per cent of men were engaged in agriculture. The proportions in industry and services were 6 per cent and 15 per cent for females and 6 per cent and 16 per cent for males. During the 30 years between 1950 and 1980, both women and men moved out of agriculture into the non-agricultural sectors. Between 1950 and 1980, the proportion of females in agriculture declined to 59 per cent. For males, it declined to 60 per cent. During the same period, the proportion of all economically active females in industry increased from 6 to 13 per cent, while that of males increased from 6 to 14 per cent. The female proportion in services increased from 15 to 29 per cent and the male concentration increased from 16 to 26 per cent.

Females and male shares make it possible to explore the female-male position in each sector. The female share in agriculture is projected to decline slightly from 36 to 34 per cent during the second half or the twentieth century. During the 30 years between 1950 and 1980, the female share increased in both the industrial and services sectors. Projections for the year 2000, however, show a moderate decline from 39 to 38 per cent for the female share of the non-agricultural sectors. These data show that opportunities for activities for women need to be expanded in the three sectors, namely agriculture, industry and services, in conformity with Alternative II projections.

Middle South Asia

In 1950, 89 per cent of all females were in the agricultural sector. This figure had declined to 77 per cent by 1980 and to 74 per cent by 1985 and is projected to decline to 64 per cent by the year 2000. The proportions of males in agriculture were the following: 74 per cent in 1950, 65 per cent in 1980, 64 per cent in 1985 and 59 per cent in 2000. Clearly, women are currently more concentrated in the agricultural sector than are men in middle South Asia. Male-female differences are also apparent for the non-agricultural sectors. First, more of the economically active males than economically active females are estimated to be in these sectors, e.g. 35 as compared to 23 per cent in 1980. Men, however, tend to be more concentrated in services while women are more evenly distributed between industry and services: of the economically active women in 1980, 11 per cent were in industry and 12 per cent were in services. Twenty-one per cent of economically active males were in services as compared with 14 per cent in industry.

The male and female shares take into account the number of economically active males and females in each sector. The female share of agriculture is projected to be 23 per cent at the end of the twentieth century. This figure is the result of a steady decline in the female share dating to 1950 when it was 31 per cent. During the same 50-year period, the male share is projected to increase from 69 to 77 per cent.

The female share of the non-agricultural sector is projected to increase from 18 per cent in 1975 to 19 per cent in 2000. Increases are estimated for the 30 years between 1950 and 1980 for the female share of both industry and services: it increased from 15 to 20 per cent in industry and from 13 to 15 per cent in services. Even so, in 1980 the male shares were 80 and 85 per cent, respectively. These data suggest the importance of expanding economic opportunities for women in all sectors of the economy in middle South Asia. Since the male share of each sector is approximately 80 per cent, intensified efforts are essential to expand opportunities for women in all sectors, and in particular in the non-agricultural sectors.

Western South Asia (Excluding Non-Arab Countries)

The majority of economically active females and males are projected to be in the non-agricultural sectors at the beginning of the twenty-first century. In 1950, women were more concentrated than men in these sectors: 38 per cent and 34 per cent respectively. By 1980, however, the situation had reversed. Now men were more concentrated than women in the non-agricultural sectors: 67 per cent and 51 per cent respectively. In 1950 both women and men were more concentrated in services than in industry: 28 per cent of economically active females were estimated to be in the services sector, while 9 per cent were in industry. During the next 30 years, females became more concentrated in services, their share increasing from 28 to 41 per cent, while that in industry remained about the same—10 per cent. During the same period, the share of males increased for both sectors, from 20 to 33 per cent in services and from 14 to 24 per cent in industry.

An estimated 24 per cent of all economically active females are projected to be in the agricultural sector at the end of the twentieth century. The share of females in agriculture is projected to be slightly higher than that of males by the year 2000. This trend can be traced to changes during the 1950-80 period in the distribution of males and females by sector. In 1950, 62 per cent of all economically active females were in the agricultural sector. By 1980, the share had declined to 49 per cent. During the same period, the male share in agriculture declined from 66 to 43 per cent.

An examination of the female and male shares of the various sectors reflect the low levels of economic activity recorded for females in western South Asia and Oceania. In the year 2000, women are projected to make up 21 per cent of the agricultural and 17 per cent of the non-agricultural sectors. Correspondingly, males will comprise approximately 80 per cent of these sectors. Estimates for the 1950-80 period for the services and industrial sector suggest an even greater female-male differential. In 1980, 94 per cent of the active population in industry were male and 6 per cent were female. In services, 88 per cent were male and 12 per cent were female.

These data suggest the importance of making special efforts in western South Asia and Oceania to examine the current real work of women in the light of new recommendations for economic activity, particularly those changes which expand the inclusion of unpaid family workers as economically active. Intensive efforts are also necessary to create opportunities for gainful activities in all sectors of the economy. Since between 80 and 90 per cent of those active in agriculture, industry and services are male, efforts need to be accelerated to create opportunities for women in all sectors of the economy.

East Asia

In the year 2000, the majority of economically active females and males are projected to be in the agricultural sector of the economic of East Asia. This projection in based on trends dating to 1950, when 91 per cent of all females and 85 per cent of males were in the agricultural sector. By 1980, these concentrations had been reduced to 77 and 69 per cent, respectively. During the same period, the female share in the non-agricultural sector increased from 9 to 23 per cent while the male share increased from 15 to 31 per cent. The continuation of these trends to the twenty-first century means that more women than men will be concentrated in agriculture, and vice versa for non-agriculture.

An examination of female and male shares of the active population in each sector highlights some of these differences. In the year 2000, 47 per cent of those active in agriculture are projected to be female, an increase from the 41 per cent share in 1950. Projections for the female share of the non-agricultural sector suggest an increase from 36 per cent in 1985 to 39 per cent in 2000. Data for 1950 and 1980 show increase in the female share of both industry and services. In 1980, this share was approximately one-third of both sectors. These data suggest that efforts in East Asia should be concentrated on creating gainful activities for women in the non-agricultural sectors of the economy. Since nearly two-third of the active population in both the services and industrial sectors are male, these two sectors should be targeted by governments. Intensified efforts in the non-agricultural sector would further contribute to decreasing the disparity between women and men.

5

An Assessment of Women Employment

Women are mostly engaged in household activities which are not considered "economic" and therefore, do not get counted as workers under conventional measures of employment. Market-oriented concepts of income and employment do not capture a large part of women's economic activities as these activities consist of production of goods and services for the use of their own households. Even women's work in the production of goods and services for the market often gets ignored because of its being intermitant and subsidiary to their non-market and "non-economic" household work. [Papola 1992]. Sample surveys of the National Sample Survey Organization (NSSO) and Population Censuses have tried to devise ways to reduce underestimation of women's work and such attempts have to continue. Comprehensive information on trends in the structure and levels of women employment is available from two sources, namely, the 1981 and 1991 population censuses and the quinquennial surveys on employment and unemployment of the National Sample Survey Organization (NSSO) conducted from 1972-73.

The two censuses had broadly comparable concepts of workers, but during the 1991 census, additional probing questions were put to informants so as to identify workers among women so as to minimise underenumeration of women workers. Trends during the period 1981-91 revealed by the two censuses, therefore, need to be treated with caution. The three NSSO sample surveys conducted in 1977-78, 1983 and 1987-88 are based on comparable concepts and, therefore, enable an analysis of trends over the period 1987-88. These surveys also provide comprehensive information on the trends in the levels and structure of unemployment making uses of concepts designed to suit the specific features of a predominantly agricultural economy. Data on trends in employment in the organized sector of the economy are available from the Employment Market Information (EMI) programme of the Ministry of Labour (Directorate General of Employment and Training).

Economic Activity and Women Participation

The Labour Force Participation Rate (LFPR), namely, the percentage of labour force to population, is a measure of the extent of participation in economic activity. These rates for women show that a majority of women, even in the working age groups, are outside the labour force. LFPR for women in the age group (15-59) is only 26.5% compared to 87.6% for men according to the NSSO 43rd Round (1987-88) survey on employment and unemployment. The rural-urban differential in the extent of women's participation in economic activity is substantial, LFPR for rural women being twice that of urban women (41.2% and 20.2%). On the other hand, LFPR for men is much higher in both rural and urban areas and not much different form each other (89% and 83.3% in rural and urban areas respectively). LFPRs for women in the age group 5+ are similarly quite low both in rural (29.3%) and urban areas (14.7%), the overall rate being 26%; and these are substantially lower than the corresponding rates for men. LFPR for women have also been stagnant over the eighties, according to the 38th and 43rd Round (1983 and 1987-88) NSSO surveys. The low level of participation rates for women has also meant a low and stagnant share of women in total workers (28.%) over this period.

Trends in Levels and Structure of Unemployment among Women

The conventional and the most commonly used concepts of unemployment measure involuntary idleness but not 'invisible' unemployment and underemployment, which is a problem of a much larger magnitude in India. Involuntary idleness is measured in NSSO surveys of employment and unemployment using three concepts—Usual Principal Status (UPS), Current Weekly Status (CWS) and Current Daily Status (CDS). A person is considered unemployed on UPS basis if he/she was not working but was seeking or available for work for a relatively longer time during the reference year. A person is considered unemployed on CWS basis if he/she had not worked for even one hour during the reference week. Unemployment on CDS basis measures unemployment by aggregating unemployed days of all persons in the labour force during the reference week. UPS and CWS concepts estimate open unemployment, while the CDS concept, which is the most inclusive one, provides a measure of visible underemployment. An idea of invisible underemployment could be had by comparing these rates with poverty levels.

Incidence of unemployment is higher among women than among men, according to the 43rd Round (1987-88) survey of NSSO. The rates for women are estimated to have been 4.19% (of the labour force) on UPS basis, 4.92% on CWS basis and 7.61% on CDS basis (see Table 1). In absolute terms, unemployment is estimated to have been 3.61 million women, 3.99 million women and 2084 million women-days respectively during 1987-88. These respectively accounted for 31.%, 28% and 32% of total unemployment on the basis of each of the three concepts. The rates for different groups in different years estimated on the basis of the three concepts (see Table 1) show that underemployment is a much higher proportion of unemployment among women than among men. There is also a shift in the structure of unemployment from a state of widespread underemployment towards greater open unemployment. This trend is stronger in rural areas and in the case of women (Planning Commission 1992). Greater attention has, therefore, to be paid to creation of regular employment opportunities for women than to temporary, off season public works employment.

Incidence of unemployment among educated women is higher (27%) than that for men (10%). Among all the educated unemployed 27% are women. Incidence of unemployment among educated women has declined from 32% to 27%; and the share of women among all the educated unemployed has come down from 42% to 27% over the decade 1977-78 to 1987-88.

Trends in the Growth and Structure of Employment of Women

Overall women employment has grown at the average annual rate of 1.90% over the period 1977-78 to 1987-88 according to NSSO surveys. The rate of growth has been more or less the same (1.97%) as that of employment of men during the period and as a result, the share of women in total employment has remained at the level of 28% over the period. Women employment has grown much faster in urban areas (3.62%) than in rural areas (1.66%). The rate of growth of urban employment has been more or less the same for men (3.66%) and women but in rural areas women employment has grown faster than employment of men (1.48%). While the share of rural areas in total employment has declined from 82.% to 78.% the share of rural areas in total women employment declined less sharply from 89% to 87.%; and the share of rural women in total employment fell only slightly, from 24.9% to 24.2% (NSSO 1981-1990). Women employment thus continues to be predominantly rural.

Although the share of women in total employment has been stagnant at 28.%, and in agriculture at 32%, it has increased in construction (from 14% to 24%) and in finance, insurance and real estate (from 4.5% to 7.5%) and has declined in trade and commerce (14.%) to 13.%) during 1978-88. The average annual growth rate of employment of women has been higher than that of overall employment in agriculture (1.1% against 0.9), construction (16% against 10%), electricity gas and water supply (10% against 5%) and finance, insurance and business services (13% against 7.5%) (NSSO *ibid*). As the last two are small sectors in terms of employment shares, major gains in employment for women would appear to have occurred in sectors mostly offering insecure and unstable employment, namely, agriculture and construction.

Differential rates of growth of employment of women in different sectors have brought about some changes in the structure of women employment. The share of agriculture in women employment fell from 80% in 1977-78 to 75% in 1987-88 and the shares of each of the other sectors in women employment increased. Construction registered the most significant increases, from 0.93 to 3.33% but the shares of sectors like manufacturing, trade, transport and services in total women employment increased slightly. On the other hand, the share of agriculture in employment of men fell more sharply, from 67% to 59%; and that of construction increased less significantly, from 2.18 to 4.17% (NSSO *ibid*).

An analysis of trends in the structure of employment by category of employment, reveals a shift from self employment to casual work, with the proportion of regular wage/salary earners remaining unchanged, but in the case of women workers, the shift is more towards regular wage/ salaried work 54.8% of women workers were self employed, 6.6% regular wage/salaried workers and 38.6% casual workers in 1977-78, while the corresponding proportions were 53%, 8% and 39% respectively in 1987-88. On the other hand, the share of the self employed in employed men declined from 58.% to 54%, and that of casual workers rose from 24% to 28% while the share of regular wage/salary earners remained at 18% during this period (Planning Commission 1992). Although a larger proportion of women workers are casual workers and a smaller proportion regular wage/ salary earners than male workers, on the margin, women have been able to secure regular jobs better than men and avoid increase in the degree of casualisation.

Average annual rates of growth of overall employment as well as women employment are higher according to the 1981 and 1991 Census (2.4% and 3.4%) than those revealed by the 32nd and 43rd Round NSSO surveys (1.95% and 1.90%). The same is the case in some sectors, namely, agriculture, trade and commerce and 'other services' (other than transport etc.). Census rates of growth for overall and women employment are lower than NSSO rates in other sectors, namely, construction, mining and quarrying and transport, storage and communications. In all sectors except construction and trade and commerce, however, employment growth rates for females are higher than those for overall employment during the period

1981-91. The share of females in total employment has, therefore, risen from 20.3% in 1981 to 22.5% in 1991, though the share according to Census data is smaller than that revealed by NSSO surveys. Census data also reveal, like NSSO data, a slower shift away form agriculture in the structure of female employment (81.3% to 80.8%) than is the case with the structure of male employment (65.6% to 62.7%) (Registrar General, India 1993). The shift noticed from Census data is also much smaller than shown by NSSO data. The low growth of employment of females in construction and the fall in the share of construction in total female employment as well as in the share of females in construction employment during 1981 to 1991, is, however, contrary to the trends during 1977-78 to 1987-88 revealed by NSSO surveys. All these trends have to be examined in detail, taking note of the reasons mentioned earlier as also other relevant factors.

Work in the unorganized sector is the more predominant mode of employment of women than of men. The share of the organized sector even in overall employment is only 10%; but the share in the case of women employment is much less, only 3.2%. Employment of women in the annum) than that of employment of men 91.5% per annum); and as a result, the share of women in organized sector employment has increased from 12% in 1979 to 13.6% in 1989. Employment of women has grown relatively faster in certain subsecotrs of the organized sector, like financial services (8.8% per annum), transport, communications (6.8%), electricity, gas and water services (7.7%) and community services (4.6%). It registered an absolute decline in manufacturing and mining and grew slower than employment of men in agriculture and construction. Such deferential growth rates have led to changes in employment shares of women in different subsectors of the organized sector and in the structure of organized sector employment during the period 1979-89. Employment shares of women have risen fast in financial services (8% to 11%) and community services (16% to 20%); and the share has declined in manufacturing. In 1979, half of the women employed in the organized sector were in community services and a little over one-fifth in manufacturing; and in 1989, the corresponding shares were 57%

and 16% (Ministry of Labour-successive Annual and Quarterly Employment Reviews).

Public sector has been the main contributor to the growth of organized sector employment, with the public and private organized sector employment levels registering average annual growth rates of 2.35% and 0.36% respectively. Employment growth rates have been higher for women than men in both the public sector (4.8% against 2.1%) and the private sector (0.85% against 0.25%) (Ministry of Labour, *ibid.*).

Employment of Educated Women

Employment of educated women has grown faster (almost 10% per annum) than overall women employment and also faster than employment of the educated in general (7.5% per annum) during the period 1977-78 to 1987-88. The share of the educated in total women employment has consequently increased from 7.5% to 1.5% during this period, but the increase in the share of the educated in total women labour force has been sharper, from 19% to 33% (NSSO 1981, 1990).

Quality of Women's Employment

It has been seen that (i) women's employment is more predominantly rural than that of men's employment, (ii) the share of women workers has increased mostly in sectors offering only low paid, insecure and unstable employment (like agriculture and construction), (iii) the shift from agricultural to non-agricultural employment has been less marked and that to construction is more marked in the case of female workers than of male workers, and (iv) the proportion of casual workers among female works, though stagnant over the Eighties, is still higher than for male workers. These show that the quality of women's employment is not only relatively much lower than that of men but also that it has not improved over time.

Data on earnings of male and female workers from NSSO surveys on employment and unemployment confirm these trends. Notwithstanding the Equal Remuneration Act, average earnings of female workers continue to be less than those of male workers; and the disparity in earnings between male and female workers, regular or casual, has worsened over the Eighties in the agricultural sector except in rural public works. The disparity has reduced somewhat in the non-agricultural sector, and more sharply in urban sectors than in the non-farm rural sector. Further, the disparity between average daily earnings of male and female casual workers even in 1987-88 is greater that in the case of regular wage/salaried male and female workers.

Conclusions

Obviously, we witness:

(i) unemployment rates are higher for women than men.

(ii) the level of participation, of women in economic activities is low; and this has meant a low and stagnant share of women in total workers (28%) over the years.

(iii) Work in the unorganized sector is the more predominant mode of employment of women than men.

(iv) visible underemployment is a much higher proportion among, women than among men.

(v) Incidence of unemployment among educated women is much higher (27.%) than that for men (10%). A little over one-fourth of the educated unemployed in 1987-88 are women, though this share has come down from 42% to 27% in the Eighties.

(vi) The trend towards an increase in the incidence of open unemployment and a decline in that of (visible) underemployment, has been stronger in the case of women than in the case of men.

(vii) Employment of women is more predominantly rural than of men.

(viii) The share of women in overall employment has increased mostly in sectors offering only low paid, insecure and unstable employment; but here is also a trend towards an increase in some smaller sectors characterised by stable employment (namely, financial services and electricity).

(ix) Average daily earnings of female workers continue to be less than that of male workers, the disparity being greater in the case of casual workers then regular wage/salaried workers. The disparity has worsened over the Eighties in the agricultural sector except in rural public works. It has reduced somewhat in the non-agricultural sector, and more sharply in urban sectors than in the non-farm rural sector.

(x) Quality of employment of women is, as seen from the foregoing, not only relatively much lower than that of men but also that it has not improved much over time. However, (viii), (x) and (xi) above indicate a trend towards some improvement.

(xi) The shift in the structure of employment from agricultural to non-agricultural employment has been less marked, and that to construction has been more marked, in the case of female than of male workers.

(xii) There has been an increase in the stability of women's employment, in terms of proportion of regular wage/ salary earners among workers; the proportion has slightly declined in case of men. On the other hand, while proportion of casual workers has significantly increased in the case of males, it has remained unchanged in the case of female workers.

(xiii) Women have been able to secure an increase in the organized, particularly public sector jobs much faster than men. A major part of this increase is accounted for by community services and financial services.

6

Working Women in Socialist Countries

In recent centuries, the changing role of women has been closely interrelated with other aspects of the development of society, such as industrialization, urbanization, demographic revolution,[1] etc. The most characteristics feature of developed countries for roughly the past two centuries has been the growth and change of all social structures. It is necessary to see changes in the position, status and roles of women in society, together with changes in the levels of fertility, etc., in the context of this complex global revolution, as the position of women is deeply rooted in other social processes and has relatively little autonomy. The relationship between the status of women and fertility levels has been cogently expressed by a well-known demographer: "...Our past success at population replacement, throughout all of human history, has been conditional on the discriminatory treatment of women" (Ryder, 1979, p. 366).

This relationship is, however, two-sided. It is difficult to answer even the simple question of whether women have fewer children than in the past as a consequence of their emancipation or whether they are emancipated because of fewer children. And yet the emancipation of women has often been mentioned in the past as an important cause of the decline in fertility levels, along with factors such as social mobility, rising standards of living, urbanization, the rise of individuality, the curtailment of parental power, the decline of mortality (in particular that of infants), compulsory school attendance and changes in the economic importance of children to the family.

Fertility levels decline during the past two centuries has been relatively well explained by the theory of demographic revolution. It is both a part and a consequence of the economic, social and socio-graphic changes which make up a global revolution. Changes in the position, status and roles of women are another aspect of this complex process. The period of increased birth rates lasted in the Czech regions until 1951, and in Slovakia for five years longer. This period is also marked by the start of socialist development which, with the introduction of a new social policy and population measures, influenced people's lives in many ways.

Though the Workers' Health Insurance Act had provided maternity benefits to insured women since 1888, and various financial measures designed to help mothers and families had been introduced after the First World War, the most important social policy measures were not implemented until after 1948. Family allowances for all employed persons, covering all children and increasing for every additional child until the fifth, were introduced in 1948. The National Insurance Act No. 99/1948 Sb. stipulated a uniform adjustment of all maternity benefits. Maternity leave was extended to 18 weeks, with maternity benefits to be paid for this period according to the wage or salary and the length of employment. These measures were not expected to affect the level of fertility, as this was considered satisfactory after the Second World War. However, they benefited employed women and families with children, as did the post-war rationing of goods and clothing.

There was a renewed decline in the level of fertility, accompanied by a change in the age structure of mothers, in the 1950s. In the Czech regions, the proportion of children born to mothers under the age of 30 years was 65.6 per cent in 1947, 70.0 per cent in 1950 and 83.1 per cent in 1960, while in Slovakia the proportion rose from 61.9 per cent in 1947 to 67.6 per cent in 1956 and 72.2 per cent in 1962. The reduction in the average age of mothers was no longer sufficient to compensate for the generally decreasing trend. However, in Slovakia, due to the postponement of the end of the demographic revolution, the level of fertility in 1962 was approximately the same as in the Czech regions ten years earlier.

The decrease in the birth rate from 1958 was also affected by the new abortion law which permitted induced abortion on social grounds. It can be assumed that as a result of this law the number of higher-parity births and the birth rate as a whole declined slightly, but its adoption resulted in no marked step in the overall trend towards lower birth rates during that period. This suggests that, on the one hand, illegal abortions had been available before the adoption of the law and, on the other hand, the social causality of fertility development after the demographic revolution was so complex that the existence or non-existence of such legislation was of secondary importance. In 1953, rationing was abolished and a currency reform was carried out. Although family allowances were increased simultaneously, incomes per head began to increase faster in childless households or in families with one child than in larger ones.

From 1963 to 1972, both in the CSR and the SSR, the birth rate oscillated slightly, though on different levels for the two populations. After the low point in 1960, the fertility level rose slightly in the CSR until 1964, before falling again to reach the lowest post-war gross reproduction rate (GRR)[2] of 0.09 in 1968. Fertility in the SSR wavered only in 1963 and 1964, and to a much lesser degree. After 1968, the fertility level increased again in the CSR and the GRR reached a peak of 1.20 in 1974. A similar peak in the GRR occurred in the SSR in the same year at the level of 1.27, narrowing significantly the difference between the two parts of Czechoslovakia. Such an evolution has prompted a good deal of discussion. The population measures discussed in the following section no doubt had some effect but a closer analysis also demonstrates the limits of these effects.

While the quantitative effect of the political and economic stabilization after 1968 cannot be measured, it probably played a very significant role in the increase in fertility levels. In large part, however, the upward trend seems to have been due to a change in the timing of birth (i.e. births delayed from an earlier period or those originally planned for the future). Such an evaluation is based on an analysis of the population climate, on the birth order of children born, and on generational fertility trends.

Measures for Population Policy

The downward trend in fertility levels at the end of the demographic revolution and in the following decades gradually led to an increase in attention to population-development issues. Further measures to benefit mothers and larger families were adopted, and for the first time these measures clearly supported fertility. In 1956, maternity leave benefits were amended; leave remained at 18 weeks, but maternity benefit was made the same for manual and white-collar workers: for employees with less than two years' prior employment, 75 per cent of their wage; for those with two to five years' employment, 80 per cent; and for all other employees, 90 per cent. In addition, all women workers and employees as well as economically inactive women were to receive a birth grant of 650 koruna (Kcs) i.e. approximately 60 per cent of the average monthly wage of women at that time). Price reductions after the currency reform provided further help for families with children. Moreover, with the price reduction of 1959, children's clothes and shoes were greatly reduced; this price subsidy was abolished as economically unjustifiable only in the 1980s.

By the middle of the 1960s, population and population measures had become an important political issue. The 11th Congress of the Communist Party of Czechoslovakia, held in 1958, called for an increase in the personal spending capability of families, especially those in the lower income brackets with several children. The 12th Party Congress in 1962 dealt with this problem in greater detail. In the resolution on the main lines for development, pre-school and out-of-school care for children was stressed, as well as school meals and the further establishment of nurseries and kindergartens. The following Congress held in 1966 spoke of further support for families and working women and the supply of nurseries, kindergartens and dwellings for young couples.

Since the school year 1960-61, pupils in general educational schools up to high school level have received all textbooks and educational supplies free of charge. In 1959, family allowances were raised once more for third and subsequent children. In 1964, a differential pensionable age for women was introduced, dependent on the number of children raised. At the same time, a special compensation allowance was introduced for women transferred to lower-paid jobs during pregnancy or motherhood.

Since 1964, rent reductions have been granted in state-owned dwellings according to the number of children in a family. Act 58 of the same year introduced a significant increase in welfare during pregnancy and motherhood: maternity leave was extended to 22 weeks. For the first time, preference was given to single mothers; their paid maternity leave was extended to 26 weeks, provided that they dependent on their own earnings.

Maternity leave and cash maternity benefits were also accorded to women who took into their care another woman's child for later adoption or because of the mother's death. The Act also affords women legal claim to further leave, up to the end of the child's first year. The employer is obliged to re-employ the mother after this period has elapsed, in the same capacity and under the same financial and legal conditions as before the birth.

Also in 1964, the co-operative farmers' social security scheme was improved: family allowances and birth grants were provided under the same conditions as for wage earners. Family allowances were increased again in 1968. Maternity leave was extended from 22 to 26 weeks and in 1970 the amended Labour Code increased unpaid maternity leave until the child reaches 2 years of age. On 1 July 1970, a so-called maternity allowance came into force, amounting to Kcs500 per month, to be paid to employed mothers, with at least two children, who decide to stay at home after their paid maternity leave has elapsed in order to look after their children until the youngest child has reached 1 year of age.

The 14th Congress of the Communist Party of Czechoslovakia, held in 1971, emphasised new population policy measures designed to increase family size and to support young married couples and families with young children. From 1 November 1971, the period of the maternal allowance increased to two years after the birth of the youngest child and was made universal for all mothers, including housewives. From 1 January 1973, allowances for second, third and fourth children were increased and credits were established for young married couples to furnish their households after the birth of children.

Apart from an increase in family allowances in connection with price regulations in 1982, there have been no other major changes in population policy. Contemporary population policy, which is made up of a series of social and economic measures, was formed gradually during the first stage of socialist development. It is aimed primarily at improving the economic situation of families with children and of young people after marriage and the birth of the first child, the living conditions of employed women, etc. Attention is also given to services available for families with children, to the working conditions of women, especially mothers, and to mother-and-child welfare.

Impact of Population Policy Measures on Fertility Levels and Population Climate

The influence of the population policy measures can be seen both in the fertility levels and in changes in the population climate. The population climate may be distributed into two components: the basic component, which changes very slowly and which is related to certain social norms as to the most suitable (ideal, planned, desirable) size of the family in a given population; and the secondary component, which concerns the most suitable timing or spacing of children. The secondary component, though it does not directly affect the total number of children desired, can have an important impact on the CBR and GRR over a period, by concentrating births into one year or by postponing them to a later time.

First survey of the population climate was organized in Czechoslovakia in 1956 and several further surveys were carried out in the next 25 years. The number of desired children ranged from 2.1 to 2.4 in various years and was always considerably higher in the SSR. Apparently it was not affected by population policy measures.

It can be concluded, therefore, that these measures influenced mainly the secondary component of the population climate which was not shown by the surveys (Pavlik, 1977). The oscillating fertility levels after the demographic revolution may be illustrated by an analysis of birth intervals. Parallel to falling proportions of childless families, there is a shortening of the interval between marriage and the birth of the first child, both in the CSR and the SSR. This is partly connected with increased proportions of premarital conceptions among first children. On the other hand, the intervals between the first and second child, and the second and third child have been increasing, hence the oscillation of period rates.

Major reason for the increase in the CBR around its peak in 1974 was due primarily to first births, then to second births and much less to third births; higher parities did not significantly affect the increase. This was evident, in particular, in a fuller and perhaps even more rapid realization of the number of children planned but was not influenced by changes in the planned family size. The data were also affected by the age structure of population. But in spite of this their meaning is clear. Furthermore, the available analysis of cohort fertility has shown that generations with completed childbearing after the demographic revolution differ little in terms of completed fertility (Lesny, 1978, pp. 106-116).

PARTICIPATION OF FEMALE LABOUR FORCE

The Increase in Women's Economic Activity

The economic and social development of Czechoslovakia continued under socialist conditions after the demographic revolution. Changes in the structure of the economically active population between 1961 and 1970. In particular, notice that the share of agriculture has continued to decrease and that the economic structure of the SSR is approaching that of the CSR.

The proportion of economically active women among all women of productive age (15-54 years) is very high: it reached 76.9 per cent in the CSR and 62.7 per cent in the SSR in 1970; comparable percentages for men were 86.4 and 83.7 (Statisticke a evidencni vyadavatesltvi tiskopisu (SEVT), 1975, p. 119). In spite of the high level of economic activity among women in 1961, the level increased even further in 1970 and 1980. The largest increase was in the 25.34 year age group, when women up to the age of 30 years are still in the most intensive childbearing period or have young children. In 1980, the proportion of economically active women was high among married women, although it was slightly higher in the CSR than in the SSR. The decrease in economic activity in the 15-19 year age group was due mainly to the higher attendance of girls at secondary schools and at universities.

There is no doubt that the increase in the level of women's economic activity in Czechoslovakia during the past two decades has been very striking. Women are becoming almost as important as men in the total labour force. However, there are only two periods in women's lives when their situation is fully comparable with that of men: before the first child is born and after the youngest child leaves school. During the period when women are pregnant or looking after small children, they represent a specific kind of labour force as their economic activity in conflict with their maternal duties.

The increase in the proportion of economically active women after 1961 can be explained by two contradictory factors: the fall in the fertility level in the 1960s and the population policy measures in the 1970s aimed at overcoming the conflict between maternal duties and economic activity (women on maternity leave are considered as economically active). It is not easy to say which factor was more important. Hard evidence is difficult to obtain and various results from sample surveys can be interpreted in different ways; they depend very much on the methodology of the survey (for example, the formulation of questions, the self-censorship of respondents, not weighting the various factors which affect the respondent).

Differences between the CSR and the SSR can also be seen here. The far higher proportion of women working in industry in the

CSR explains the higher proportion of the socio-occupational group "workers" (i.e. production workers) in the CSR in comparison with the SSR. However, the gradual economic equalization between the republics is clearly shown by the similar proportion of women working in commerce, transport and communications, and by women who are "employees" (i.e., white-collar workers).

As a result of previous changes in the national economy, the age structure of these women in the SSR is considerably younger than that of the CSR. This holds for all branches of the economy, apart from agriculture and forestry where both republics are very similar. In spite of the fact that apprentices are not considered as economically active, the youngest age structure is found in industry. More than 41 per cent of women economically active in industry in the CSR and more than 52 per cent in the SSR were under the age of 30 years in 1970; the corresponding figures for agriculture and forestry were below 19 per cent for both republics.

The oldest age structure is characteristic for co-operative farmers and independent farmers. The latter group will obviously become even less important in the future; almost 46 per cent of women in this group in the CSR and 29 per cent in the SSR were aged 55 years of above (i.e. of pensionable age) in 1970, and represented only 0.33 per cent of women in the CSR and 2.44 per cent in the SSR. The age distribution of economically active women depends largely on the age distribution of the whole population; however, certain features already noted can be confirmed. The proportion of working women is often lower in the age group with the highest fertility, and when children are very small, than before and after, and this decline occurs more among workers than among employees and other groups. The small size of these differences suggests a rather quick return to work if the mother does not return immediately after maternity leave.

As can be expected, the branches of the economy where the proportion of women is highest fall within the sphere of non-material activities—mainly in social care, health services and education, followed by commerce. The lowest share of women is in construction and in transport and communications. The differences between the CSR and SSR are rather small.

Czechoslovakia is one of the few countries in which population policy measures have been extensive. This might explain why the level of economic activity during the whole productive life of women is so high and is still rising. Although economic activity has always been high among unmarried increase among married women . The increased proportion of women in the labour force has been a decisive factor in the increase in the total labour force in Czechoslovakia in the past decade.

Women's Attitudes Towards Labour Force Participation

The attitudes of women towards their economic activity can be characterised either objectively by their behaviour or by the opinions of women themselves. The most significant objective characteristic is the high economic activity rate and the relatively quick return to work after maternity leave. According to a survey carried out on, 6,176 women in 1962 (Srb, 1967, pp. 246-247), about one-third of women returned to work immediately after maternity leave; the remainder asked for unpaid leave or ceased working. The situation changed dramatically after 1968 and 1971, when maternity leave was extended and the maternal allowance introduced. Although no similar survey has been carried out since 1962, the proportion of women staying at home after their maternity leave has been considerably reduced

In another survey, carried out in 1977 (Srb, 1979, p. 308), women were asked what was of greatest help to a working mother. In the first place they gave the understanding of their colleagues (30-49 per cent; more in the SSR than in the CSR); next was more places in creches (21-40 per cent; more in the cities and in the CSR). Other reasons were mentioned by smaller proportions of women—more time for children, a better financial situation, better services, etc. A fertility survey carried out in Czechoslovakia in 1981 (Dvorak, Srb and Ales, 1983) by and large confirmed the previous results.

Problems of families and the position of women were the main topic of a survey which was carried out in Czechoslovakia in 1979 (Bauerova and Bartova, 1980, pp. 3, 11). A standard interview was held with 2,228 inhabitants of different ages, nationalities and socio-occupational groups. The question which is of most interest here was formulated as follows: "Should a woman work outside the home or should she stay in the household and take care of the children?" The attitudes of the population towards the economic activity of women were generally positive. It is worth mentioning that women more often than men answered that women should work outside the home in any case. Older people preferred that women should stay at home. Workers and employees preferred that women should work, while the agricultural population declared the opposite. People in small cities and with the lowest educational level were the most conservative.

But how long should the woman stay at home with small children? The limit that was given most frequently was 3 years of age of the child (about 40 per cent); when the child is old enough to go to nursery school, the mother can go to work. Only about 30 per cent of the people interviewed put the limit at 6 years of age. This survey also gave an interesting picture of the use of time in the family (see further in "Women's time use and division of labour in households", below).

THE EFFECT OF EDUCATION AND NUMBER OF CHILDREN ON WOMEN'S ECONOMIC ACTIVITY

Education

A significant increase in the number of female students at all educational levels has been characteristic of socialist development. Girls now form a definite majority at universities and at many kinds of high school. An especially high proportion of girls attend gymnasia, which mainly prepare students for university-level education.

The increase in the educational level has also been significant among production workers. The proportion of skilled workers among all workers has risen considerably in recent generations, and the difference between the CSR and the SSR has practically disappeared among those below 30 years of age. Although the same process has occurred among women workers, they are still significantly behind men in terms of skills. This should always be kept in mind if comparing, for instance, the level of wages.

According to this micro-census, university-level education is still twice as frequent among men but all other levels, with the exception of apprenticeships, show a higher proportion of women. The vertical socio-occupational distribution indicates the high level of women's participation in professional activities. Men are slightly more frequent among higher professionals (leading positions, university teachers, scientific workers, physicians, etc.), but women predominate among middle-grade professionals (professionals in the central administration, teachers, nurses, etc.). Men are more frequent among technicians and skilled workers, but women predominate among other employees. Such a distribution, which will change only slowly in the future, raises the following question: what degree of equality between men and women will be reached in the future under socialist conditions given the different roles and duties of each sex in reproduction and in social life?

Number of Children and Women's Economic Activity

In studying the relationship between the level of economic activity, education and fertility, we should start with the objective finding that economically active women have fewer children than inactive women. In 1961, economically active women in Czechoslovakia had on average 1.72 children below 14 years of age, while economically inactive women had 2.03 children . However, women with one or two children below the age of 14 (were more likely to be economically active than inactive; this proportion was reversed among women with more children.

The differential fertility evident at the period of transition has been maintained until very recently. The differences have remained not only between the CSR and the SSR, but also among various socio-occupational groups. The group of employees, which consists mainly of white-collar workers, had by far the lowest fertility level in 1970, while the highest number of children was still found among women in agriculture. (In the CSR in 1961, 42.4 per cent of women among workers were economically active, 50.2 per cent among employees and 52.4 per cent among co-operative farmers; the corresponding percentages for the SSR were 35.6, 49.4 and 45.3.)

The level of economic activity, both among married and unmarried women, has increased significantly since 1961. The magnitude of this increase for married women; it rose by more than 20 percentage points among women below the age of 35 years with one or two children between 1961 and 1970, and only a little less among women with three or more children. As has been mentioned, the comparative significance of population policy measures and of the decrease in the fertility level cannot be measured from these data. Because of the fertility changes, a higher proportion women had children over 6 years of age in 1970 than in 1961, and most of these women would have gone to work anyway.

In general, the significance of the relationship between the number of dependent children and women's economic activity decreased between 1970 and 1980, particularly for women whose youngest child was under 6 years of age. In 1970, mothers of young children were more likely to be inactive the more children they had. In 1980, this trend had almost disappeared except for those with three or more children. The increase in the level of women's economic activity between 1970 and 1980 occurred in all groups but was most marked for mothers of young children. In 1980, women with children under 2 years old were benefiting from the 1970 measure which extended unpaid maternity leave until the child reaches this age. (In 1980, there were 265,763 women in the CSR and 114,027 women in the SSR on child-care leave, representing approximately 11 per cent of the active female labour force in each republic.) Since activity rates do not decline for mothers whose youngest child is 3-5 years of age, compared with those whose youngest child is 0-2 years of age, most women seem to return to work after the end of their maternity leave. It should be noted that the data concern only the CSR, where this process was the most pronounced. Here also one of the main findings is confirmed: economically active women have somewhat fewer children on average than inactive women, taking into account education and marital status. Women with the highest educational level have fewer children than other women, and non-married women (mostly divorced) also have fewer children than married women; however, the proportion of single women plays a particular role here.

WOMEN'S TIME USE AND DIVISION OF LABOUR IN HOUSEHOLDS

Such factors as economic activity, socio-occupational group, education, fertility level, etc., are objective conditions of social development which are inter-related. Many more factors may be defined, but they are less often documented statistically; in other words, only soft data on them is available. Such data include women's attitudes towards their participation in the labour force, already mentioned above, and women's time use and the division of labour in households.

With the increasing level of female economic activity, the situation of women in households has not changed substantially in spite of the fact that after the demographic revolution the number of children decreased, usually to one or two. Even under socialist development, many traditional features of the division of labour between men and women in families still persisted. As early as 1959-60, a survey was carried out which aimed to describe the daily routine of women in one factory (Srb, 1967, pp. 232-233). The average daily work of a woman in the household (i.e., not at the factory) was very time-consuming (5-5.5 hours, including 1 hour for shopping and 2-3 hours for the preparation of meals; the rest was devoted to other work such as washing, sewing and looking after the children).

The results of this survey did not answer the question of whether women had enough time to cope with all their duties. The rest time of women was dependent on the number of children. Women without children rested 7.2 hours on average, with one child 6.6 hours and with two or more children 6.2 hours. The greater the time spent on caring for the children, the less the woman rested. These results are rather striking, but it should be kept in mind that one factory is not a very representative example.

Another, survey was carried out in 1960; it covered 5,964 people from the whole of Czechoslovakia, 2,918 of whom were men and 3,046 women (Srb, 1967, pp. 238-241). The difference in time use was far greater between men and women than between various socio-occupational groups. In particular, work in the household amounted to only a little less time than work outside the home (with the exception of women staying at home). Economically active women had a second shift at home and therefore had significantly less free time and rest time than men.

Twenty years later, a similar survey showed comparable results. Differences can be explained mainly by the division of time use into working days and days off in the latter survey. In addition, a more detailed classification of activities was used. The division of labour between men and women was much more pronounced than among men, women or various socio-occupational groups. The differences among workers, employees and members of the uniform agricultural co-operatives (UAC) were very small. As might be expected, women staying at home had the most different system of time use. However, they had almost as little free time as women workers and employees and they had even fewer days off. Apart from essential personal needs, they devoted a considerable amount of time to cooking, cleaning, sewing, shopping and caring for the children. The time they devoted to themselves was less than in all other groups.

It is interesting that the amount of household did not depend greatly on the number of dependent children (this amount rose only among women staying at home and among employees). Time spent in care of children did not depend on their number either. Some results were rather surprising and suggest a certain heterogeneity in the sample. Why do workers with three children have more free time than workers with one or two children? Why do workers and employees with five or more children devote less time to their care than all other women? Do these women perhaps belong to the gypsy (Romany) population or do older children help care for younger ones in these families? However, the main results correspond quite closely with the results of the previous survey.

A recent survey (Bauerova and Bartova, 1980, pp. 3, 11) also confirmed that the greater part of the work in the household is done by the woman; only in younger families does the man participate more in work at home. In many of these families, a grandmother provides considerable help to an economically active woman. All the persons questioned evaluated the time, and the physical and psychological demands on women related to their care of household and family, as great or very great. The women worked at home 25.5 hours a week, the men 14.5 hours; however, the amount of time for women was lower and for men higher than in the previous survey. Older people, people with lower education and those living in the country did more work at home than the others. Men considered work at home as somewhat demanding. The higher participation of men in work at home shown in this recent survey indicates the more democratic character of the family, and it is usually related to other attitudes and ideas. The persons questioned were more likely to think that the care of children should be divided equally between the man and the woman and that both partners should participate equally in family decisions. Only 7 per cent of men did not participate in work at home at all.

TABLE 1

Reasons Why Women Work by Number of Children in Czechoslovakia, 1961 (Percentage)

Reason for work	*No. of children*				
	1	*2*	*3*	*4*	*5 or more*
Financial reasons	79.1	81.6	85.6	89.0	90.4
Importance of the work for society	23.2	24.0	23.9	22.9	20.7
Woman wants to be independent	36.1	26.3	16.5	18.0	9.1
Other reasons	4.9	4.6	5.1	4.9	4.8
(More than one reason was accepted.)					

Source: Srb, 1967, p. 243.

This recent survey showed one interesting feature which should not be overlooked. With the increased participation of men in home activities, the participation of children seems to be decreasing; it is higher in traditional families than in modern ones where the father shares the family duties. This could have negative consequences in the future when a new generation starts to build its own families.

Standard of Living of Families with Children

Standard of living and especially its material components are closely related to other social factors. In one survey carried out in 1961 (Srb, 1967, pp. 242-245), 7,955 women were asked why they worked. Such a conclusion can be made in spite of the significant increase in the standard of living in Czechoslovakia since the Second World War. According to selected indicators of increase in the standard of living, real wages rose from 100 to 255.8 between 1937 and 1980. Other indicators also show a considerable increase. National income per head rose more than 5 times between 1948 and 1980, while the yearly income per person rose 3.6 times between 1953 and 1980. The number of children in nursery schools and in creches also rose very markedly, as did the number of cars and other consumer goods.

The differences in standard of living among various socio-occupational groups were very small, and they are still gradually decreasing.

7

Work Participation of Women

Defined in conventional terms, women make up one third of the labour force. When women, engaged in the collection of fuel and fodder, or in dairy, poultry or kitchen garden production for the family, are added, the female labour force participation rate increases to 51% from 39% (only 13% lesser than the male participation rate of 64%).

This is further elaborated in the Document of the World Bank is follows:

> "Conventional definitions of economic activity would suggest that most Indian women are "housewives" but as the definitions and methods of measurement become more precise this picture comes into better focus. According to the 1981 Census, only about 20% of the women in India were in the labour force; when the broader definitions of work and the more intensive survey methods of the National Sample Survey (NSS) are used, this percentage increases to around 39%. Yet even this figure is acknowledge to miss a significant portion of women's gainful economic activity in the subsistence sector."

'Work' Defined

The different definitions of 'work' become relevant for quantifying employment or unemployment.

Census Definition

The Census of India recognises production for own consumption in cultivation as economic activity. The term cultivation in the Census, covers only growing of certain crops such as cereals, millets, sugarcane etc. Growing of plantation crops, vegetables, flowers and other crops are not included under cultivation. Growing of such crops if done, exclusively for home consumption, is not considered as economic activity in the Census.

Processing of primary commodities for own consumption and own account production of fixed assets are also excluded from the purview of economic activity in the Census. In other worlds, with the exception of cultivation, the Census does not include the *non-market economic activities* as work. Consequently persons working for the household in non-market activities would not be 'workers'.

NSSO Definition

The NSSO has defined 'work' or 'gainful activity' as the activity pursued for pay, profit or family gain or in other words, the activity which adds value to the "rational product." Normally, it is an activity which results in production of goods and services for exchange. However, all activities in the agricultural sector (Division '0' of the NIC) in which a part or whole of the agricultural production is used for own consumption and does not go for sale are also considered as gainful. In short, work is defined as any market activity and any non-market activity relating to the agricultural sector.

Both census and NSSO do not include attending to household chores as work or gainful activity.

The NSSO, therefore, introduced a new, additional code (code 93) in its occupational classifications for the 32nd round (1977/78). This new code allowed the survey respondent to distinguish between the performance of conventional 'domestic activities" (code 92) and domestic activities and also free collection of goods (vegetables, roots, firewood, fish, cowdung, cattle feed etc.), maintenance of kitchen gardens, orchards, etc., work in poultry or dairy, sewing, tailoring, weaving, etc., for household use, water collection and tutoring of children" (code 93)." The results are shown in Table 1.

TABLE 1

Work Participation Rate, 1983/84 (Conventional and Expanded Concepts)

Labour Force Concept	*Rural*		*Urban*	
	Male	*Female*	*Male*	*Female*
Conventional	63.22	38.74	57.71	17.31
Expanded/a	63.83	50.97	57.88	25.06

/a: Includes persons engaged in "Code 93" activities.

Source: Kalpagam, *Women in the Labour Force: An Analysis of NSS Data*, 1998.

This document has further established that it is necessary to goby the various micro-level studies that have captured women's work to find where the women work. A major part of the work is unpaid domestic work and is, therefore, considered as non-labour force activity-particularly domestic work. If domestic work is included in the concept of work participation, 55% of the female population above age 5 would get included.

Measurement of 'Work' in Censuses and Other Surveys

Data on the economic activity of the people collected upto the 1951 census was based on 'income' and 'dependency' concepts. From the *1961 census* onwards, the concept of work measured in terms of time or the labour force concept has been followed. This is in accordance with the recommendations of International Labour Office (ILO) and is generally followed in most of the countries. The classification of population as 'workers' and 'non-workers' based on the concept of work was introduced in the 1961 census.

In the *1971 census* every person was asked what his 'main activity' was i.e. how he or she engaged himself mostly. On the basis of this question, the population was divided into two broad streams of main activity as *'workers'* and *'non-workers'*. The reference period adopted was one week prior to the date of enumeration in the case of regular work in trade. A person was a main worker. If he had participated in any such regular work on any one of the days during this reference period and this had been treated as his main activity.

In the case of seasonal workers, a person's main activity was ascertained with reference to such work in the last one year, even if the person was not economically active in the week prior to the enumeration.

With these changes in the concepts, the 1971 census registered a sharp decline in the work participation rate (WPR) defined as the percentage of workers among the total population, as compared to the 1961 census. In the *1981 census,* the economic questions were formulated so as to first divided the population into: (i) workers, those who had worked any time at all during the year preceding the census; and, (ii) non-workers those who had not worked at all during the year.

Having classified the population into these broad groups, an attempt was made to sub-divide those who had worked anytime into two groups. (i) 'Main workers' i.e. those who had worked in some economic activity for the major part of the year i.e. for a period of six months (183 days) or more and; (ii) 'Marginal Workers' i.e. those who had worked for some time during the last year but not for the major part.

An attempt was also made to find out whether those who were non-workers or those who were marginal workers—were seeking or available for work.

Thus, a trichotomy of persons into mutually exclusive groups of *'main workers', 'marginal workers'* and *'non-workers'* was introduced in the *1981 census.* A uniform reference period of *'one year'* preceding the enumeration was adopted for recording activity status in the 1981 census, irrespective of whether the activity was 'seasonal' or 'regular'.

While formulating the economic questions in the *1991 census,* it was decided to adopt the same long reference period of 'one year' for both seasonal and regular activities besides continuing the concepts and definitions used in the 1981 census. Further it was also adopted *to incorporate the words 'including unpaid work on farm or in family enterprises' to the main question relating to the work—with a view to capture the unpaid contribution by women and children in their family farms and family enterprises.*

In order to capture women's work in the informal sector falling within the Census' definition of work, special efforts were made during the 1991 census by improving the economic questions in the household schedules and by training the enumerators for capturing the information. Wide publicity was given in the print and electronic media to sensitise the women respondent in the census enumeration. This paid of dividends in terms of increased female work participation rates.

In order to ensure that the economic activity of unpaid workers on farm or in family enterprise (women and children are the predominant constituents of this workforce) is properly enumerated in the 1991 Census, the instructions to census enumerators were expanded and emphasis was laid on the need to ask 'probing questions' regarding the work done at any time at all last year or any of the seasons in the reference period especially in the case of women. The concepts adopted in the 1991 census are described below to facilitate ready reference.

> *Work* is defined as 'participation in any economically productive activity. Such participation may be physical or mental in nature. Work involves not only actual work but also effective supervision and direction of work. It also includes unpaid work on farm or in family enterprise.
>
> *Reference Period* In all the questions except Question 16B, the reference period is one year preceding the date of enumeration. For Question 16B, the reference period is any time before the date of enumeration.
>
> *Main Workers* are those who had worked for the major part of the year are termed as main workers. By major part of the year is meant 6 months (183 days) or more.
>
> *Marginal Workers* are those who had not worked for the major part of the year, i.e., those who had worked for less

than six months (183 days) in the year are termed as marginal workers.

Comparison with ILO's Concept

According to Resolution No. 1 of the 13th International Conference of Labour Statisticians 1982, the 'economically active population comprises persons of either sex, who furnish the supply of labour for the production of economic goods and services as defined by the United Nations systems of national accounts and balances, during a specified time reference period. According to these systems, production of economic goods and services includes all production and processing of primary products whether of the market, for barter or for own consumption, the production of all other goods and services for the market and, in the case of households which produce such goods and services of the market, the corresponding production for own consumption.

Thus according to this definition, economic activities can be market activities or non-market activities. Market activities are those in which one produces goods or services for pay or for profit. The non-market economic activities are:

(i) Production of primary commodities for own consumption.
(ii) Processing of primary commodities for own consumption.
(iii) Own account production of fixed assets.

The Census of India recognises production for own consumption in cultivation as economic activity. The term *Cultivation* in the Census, covers only growing of certain crops such as cereals, millets, sugar cane etc. Growing of plantation crops, vegetables, flowers and other crops are not included under cultivation. Growing of such crops if done, exclusively for home consumption, is not considered as economic activity in the Census. Processing of primary commodities for own consumption and own account production of fixed assets are also excluded from the purview of economic activity in the Census. In other words, with the exception of cultivation, the census does not include the non-market economic activities as work.

Comparison with the Concept of "Work" Adopted by NSSO

The NSSO has defined 'work' or 'gainful activity' as the activity pursued for pay, profit or family gain or in other works, the activity which adds value to the 'national products. Normally it is an activity which results in production of goods and services for exchange. However, all activities in the 'agricultural sector' (Section 0 of the NIC) in which a part or whole of the agricultural production is used for own consumption and does not go for sale are also considered as gainful. In short, work is defined as any market activity and any non-market activity relating to the agricultural sector.

As in the Census, attending to household chores does not constitute work or gainful activity in the NSSO. Further, both in the Census and in the NSS, beggars, prostitutes etc. are not considered as workers even though they may have some earnings. The NSSO have adopted three differenι approach to measure employment and unemployment. The three approaches are:

(i) usual status approach with a reference period of 365 days preceding the date of survey.

(ii) current weekly status approach with a reference period of seven days preceding the date of survey.

(iii) current daily status approach with each day of the seven days preceding date of survey as the reference period. Strictly speaking, this approach attempts classification of person days and not persons.

Of the above approaches, the measurement of employment and unemployment based on the usual status approach is the one that can be broadly compared with the Census. The usual status approach has a reference period of one year. In this approach, the activity on which a person had spent relatively longer time of the preceding 365 days prior to the date of survey is considered to be the principal status of the person. Accordingly, a person's principal usual status is considered as working or employed, if he or she was engaged during the reference period of 365 days, in any one or more of the work activities. A person is considered as 'seeking or available for work' or 'unemployed', if he or she was not working but was either seeking or was available for work for a relatively longer period of the specified reference period. A person is considered as 'not in labour force,' if he or she was engaged for a relatively longer period in any one of the non-gainful activities. Within the two broad activities, 'working' and 'not in labour force,' the detailed activity category is determined on the basis of time spent criterion. A person categorised as 'worker' on the basis of his or her principal status is referred to as 'principal status worker'. A 'non-worker', who pursued some gainful activity in a subsidiary capacity is referred to as 'subsidiary status worker'. Principal status workers and subsidiary status workers together constitute 'all workers' according to the usual status classification of the NSSO.

As will be apparent from the foregoing description of the classification of workers by the NSSO according to the usual status approach, there is a subtle but important difference in the concept of 'work' adopted by the Census and NSSO, particularly in the case of non-market activities and also in the minimum period in the year for which a person should work to be labeled as employed. In view of the differences it is not proposed to compare the results of the NSSO's 43rd round with the provisional results of the 1991 census in this paper. When the final figures regarding persons seeking/available for work based on the 1991 census tabulation are brought out, a comparison of the labour force as per the 1991 Census and the NSS data could be attempted.

Estimates of Value Added to GDP if Women's Unpaid House-work were Included

The *World's Women—Trends and Statistics,* 1970-90—quotes the estimated value of the unpaid house work in India as 33 per cent of GDP in 1970. It also records 35 per cent in Pakistan in 1975; 11 per cent in Philippines in 1982; 23 per cent in Canada; 60 in Denmark; 81 in Finland in 1979; and 24 per cent in USA in 1980. The Indian estimate of 33 per cent made by Mukherjee, in his study on "Contribution to and use of social Product by Women" (1988) which appeared in ILO's Report on "Economic Evaluations of Unpaid

Household Work: Africa, Asia, Latin America and Oceania—Women, Work and Development-14 (1989)". The method followed by Mukherjee to estimate the value of house-wise' services, is as follows:

— No. of House Wives: 90 million (1981 census)
(multiplied by)

— Average Annual Contribution per worker to NDP: (Computation of CSO India, 1981)

(a) NDP per worker in agriculture	:	Rs. 1282
(b) NDP per worker in overall national	:	Rs. 1884

To conclude, unpaid work down by women at home and on the farm could push up net Domestic Product by 49% and only on the farm by 33%. Surely this is a very substantial value of women's work.

8

Women Labour Pattern

The majority of the women had followed in their employment careers a pattern which has been well documented by sociologists and recognized by policy makers as the conventional one for married women. Broadly, it consists of entry into the labour force as a full-time employee on leaving school or college, and continuing this formal participation in economic life through the period of courtship and marriage, leaving the labour force only when the birth of the first child is expected. There then follows a shorter or longer spell devoted exclusively to household responsibilities, and above all to child rearing which is followed by a return to participation in the formal labour market, sometimes as a full-time, but very frequently as a part-time employee. A significant minority of the women in the study (25 per cent) broke with this more conventional pattern: their employment careers are discussed in detail later in this chapter. The fact that most followed the 'dominant' pattern described above should not mislead us into thinking there is nothing to be said about them, however, and in the section which follows we present sociologically significant information about their employment careers.

THE DOMINANT PATTERN OF WOMEN'S EMPLOYMENT CAREERS

The First Phase: Employment Patterns before Birth of First child

Most of the forty-eight women in this group left school at an early opportunity with no formal qualifications and immediately entered employment, although a few passed some examinations or went on to some form of higher education (Tables 1, 2, 3, and 4). A quarter of those who entered the labour force on leaving school stayed in their first job until they left employment several years later when expecting their first child. Only two of these had any educational qualifications, and all but one gave up her job when expecting her first child. (In most cases this first pregnancy was unplanned.)

How did they feel about their fist jobs? Most claimed to have enjoyed them, although with the benefit of hindsight, some respondents were able to recognize the limitations of their jobs:

> *Heather (on clerical work):* 'I enjoyed it while I was there...looking back on it...it was completely unproductive with no room for initiative or anything like that.'

The majority had received some form of training in these initial jobs, with the exception of two factory workers (who had less positive memories of their jobs) and one of the clerical workers.

TABLE 1

Age of School Leaving—Dominant Pattern

School leaving	*Number*
Left at 15	28
Left at 16	14
Stayed beyond 16	6
All	48

TABLE 2

Destination on Leaving school—Dominant Pattern

Destination	*Number*
Employment	40
Secretarial college	6
Teacher training college	1
University	1
All	48

Three-quarters of the direct entrants to employment, however, changed their jobs at least once before leaving the labour market to raise children. Table 5 indicates the reasons given by these thirty women for their job changes. I have categorised the reasons given for changing or leaving jobs as follows: *instrumental* (for better pay and/or benefits), *family* (in order to fulfil obligations to parents or husbands, or to care for dependent children), *dissatisfaction* (because dissatisfied with working conditions, treatment at work or nature of duties), *travel* (to obtain more conveniently situated work), *social* (because dissatisfied with social contacts at work), *sexual harassment* (to escape unwanted sexual attentions at work), *redundancy, education* (to obtain further education or training), and *health* (of the woman concerned).

TABLE 3

Formal Qualifications Before Entering Employment—Dominant Pattern

*Level of qualifications**	*Number*
No qualifications	31
Secretarial qualifications only	3
CSE grades only	1
One or more GCE 'O' level pass	10
One or more gce 'A' level pass	3
All	48

* Highest qualification obtained.

For many (seventeen of the thirty), changing their job had also involved changing their occupation. The case of Caroline, who began a hairdressing apprenticeship on leaving school, but was unhappy in her job and left, before completing her training, to become a sales assistant, illustrates this kind of job change. Those who changed jobs were mostly motivated by instrumental and family reasons, but other reasons were also important, as can be seen in Table 6 and 7 overleaf.

TABLE 4

First Occupations of direct Entrants to the Labour Force-Dominant Pattern

Occupation	*Number*
Clerical workers	14
Sales workers	10
Factory operatives	6
Hairdressing apprentices	3
Miscellaneous*	7
All occupations	40

* Miscellaneous = telephonist, waitress, children's nurse, dressmaker, window-dresser.

TABLE 5

Reasons for Job Changes*—All Direct entrants to The Labour Force

Reason for change	*Number of changes*	*Number of respondents*
1	*2*	*3*
Instrumental	21	13
Family	18	14
Dissatisfaction	8	7
Travel	7	7
Dismissal	6	2
Social	5	4
Sexual harassment	3	3
Redundancy	3	3
Don't know/miscellaneous	5	5
Total	*76*	*30*

* Taking the 'main' reason given; obviously changing jobs may be the result of a variety of complex casual factors.

As already suggested, eight of the forty-eight women did not enter the labour force directly on leaving school, but engaged in some form of further education. Did their experience differ in any

other important ways from the rest? The most striking differ in any
other important ways from the rest? The most striking difference is that none of these eight women moved from one type of work to another during their first phase of participation in the labour force. All but one, however, changed her job at least once over this period, during which time the eight women had between them a total of twenty-three jobs. The six who went to secretarial college all found employment in clerical and secretarial jobs, and Jenny, who went to teacher training college, worked as a teacher. Frances, who went to university, dropped out at the end of her first year, partly because she failed her examinations, and partly because she had married. Her two spells of employment following this, and prior to the birth of her first child, were both in sales jobs. Another important difference between this group and the other women who had changed their employment during the first employment phase, is that *family* reasons were overwhelmingly the ones given for their job changes (see Table 8). These related primarily to marriage and husbands' job changes, but parents' job changes and health also played a part. Instrumental reasons, the most important explanation of job changes

TABLE 6

Reasons for Job Changes—Direct Entrants to the Labour Force who had more than One Occupation

Reason for change	*Number of changes*	*Number of respondents*
Family	12	10
Instrumental	11	8
Dismissal	6	2
Dissatisfaction	5	4
Travel	4	4
Redundancy	2	2
Social	1	1
Sexual harassment	1	1
Education	1	1
Health	1	1
Don't know	1	1
Total	**45**	**17**

for the other thirty women, played a very significant part in shaping the early employment patterns of those who had gone on to further or higher education.

TABLE 7

Reasons for Job Changes, by Type of Work—Direct Entrants to the Labour Force who had Only One Occupation

	Number of Changes				
Reason for change	*Clerical workers*	*Sales workers*	*Factory workers*	*Number of all*	*Respondents*
Instrumental	7	3	0	10	5
Family	2	3	1	6	4
Social	3	1	0	4	3
Dissatisfaction	2	1	0	3	3
Travel	3	0	0	3	3
Sexual harassment	0	1	1	2	2
Redundancy	1	0	0	1	1
Don't know/ Miscellaneous	1	0	1	2	2
Total	**19**	**9**	**3**	**31**	**13**

TABLE 8

Reasons for Job Changes—Women who Engaged in Further or Higher Education

Reason for change	*Number of change*	*Number of respondents*
Dissatisfaction	2	2
Social	2	2
Redundancy	1	1
Instrumental	1	1
Total	**15**	**7**

The detailed information given above (Table 5, 6, 7 and 8) is summarised below in Table 9, which indicates the relative importance of the various reasons for changing jobs given by all those in the 'dominant' group who had two or more jobs during this first phase of their employment careers.

TABLE 9

Reasons for Job Changes—All Those Who had More Than One Job

Reason for change	*Number of changes*	*Number of respondents*
Family	30	21
Instrumental	22	14
Dissatisfaction	10	9
Travel	7	7
Social	7	6
Dismissal	6	2
Redundancy	4	4
Sexual harassment	3	3
Don't know/miscellaneous	5	5
Total	**94**	**37**

Leaving the Labour Market to Raise Children

If the process by which women leave the labour market in order to raise children is to be understood, it is important to know to what extent, if at all, their departure from paid employment has been a consciously planned event. Women in the study were therefore asked to disclose whether the birth of their first child had been 'planned' or not. Twenty-three of the women in this group said their pregnancies had been planned, while twenty said they had been 'unplanned'. (The five women who did not give this information, or who claimed to have left the matter to 'chance' are not discussed in this section.)

All but four of those who had planned their pregnancies had conceived their first child at roughly the time they desired (The remainder all had some years to wait). On average, they had been in the labour force for about seven and a half years when they left to have their first baby. The plans which these women had made (often jointly with their husbands) frequently took into account such factors as a desire to have children whilst they were still relatively young, and a recognition that they were 'settled' as a couple.

> *Christine:* 'We had decided about then—we had our own house as soon as we got married, and we gradually sort of spent the four years...getting it all together...and we had decided that the time had come to start a family.

Some of the women had mixed feelings about giving up their jobs to start a family, recognizing the passing of a relatively carefree phase of their lives, whilst others had looked forward to motherhood without reservations.

> *Tessa:* 'I was really pleased—I couldn't wait to leave work. I think it was—at that particular time—it was really what I wanted. I wanted the home and the family and I wasn't interested in going out to work or earning a living or anything.'

> *Elizabeth:* 'I was a little bit reluctant to leave [my employers], but, you know, it was just one of those things, I mean I wanted a family just as well, so I had to make the choice.'

Only Carol disclosed that at the time having a baby was more her husband's wish than her own.

> *Carol:* 'We got to the stage that I was doing supervision and my husband could see the point that if I didn't soon leave, I wouldn't want to leave at all. There were people [at work] that were saying "You could go a long way...there's a lot you could do.... 'And he could see the point that I wouldn't want to leave—I would turn into a career person. He said, "I think we ought to start a family."'

Whilst their pregnancies and withdrawal from the labour force were thus in some sense 'planned', the idea of also planning for a return to employment had clearly not occurred to most of them.

> *Teresa:* 'I didn't [think about it] at that time, no...I suppose I thought when my children were off hands I would go out to work.... But I didn't even think of it then.

Several had thought of returning to employment when their children started school or were old enough to look after themselves, and one or two seven said that they had definitely intended to seek a job at this stage. However, none had made any plans about how she would organize this. Nevertheless, the average length of time spent out of the labour force before the first return to paid work was just under three years, and almost a third had less than eighteen months out of employment.

There were four women whose first child was 'planned' but who had to wait a number of years before conceiving. By the time these women left the labour force to raise children, they had been members of it for, on average, almost eleven years. All had been very happy when, after what was often a rather distressing period in their lives, they finally became pregnant. Although one began doing seasonal farm work when her child was only a few months old, the other three all had a much longer break of between four and a half and six and a half years out of the labour force.

Twenty of the women in this group had a first child as the result of an unplanned pregnancy. The average age of these respondents on the birth of their first child was just under 20 years, and the average length of time spent as members of the labour force before the child was born was just over four years. Five of the women in this group disclosed that they had become pregnant before marrying, and of these, two did not marry until after the child was born.

Despite the fact that their pregnancies had been unplanned, the women in this group expressed views about having a first child and giving up their jobs which were very similar to those expressed by the women whose first pregnancies had been planned. Many accepted their situation quite happily, and most either expected to be out of the labour force for some years, or had no thought about any future return to work.

> *BARBARA:* 'Well, I'd always wanted children.... I thought perhaps that eventually I might get another job, but I didn't intend to work when the children were small. It was a struggle,

> butt didn't intend to anyway...it was...just a matter of drifting along.'
>
> *Pru:* 'No, I didn't...it was purely accidental—I was quite shocked—it always happened to somebody else...quite honestly, I was on cloud nine—I thought I would never have to go to work again in my life.'

The main difference between the women with unplanned pregnancies, and the women who had planned their first child was that a minority (four of the twenty) had experienced very negative feelings about their situation. In some cases the feelings stemmed from a sense of being unprepared to start on family life, in others from a reluctance to give up a job.

> *Margaret:* 'I felt terrible. I felt I was too young to have a child really. I liked my job so much and I wasn't really very happy about having a baby at all.'
>
> *Jenny:* 'Not very happy—we were living in a rented flat, and it wasn't big enough to 'bring up a baby in...we wanted to own our own house, it came a bit soon.... We didn't know what we were going to do...eventually, it got round that we could afford to buy a house, and it just arose, really, that I was going to go back to work' (Jenny did not leave the labour force until the birth of her second child.)

Return to the Labour Force

By definition, the women whose employment careers had followed the 'dominant' pattern all moved from the first employment phase (described above) into a period outside the paid labour force. During the latter period, they were almost exclusively engaged in domestic labour, principally the bearing and rearing of young children. In considering their subsequent return to the labour force, as mothers seeking employment, it becomes necessary to distinguish between three groups, each of which has a different set of experiences.

The first consists of women who have only one child. Their return to paid employment is a relatively straightforward affair often a once-and-for-all event. The return to paid work came sooner than many had originally anticipated, in most cases within three years. The initial return was usually prompted by either financial pressures or a perceived need for social contacts, or a combination of both.

For many of these women, some unanticipated aspect of their lives as young, mothers prompted an early return. Gail was separated from her husband when her child was about a year old, and decided then to return to full-time employment.

> *Gail:* 'I decided that if I ever wanted to be as independent... I would have to go back to work and get some money together.'

Another young mother found to her surprise that she was not perfectly content with being at home all day with a small baby.

> *Shirley:* 'I don't like a lot of female company, so coffee mornings, tupperware parties—all of that—I just couldn't take, and basically that's the only thing you can do when you're at home with a baby...and nothing annoyed me more than somebody coming round and talking about how they washed their nappies, or something—it's just not me... I couldn't stand it...plus, I didn't like not being able to barn my own money.'

For others, the decision to take a paid job was prompted by both financial difficulties and a desire to escape the isolation of housework.

> *Alison:* 'Mainly it was the money—we needed the extra money—and I was bored to tears at home, although I had my daughter, it seemed I'd never, ever seen anybody, I was indoors with my daughter all day.'

One of the women, however, was prompted to return to paid work after only six months out of the labour force because of financial circumstances alone.

> *Marion:* 'The only reason I've come back out again is because (my husband's] overtime was cut... I didn't have any choice...we were on a tight budget anyway, so there was really no question—either he had to get another job, or I did. And it seemed better that I should, because he already works six days, and for tax reasons as well...it was better that I did.'

About a third of these women took temporary or seasonal jobs at first, but once the return to permanent jobs had been made, job changes tended to be prompted by a variety of factors: instrumental family, redundancy, personal health, and dissatisfaction. Wendy's account provides several illustrations of why women may change their jobs. She explained her move in 1971 from a part-time job as a shop assistant, to a full-time one in the school meals service.

> *Wendy:* 'Well, we'd had a lot done to the house, and we'd used up any money we'd had, and really more than 2 a week was needed then—so someone said, "Try school meals", and at that time they were very short of staff and they were glad of anybody.'

Wendy stayed in the school meals service for eight years, accepting promotion to assistant cook during this time. Why did she eventually leave to become a full-time sales assistant?

> *Wendy:* 'Well, school meals is really going down...and down...and down. When I first went in, the meals were—they had the best of everything and skimp.... I know school meals have always had a bad name, but it's not a case of how the meals were cooked. I mean, a lot of care and a lot of pride was taken in the meals themselves, especially where we were...and I enjoyed it like that, it was excellent, and the money was good...but then the money didn't alter, and I mean the conditions got worse...staff left...they were not replaced, and so your conditions were worse...equipment wasn't replaced...and the pride.— I mean to them it didn't matter any more — you made do and mend...and now instant

> things are coming in...and what really made me decide to get [another] job was I was in charge, and I think we were really short of staff, and six came from...top level and walked into the kitchen, purely looking at how we were working, and not one single one spoke. They looked round the kitchen, noses in the air, and they were just standing there, and I thought "this is it, out!"—no way do you have to work under those conditions.'

Wendy's vivid description of her progressive disillusionment with this job demonstrates her active membership of the labour force. Pride in her work, the need for her skills to be recognized, unwillingness to put up with being treated as if she were a machine rather than a person, all suggest a commitment to her job which breaks with the more conventional image of female employees as very passive members of the labour force. This attitude was by no means uncharacteristic of the majority of my respondents.

Clare's account of her employment career illustrates the commitment felt by many of my respondents to both their families and their job responsibilities. She explained why she resigned her job as a sales assistant when she was finding it necessary to have frequent time off because of her daughter's health.

> *Clare:* 'I worked from May until...December, then again (my daughter] started having trouble, and I gave my notice in and said it wasn't fair—although [the Staff Manageress] did say to me that they would be prepared for me to have time off whenever she was ill, but I didn't think it was fair to the other girls. I mean, it wasn't a long-term illness, but it used to spring up overnight and she'd be really ill for three or four days, and then be OK again.... I just didn't think it was fair to the company or to the girls I worked with to have to cover me.'

For almost all of those with one child, the kind of employment obtained after the break for childcare was of lower status and less well paid than that held beforehand. The post-childrearing phase typically included agricultural, domestic and catering, and sales employment, while the pre-childrearing phase had typically included clerical and secretarial, and sales employment.

The experience of women with larger families was different in several important respects, and these women form the second and third categories in the discussion here. The second group consists of those who took paid jobs in between the births of at least two of their children (about two-thirds of those with two or more children). For them, the 'return' to employment was not a single event, but involved a series of moves in and out of the tabour market.

The majority of them had two children, while others had three or four. For most of those with two children, there had been only a short gap (of between eighteen months and three years) between the two births. However, in a few cases the gap was longer, either because the second child was unplanned, or because there was a child from each of two marriages. For the women with three or four children, the longest gap between births was normally that preceding the last child—which in several cases represented an unexpected, and initially unwanted, addition to the family. Nearly all the women took paid employment between the births of each of their children. Most commonly this work was agricultural labour ('field-work'), often of a seasonal and casual nature, or domestic and catering work. Factory jobs, and sales and clerical employment were also quite common. Most jobs were taken on a part-time or seasonal basis, and usually the first return to employment occurred within a year.

Overwhelmingly, the motivation for taking a job at this stage was the need to supplement the family's income. At this point in their lives, most of the women were married to men in relatively poorly paid or insecure occupations—construction workers, semi-skilled manual workers, tradesmen, drivers, etc. The few husbands who were in occupations with relatively good potential earning power (police officers, technicians, and a surveyor) were all at the outset of their careers, or in the process of moving into those jobs from less secure ones, and thus not earning high wages when their children were small. Most of the women were quite frank about their reasons for taking a paid job at this time.

> *Maria:* '[My son] must have been about three or four months...and then I went out to work again...it was a situation where we bought our own home, and financially he needed support, so I went out to work...a part-time job, to help towards the home.'

> *Cheryl:* 'I had an early morning job when I used to take my eldest one with me. That was cleaning in a pub.... She was about fourteen months, we needed the money...my husband's wage was about £18 a week then (1968).'

Several women had been unsupported by a husband at this time, either because they were as yet unmarried, or because their marriages had broken down.

> *June:* 'I did a little cleaning job, which was three days a week...for about two hours, I suppose, every morning...and then from there I used to go on the strawberry fields. [My daughter was] about three, I would say, she used to come with me.... At this time I was on my own.

Some acknowledged that for them there were other motivations besides purely instrumental ones:

> *Elizabeth:* 'She was ten months [when I went back to work] money got tight, there wasn't that much to keep me occupied really, and she was a devil when she was a baby, so I was quite glad to leave her in some ways.'

For those women who had more than two children, the arrival of a third or final child sometimes disrupted what had been the mother's gradual return to full participation in the employed labour force. Dawn, for example, had only just returned to her career in hairdressing after a seven-year break, when she had to leave because of a third, unplanned, pregnancy. She has not since returned to this occupation, feeling that her skills have subsequently become 'rusty' and old-fashioned. Pat's fourth pregnancy and temporary withdrawal from paid work came just as she had established herself in a permanent part-time job as a hospital bed-maker, following a number of years when she had only been able to undertake evening or seasonal work because of her family's needs.

Thus for two-thirds of those with two or more children, raising a family had by no means meant a complete withdrawal from the employed labour force. Much of the employment discussed above will not, of course, have been included in any official statistics on employment, but it is no less real or important for that. It should, however, serve as a reminder of the need to exercise great caution in interpreting official data about women's paid employment. For these women, finding a way of supplementing the family's income, by selling some of their labour power for wages, was an important part of what they saw as their family responsibilities. Most were only too well aware that if they were not earning their families' standards of living would drop significantly and they might well sink into poverty.

The third category contains women who remained out of paid employment until they had completed their families, just over a third of those with two or more children. The majority of those in this category had been in employment for over four years when they left the labour force to raise children, and on average had spent about eight-and-a-half years out of the labour force looking after their families. As one would expect, the women with larger families tended to stay out of the labour force for longer than those with only two children.

When interviewed, all but two of the women were married and living with their first husband. In contrast to those in the second category, most of these women were married to men in white-collar occupations with relatively high earnings—technicians, managers, and administrators, for example. The fact that their husbands had been bringing home relatively good wages had obviously been important in enabling the women to stay out of the employed labour force whilst raising their young families, and in enabling them to adopt a particular ideology of family life.

> *Yvonne:* 'I believe that if you have children, then you should look after them, and I stopped at home until they went to school.'

I do not wish to suggest that economic considerations played no part in prompting these women's eventual return to employment. Indeed, for some, the need to earn an income was the decisive factor, placing them in a situation where they felt they had no choice but to get a job.

> *Tessa:* 'I didn't work at all until my second daughter was born. My first marriage had broken up actually when I was still only six months pregnant...and it was necessity rather than anything else. Social Security wasn't very much and my husband's whereabouts were unknown. I took a part-time job in a local estate agents...purely and simply because I needed the money.'

> *Sandra:* 'I (still] had two [pre-school children]...the youngest one and the one I foster... I got a bit fed up with being at home...actually it was a case of having to (get a job], because my husband was out of work at the time.'

Sandra's remark, made apparently only in passing, almost conceals the importance which male unemployment may have for prompting wives to seek work. She was not alone among my respondents in having this motivation.

Christine, on the other Wand, took paid employment outside the home for slightly different reasons.

> *Christine:* We were going through a very dodgy time, you know, marriage-wise, and I was trying to consider what to do...and I thought perhaps if I could get some sort of job, it would make me more financially independent; and help me decide what I would do.'

Others saw employment as a means of achieving a limited, but specific, material objective.

> *Yvonne:* 'I started in September because I wanted to get two bikes for Christmas for them...and I thought I'll just go out to work and earn the money to get that, and I got a job in a hotel, and I stopped there for five years.'

Several women-first began earning money again without needing to leave their homes, and in a few cases, husbands were active in providing their wives with income-generating work at home.

> *Christine:* 'I used to work sometimes for my husband('s firm) on a casual basis, doing their typing at home—he used to bring it home—and that all started when [the youngest one] was born...instead of getting a temp. in they'd send it home to me.

It would be misleading, however, to concentrate on financial motives for returning to employment to the exclusion of the other important factors. For a number of women, obtaining a job was a constructive means of escaping their social isolation at home and of defeating their sense of lost identity once their children began to grow older.

> *Teresa:* 'I felt I needed something at that time. I was really getting into a rut at home and I felt I needed to be out. The children were both at school, and I needed... I felt I needed something different, it was really getting me down, so I thought, well, I'd have to do something...and that's when we decided that we'd go for the Christmas period, it would be a break—which several friends had done.... I stayed on there two years.'

How did their first employment on returning to the labour force compare with the jobs they had held prior to having children? Of the seven who had been clerical or secretarial workers before having their children, only one obtained such work when she first took a job afterwards. The rest went into sales jobs, factory work, and other manual jobs. Two other women had jobs with specific skills in their first employment phase: Anne had been a telephonist, and Yvonne a dressmaker. Both re-entered the labour force as domestic workers.

The two other women who became domestic workers at this stage had previously been employed in sales and in factory work. Thus for most, the break from employment resulted in a deterioration of their occupational status. Two women, however, were to find higher status occupations on their return to work. Tina, who had originally been a factory worker, found an opening in nursery nursing, while Frances decided to train to 'be a teacher. She explains how she finally reached this decision:

> *Frances:* 'I [had always] said that I wanted at some date, when we were in a suitable place, and knew far enough ahead etc., that I would hopefully go back and do some form of further education, but, it's a very easy thing to put off unless you've got that extra bit of determination — and obviously [my husband's] leaving was the push I needed.'

The employment patterns of the women with two or more children are also of interest following their return to the labour force *and* the completion of their families. These patterns are best described in relation to the age of the youngest child, whether of pre-school, primary school, or secondary school age.

All but two of the nine women who still had a pre-school child when interviewed had returned to formal, regular employment, most working part—time: only two were in full—time jobs (one as a the other as a hospital domestic) and both of these women had previously done a spell of part-time work. Five of the seven women had been employed in domestic and catering work, and other employment undertaken included clerical and secretarial jobs, sales jobs, agricultural jobs, and childminding. Three of those in regular employment had been in clerical or secretarial jobs prior to having their families—however, when interviewed, only one had returned to using these skills, while the other two were engaged in domestic work.

Seven of the eight women with a youngest child at primary school were in regular, paid employment, while the eighth was a full-time student at a teacher training college. Four were working full-time, and three part-time, and all but one of the full-timers had previously been a part-time employee. Again, manual jobs had predominated in the post childbearing phase. Four of the seven were or had been engaged in domestic work, four in other manual work (in factories and warehouses), and two in agricultural work. However, when interviewed, the seven also included two sales workers, a clerical worker, and a telephonist. Like those with preschool children, many of these women had also been unable to return to their former skills, especially in office work.

About half of those with two or more children (eighteen of the thirty-five) had a youngest child at senior school. Some had children in their late teens, or older ones who had left home. When interviewed, half were employed part-time, and half full-time, and all but one of the full-timers had worked part-time at some previous stage. Their occupations were as shown in Table 10, although at an earlier stage (after completing their families) seven had done paid work of a seasonal or casual nature, and four had done some kind of home work. Of the eight who had some kind of job-specific skills prior to having their children (clerical, hairdressing, dressmaking, telephonist), four had not obtained work using these skills after completing their families, and a fifth had only done so after taking a TOPS course (Training Opportunities course, funded by the Manpower Services Commission.

TABLE 10

Occupations of Selected Respondent* at Time of Interview

Occupation	*Number part-time*	*Number full-time*
Sales	3	3 6
Domestic and catering	5	4 9
Clerical	1	2 3
All	9	9 18

* Respondents with a youngest child at senior school.

Although a few of the women with two or more children were unsure of their future plans, the vast majority of them fell into one or other of two categories: those who expected to stay in the job they were doing when interviewed until retirement, and who did not intend to seek or accept any promotion or greater responsibility; and those who intended to remain in paid work until retirement, but who also planned to seek promotion, further training, or simply a better job.

How did the women who planned no changes in their employment careers understand their future? Just over half were employed part-time, the rest full-time. A third were in jobs where they had some responsibility, a supervisory role, or recognized seniority over more junior colleagues, while the remainder were in the basic grade in their various occupations—primarily hospital domestics and sales assistants. Many felt that they were happy in their current job, and desired no further changes. Helen for example, a frill-time domestic supervisor in an NHS hospital, was quite clear that she did not want any further promotion. She enjoyed the close contact with staff which her job entailed and knew that any higher grade job would not have this characteristic. She expected to stay in her job 'until I retire'—a further seventeen years if she retired at 60. Nancy, also a domestic supervisor, had similar plans, but emphasised her lack of ambition in relation to her job.

> *Nancy:* '[Promotion] just sort of fell into my lap ... I've never been ambitious, to be quite honest with you, I mean, all I've lived for is my home and my children, but when you are here full-time, it's a long day, so you think...your opportunities are there, and I'm gonna take them m not one to keep changing my job—in my last job I was there eight years, I was made redundant, otherwise I expect I'd still be there I can't see me not working, quite frankly... I can't see that I'll ever be financially well enough [off]...to pack up work 'altogether.'

Teresa, a part-time deputy supervisor in a large retail store, also emphasised that her employment career had to fit into her family life.

> *Teresa:* 'I suppose really you can't be (promoted any further) because I am only a part-timer.... I think as I am now it suits my family commitments very well... I wouldn't want full-

> time work ... I'd be quite happy to continue as I am until, I suppose, retirement age.... I think if you have good working conditions, you adapt to them...that would be my only thing, if problems like that arose.'

Those who had basic grade jobs, and who were happy to stay in them, made similar comments.

> *Dawn:* 'I'm happy as I am...but, if they come and ask [if I'd like promotion]... I expect I'd say yes, I'd have a go at it.... I'd stay here, I should think [till retirement]—as I feel now, anyway.' (Dawn was a part-time sales assistant when interviewed.)

Mary would have been glad to have her experience as a part-time clerical assistant recognized by her employers, but was not ambitious in any other respects.

> *Mary:* 'Because I'm part-time, my grades don't go up—I mean, I'm doing a more responsible job within the department, than when I came—but my grades don't go up.... I know it's perhaps silly, but it would be nice for them to say "You've done well, you're now a clerk grade whatever".... I can't really see myself changing...basically, I feel that while the children are at home, you need extra money...but then, the way the situation is now, I think perhaps you'll continue to need extra money... I'll be fully happy to stay where I am.

Another respondent; a part-time domestic, put it quite simply.

> *Olive:* 'I suppose [I'll stay] until I retire...yes, I shall be working until then, yes. I don't think I'd like promotion or anything m quite happy as I am.'

All but two of the women who had no plans to alter their jobs were married women, living with their husbands. The exceptions were Maria, divorced and living with her parents and one of her two small children, and Pru, who lived with her two late-teenage sons and her 'boyfriend'. Maria was not too certain about her future:

> *Maria:* 'I should think [I'll stay] until he goes to school—I can't see myself getting another job and changing it before then...and of course if anything comes of this supervisor [training] thing, then I would stay here and do it.'

Pru also anticipated possible changes in her personal life which might affect her employment career.

> *Pru:* 'The possibilities [for promotion] could be there, but I don't particularly want it.... I don't want any hassles.... I just want... [to stay'] as I am, because it suits home life.... If I could afford to, I'd leave because I prefer to be at home...possibly if I got married again, and finances were different, then I would probably try and leave.'

Nevertheless, many of the women wanted promotion, further training, or a better job. In other words, they were seeking further integration into the labour force. They fall into two categories: those who were already working for employers who made training opportunities readily available, and in jobs where there was an established career structure; and those, mostly in domestic and catering jobs, who recognized that their current jobs held little prospect of improved working conditions or employment opportunities, and who sought a future change of occupation as a result. Tessa, a full-time telephonist, was amongst those to whom job advancement was already available.

> *Tessa:* 'I'm waiting for a vacancy to arise...because I sat an exam and a Board for promotion to Clerical Officer. I mean I could stay here *ad infinitum* and just do the same job, which I'm not really prepared to do...but I could go there as a clerical officer, and Then do another exam perhaps and become an Executive Officer or a Higher Clerical Officer...really. I would like to...it's more of a challenge, and you're using a bit more of—your brainpower.... I like this job very much, but it doesn't require a lot of initiative, as long as you're polite and tactful and know your procedures, it doesn't require an awful lot more from you.'

Heather, a supervisor in a retail store, had set her sights relatively high. She had returned to full-time paid employment once her two children were both at school.

> *Heather:* 'I shall stay here till I retire...that's twenty-five years.... [After I'd been here a while] I thought I'd like to make a career of it, I'd like to go into supervision, when I then did.... I was promoted quite quickly—I intend to go on further, too.'

Maureen, a full-time personal secretary employed by a large paper-making firm, also wanted more than 'just a job', as her discussion of future plans illustrates. She felt fairly confident of obtaining more rewarding work with her current employer.

> *Maureen:* 'I wouldn't mind staying with them (until I retire)... If I can alter my job slightly—[to one that's] a bit more interesting, a bit more involvement, then I wouldn't mind staying.'

Anne, like several other women, was currently in a 'dead-end' job at the bottom of the occupational status ladder, and hoped for better employment opportunities in the future.

> *Anne:* 'I only do what I do simply for the money, really, I don't really like the work, you know.... [I'll stay] really until I can find an alternative job that I liked...it's just a matter of if a job was available.... I should think two years would be the limit I'd stay here. It would be a different type of work altogether that I would look for. I'm going to night school in September.... I'm going to take biology—I'm very interested in nursing...that's probably what I will do.'

Pat worked full-time as a hospital domestic, and like Anne, hoped to gain access to employment in nursing at some future date.

> *Pat:* 'I love working here, but I can't say I like doing what I'm doing. Because it's all mechanical, and, well, you just

> don't need a brain.... So later on I would like to change... I thought about going as a nursing assistant.'

Although plans for the future might not be achieved, many of these women nevertheless bore little resemblance to the passive members of the labour force which women are so often taken to be. Those who lacked ambition for promotion mostly anticipated participation in the labour force until their retirement, and those who had become well integrated into their employment environment frequently demonstrated considerable determination to 'make something' of their jobs. Carol's and Cheryl's comments about their attitudes to future employment were illuminating. Both lacked the kind of aggressive career ambition which characterises the 'male' stereotype, but neither was willing to accept a definition of their work as passive and non-assertive.

> *Carol:* 'I have been asked to do supervision, but up until now I've never had the confidence to do it But now I'm thinking about it, because my children are getting older and they're [shy] like me, and I want to show them that if you tell yourself you can do it, you can.... [I'll stay] probably until I retired quite like to, because they are a good firm as regards pensions. It would pay me to stay here... I'd be silly to leave really.'

> *Cheryl:* 'I always take it stage by stage... I was an assistant and knew I could do better, and I'm aiming at supervision. When I'm doing supervision I will then contemplate whether I am capable of doing better. But I never sort of say "Oh, I want to be a Departmental Manager"—I would love to, but I've got to take it in stages to see whether I am capable—just increase it gradually come back with the intention of working till I retire.'

The Impact of Marital Breakdown

Fifteen of the forty-eight women whose employment careers had followed the 'dominant pattern' had experienced marital breakdown. Of these, nine had re-married following their divorce. All but two of the fifteen had at least one child when their first marriage ended, including in eight cases a child aged 5 years or younger. What effect, if any, did the break-up of their marriages have upon their employment patterns?

For Angela and Elizabeth, neither of whom had children, the break-up of their first marriage had little effect upon their employment careers. Angela continued working full-time as a secretary, and did not change her job. Elizabeth gave up her job as an audio-typist partly because she could not cope with facing her colleagues at work, and partly because she decided to move back to her parents' home in a different town. However, she only had a short break from employment before going back to work full-time as an office temp., and subsequently taking permanent secretarial employment.

For the eight women who had at least one child aged 5 years or under when their marriage broke down, the event either increased or prompted their participation in the paid labour force. Four had not been to paid employment: of these, two took part-time jobs, and one a full-time job when their marriages ended. The fourth began full-time training to become a teacher. Of those already doing paid jobs, two changed from part-time to full-time hours (but staved with the same employer), one continued in her full-time job, and the remaining one took on additional casual and part-time work.

The remaining five women (whose youngest children were of school age when their marriages ended) had all been in paid employment, three working part-time and two full-time. All remained with their employers, and one of the part-timers went on to full-time work, as she explained.

> *Pru:* 'I got promoted to a supervisor... I did that for about two and a half years...still 5 till 8.... Then, because of finances—I got divorced—I needed more money. I had to take demotion, to go on to the forty hours.'

Paula, a clerical worker and one of the full-timers, stayed full-time, and after her divorce went through (shortly before our interview) applied for promotion to a more senior position.

The evidence of these women suggests that the impact of marital breakdown upon employment careers is fairly straightforward. Existing participation in paid employment tends to be maintained, and is frequently increased from part-time to full-time. Where women have not been engaged in paid work, the break-up of their marriage may prompt them to seek employment Whilst instrumental motives are especially compelling at such a time, and the need to earn an income may appear to be paramount, women also recognize the social importance of their jobs at this stage, when self-esteem and confidence may be at a low ebb. The 'poverty trap' into which women who have access only to low-paid employment or supplementary benefit may fall is one of which such women are well aware. But they may still choose to be at work. One woman who worked part-time explained what had happened to her.

> *Brenda:* 'It wasn't enough to keep me and two children on… I was on Social Security, and I had a few bills that I had a job to pay, and I ended up borrowing off my parents and getting deeper into debt. In fact I went up to Social Security one day, and they turned round and said, "Well, you'd be better off not working."'
>
> *S.Y.: 'How did you feel about that?'*
>
> *Brenda:* 'Oh, I couldn't have given the job up, I had to have something to keep me going I thought it was terrible…if I hadn't worked, the actual cash in hand would have been £4 less than what I was getting by working—and bus fares and other expenses were costing more than £4…. If I did extra hours at work, Social Security stopped the extra that I'd earned, so I was no better off by doing any, and I did feel a bit trapped, but there was nothing I could do to get out of it. Even if I was working full-time, I couldn't have—well, at the time, I wouldn't have left the children alone, not for too long anyway, because they were upset as well, and I think they needed me as much as I needed them at the time.'

Brenda's account, which refers to 1976, expresses many of the tensions and ambiguities affecting an unsupported lone parent. She recognizes the need for time with her children, but also knows that her job is an important source of social contacts for her, and helps her to structure what at first appears as a shattered lifestyle. She wants to support herself, by earning what she can, but is caught by a bureaucratic social security system which lacks the flexibility to accommodate her particular needs.

A Note on Redundancy and Unfair Dismissal

In discussing patterns of women's labour, it is important to note that whilst many job changes made by women are (in the broadest sense) voluntary—women resign their jobs for personal, family, or instrumental reasons—this is not invariably the case. For the women in my sample, redundancy and dismissal (including various types of what may constitute constructive—and therefore unfair—dismissal) were also features of their employment careers. Almost a third of the forty-eight women in this group had experienced redundancy. Shops or restaurants where they had been working closed down, industrial firms cut back on staff or relocated, small companies went into liquidation. Most accepted their experience of redundancy as simply a fact of an employee's life. Rarely did women mention any kind of resistance to redundancies, and where they did, actions had been unsuccessful. I do not wish to suggest that women in general do not, and have not, put up determined and effective resistance to attempts to deprive them of employment. There are, of course, numerous examples of such action, and the case of women workers at Lee Jeans in Greenock, Scotland, who occupied their factory when threatened with redundancy, provides a recent example (Ryan 1981). However, my respondents had not been involved in such struggles.

In the interviews, women were not questioned closely or routinely about sexual harassment at work—unwanted or intimidating sexual attentions in the workplace—and it is entirely possible that some women had experienced problems of this type, but did not disclose them to me. Nevertheless, three women described incidents leading to their resignation from a job which constituted clear sexual harassment. All had been in their teens at the time of the incident, two still unmarried, and one recently married. Sheila's interview illustrates the tendency for incidents of this type to go unobserved.

> *S.Y.: 'What happened to you when you left school—did you go straight into a job?'*
>
> *Sheila:* 'Yes, I worked at [the paper] Mill—my mother got me a job. The first job I had, for four months—but it didn't work out.'
>
> *S.Y.: 'What were you actually doing there?'*
>
> *Sheila:* 'Making, well, no—sorting, paper.
>
> S.Y.: 'Why did you leave?'
>
> *Sheila:* 'I left there because—you know, they kept saying, "Oh, your Mum works here", and all this... I didn't like it...you know.'
>
> *S.Y.: 'So you think it was because of that you left, rather than because of the actual work?'*
>
> *Sheila:* 'I liked the work.... It was the foreman I didn't like...where I worked...he was dirty.'
>
> *S.Y.: 'So it was the people that you didn't really get on with?'*
>
> *Sheila:* 'Well, this particular bloke. He used to touch all the young [girls]...when the young ones used to start, they used to start in the cutter house; you know—they was all like fifteen-year-old girls, and he used to—you know—be rude to them. So... I told me mother, and she more or less smacked him in the mouth, and that was one of the reasons I left, you know.'

Barbara's experience was not dissimilar.

> S.Y.: 'What happened to you when you first left school?'.
>
> *Barbara:* 'I went to work in the dispensary at [a large chemist's store]...it wasn't what I wanted to do, so I was there a matter of three or four months I suppose.... I didn't settle in the job.... I felt that everything I did was wrong because I just didn't like what I was doing.... I was shut away in a little cubicle...plus, I didn't like the manager that was there, he was a creep.... I wouldn't have found (the work) difficult if I hadn't had this creepy manager behind me, so I think he was mainly [why I left]...you didn't have a proper office, you were just standing in this cubicle thing where they did the prescriptions, and I mean he was one of these people who'd come and smack your bottom, sort of, and in those days, you didn't turn round and tell him like they would today...he was I think the main reason why I left.'

Brenda was more direct than the other two.

> *Brenda:* 'I worked as a stock control clerk in a garage...up until I was married... I quite enjoyed it.'
>
> *S.Y.: 'You said you did that until you got married?'*
>
> *Brenda:* 'Until after I got married.'
>
> *S.Y.: 'Why did you leave the job?'*
>
> *Brenda:* 'The stores manager started getting a bit fresh...(laughs)

Thus in factory, shop, and office, these women had been subjected to intolerable pressure of an overtly sexual nature, from men in more senior positions than themselves; and this resulted in their resignation. The kinds of evidence now becoming available concerning sexual harassment[2] would seem to suggest that these three women may represent the tip of the iceberg. The optimism of Barbara's view, that 'nowadays' girls would not put up with the kind of treatment she left her job to escape in the early 1960s would appear to be unjustified by the emerging facts.

Several women disclosed that their employers had offered them an impossible choice about their working hours and conditions, which in effect constituted 'unfair' dismissal. One had been taken on to work evenings as a catering assistant, but later found her employer insisting that she work weekends also. As she had a young family at the time this left her with no choice but to resign her job. Another was forced to leave her job when her firm re-located about fifteen miles away. She was told she could travel daily to the new venue if she liked, and was prepared to work longer hours, but for a woman with both a pre-school and a school-age child, an extra burden of this kind was out of the question. A third woman, working part-time as a merchandiser; was faced with the choice of doubling her hours (to 40 hours per week) or giving up her job. Since full-time hours were impossible for her because of her family commitments, she too had no option but to lose the job.

It may be that one or more of these women would have had a case for unfair dismissal under subsequent legislation. However, it seems likely that they would not have brought a case, even if legally entitled and aware of their right to do so. One of the things employed mothers seek to avoid is 'hassle'. If they are to accommodate the demands of their families and go out to paid jobs; they must organize themselves in order to avoid spending time and effort in unnecessary ways (see subsequent chapters). Most of the women I interviewed lacked the extra energy and determination which would be required to bring legal action for unfair dismissal, regardless of their chances of success.

ALTERNATIVES: WOMEN WHO HAD NOT LEFT THE LABOUR MARKET

Six of the women interviewed had not left the labour market since joining it on completing their school or college education. When interviewed, most were in their late thirties, and all were living with their (first) husbands. Since their continuous commitment to employment breaks with the more common pattern of at least a short period at home with very young children, it is worth examining their experiences in some detail.

Three had left school at 15 with no academic qualifications, two had left at 17 with four or five 'O' levels, but had not gone on to further education, whilst one had left school at 16 with several 'O' levels and 'CSEs', and had subsequently attended secretarial college for a year.

When interviewed, most had been with their current employer for a number of years: three for over twenty years, one for thirteen years, one for five years, and one for just two and a half years. All were in white-collar jobs with established employers, five in clerical occupations (ranging from clerical assistant to accounts supervisor) and the sixth in an administrative grade which was considered to be an executive position. Three had jobs which involved supervising other staff, whilst a fourth had responsibilities which included interviewing members of the public in connection with their requirements for personal financial loans.

Interestingly, none of the six women was following an employment pattern set by her own mother. None of their mothers had been in permanent jobs whilst my respondents were children, and only two of these mothers had permanent occupations outside the home after her family had grown up.

For most, there had been a delay of some years between marriage and the birth of their first child. Two had a first child within three and a half years of marriage, but for two others there was a five-year gap, and in the remaining cases the periods were seven and twelve years. These longer than usual delays between marriage and the first child's birth were significant in explaining their employment patterns.

In three cases, the respondents had planned their families so that they could continue in employment without leaving their jobs.[3] This involved not merely ensuring that the baby was born at a convenient point, but also making arrangements for the child to be cared for once it was born, and in one case, changing her job to one with less responsibility. I shall describe each of these cases in turn.

Sara was born abroad but came to England in 1966 on marriage. Her husband has been in the nursing profession throughout their marriage, and at the time of the interview held a senior position. On arrival in England, Sara did manual work for a couple of years, before obtaining a job as a clerical assistant in a public sector company in 1968. She was subsequently promoted to clerical officer. Her first child was born three and a half years after she joined the company, and she took two months maternity leave.

> *Sara:* 'Well, we discussed it before we had children, and I've never liked the thought of staying at home, you know, I've always wanted children and wanted to work as well. So we discussed it then, you know, whether I would be able to do both. So we said, 'Well, we'll try—if we can't, then I'll pack up', you know. But as it is, we've managed.... He does his share of work, and I do my share.... We decided at first that my husband would go on night duty—we did that for a while.... He went to work at night when I got home, you know.... I found it ever so hard to leave a baby after fou weeks, to come back — but it's one of those things—I had to come back'

She goes on to describe how these arrangements were subsequently modified.

> *Sara:* 'We did that for a while, night duties, and we found out we were Just saying 'Good morning', and, you know, going out the house. So, one of my sisters came, to go to college, so he went back on normal working, the shifts—you know, they do one week a morning, one week afternoons—and so my sister was studying at home and looked after the baby for a while, and then he went to do his normal work.... The second one, we did the same—and then my other sister came and we did the same thing—she went to college and helped us out during the day. When I had the third one, she decided she was

going to get married, so I had to find a baby minder.... I used to take one to school, one to nursery...and then the other one to the minder, in the morning. But it was very hard, you know—I suppose if you want to do it, you do it.'

Geraldine left school at 15 with no qualifications and took a job as a punch operator. She worked her way up through various grades to a supervisory position, before marrying nine years later. After five years of marriage, she and her husband wanted to start a family.

> *Geraldine:* 'Now a supervisor has a lot of week-end work, a lot of overtime, so I decided to switch to be a clerk, an ordinary clerk.... I found my childminder before I was pregnant.... I used to pop over before the baby arrived, she was the first one to know when I was actually pregnant.'

When the baby arrived, in 1976, she took seventeen weeks' maternity leave. She described her feelings about going back to work.

> *Geraldine:* 'I didn't want to leave him—you don't. It's a terrible wrench. I would never advise anybody to do it—and it's hard, jolly hard, on you, because you're losing your sleep at night...of course you can't breast-feed if you're going back to work after six weeks; it's not fair on the baby, so I had to bottle-feed him.'

Both Geraldine and her husband come from large families, and have chosen to have no more than their one child.

Andrea also left school at 15 with no qualifications. Her father had recently died and she considered herself fortunate to have obtained a job as a telephonist. After about three and a half years she married, and at roughly the same time was promoted to a supervisory post which involved working shifts. Her first baby was born about five and a half years later, according to plan.

> *Andrea:* 'I'd arranged that she would go to a nursery when I came here I was on shift work then, as a supervisor—we used to do different duties, like eight till four, and either my husband

> or myself used to take her to the nursery in the morning, and one of us used to collect her at night.'
>
> *S.Y.: 'And you never considered giving up work at that period?'*
>
> *Andrea:* 'No. I'd always enjoyed work too much.'

The birth of her child was difficult, and because of this she decided not to have any more children—as she put it: 'It's best to have one that's perfectly all right.'

The remaining three women had not planned their pregnancies in quite the same way. Valerie was married for twelve years before the first of her three children was born. After a short spell as a shop assistant on leaving school aged 15, Valerie joined most of her male relatives, who already worked for the same public sector company, as a clerical assistant.

> *Valerie:* 'I think it was just pressure from Mum and Dad. You know, "You ought to get that good little job", and all the rest of it. So I applied.... It's sort of family-orientated really.'

She married a few years later and was subsequently promoted several times. Why had she sought promotions?

> *Valerie:* 'I just felt—I mean, you sort of work here, you just get caught up in it...and, I think, well, if I'm out earning, working, I want job interest...so, it was the natural...course of events to some extent...rather than...an inbuilt desire as always wanting to achieve this.'

She described how she came to decide to remain at work when she eventually had her family.

> *Valerie:* 'It was just something at the time. We'd been married twelve years then, and you sort of acquire a lifestyle, and there was no way that we could continue doing the things we'd become accustomed to doing, if you like...and selfishly

> enough we weren't prepared to give that up. Although we'd wanted a family—had it been forthcoming, you know, in our early years of marriage, when we'd planned it, I would have left work like most mums do, you know, and had the children, and then come back to work But having worked all that time, I was too old to get up and start scratching around really, because—you know, it is hard when you suddenly come down to one wage, and such like...and so we just decided that, you know..., as it happened, my mum would look after them, and so it worked out like that.'

Valerie had three children, and took four months' maternity leave from her job at each birth.

Neither Sally nor Louise had planned to start their families when they did. Before her marriage, Sally was employed for six years in a variety of jobs. A routine clerical job which she left after about a year, mainly through boredom, six months abroad as an au-pair, and several more office jobs, including assistant to a buyer in a large mail order firm, and supervisor of fieldwork in the market research department of a large company, her last job before marriage. This, she felt, was 'probably the best job I've ever had— I was in charge of the interviewers around the country.' On marriage she moved to Kent and left her job. Although she tried to find the same kind of work there, she could find nothing like it, so after a couple of months out of employment she took a job as a shop assistant in a department store.

> *Sally:* 'I stuck it for two weeks—it was utterly boring—in many ways an absolute insult to anybody's intelligence, supervised by a woman who had no sort of intelligence either. The whole thing was a complete waste of time—utterly boring— I really was bored.'

Following this, she succeeded in obtaining part-time employment as a market research interviewer, and was doing this work when she first became pregnant. However, neither this nor her subsequent pregnancy (eighteen months later), nor having two small children, prevented her from continuing this part-time work. The hours (about 20 per week) were flexible—'you just sort of did it in your own time'—and it was possible to make arrangements for the children.

> *Sally:* 'I used to strap ['the children] in the back of the car...and there were quite a few friends who would have them for the odd hour or two—and sometimes, I would take them with me.

She continued in her market research work for about six years, at the same time running her own farm shop. Once her two children were at school, however, she took a full-time clerical job with a local engineering company. She explained why she made this change.

> *Sally:* 'Really because my [self-employed] husband took a [second] job in the evenings, we did need the money—and he didn't used to get home until about half past eleven, really tired, and things got to the point where the children were both at school and realized that he just couldn't go *on* doing it And I came along here for the interview.... And I sort of took over the earnings, if you like. My husband had to take [the children] to school, and he had to pick them up and he had to make sure they were all right till I got home. That was the arrangement—if I go out to work, he'd have to accept that responsibility.'

She was still working in this clerical job when interviewed, but has subsequently, after about four years there, changed her employer, going first to work full-time as administrative co-ordinator in an advertising agency, and later, after three weeks out of employment following redundancy, taking a part-time clerical/cashier job with a building society (for 20 hours per week).

Louise went to secretarial college after leaving school and worked as a typist with a building society for six years before changing her job on marriage. She explained:

> *Louise:* 'I met [my husband] there, and you can't work for the same company' so I had to leave...[also] we moved...to London, because he got promoted.'

She described how she came to take her next job.

Louise: It was easy because it was London…I could have had almost any job but the reason—it's stupid really—but the only reason I chose [the company] was that we'd got a flat nearby and it was the most accessible place to get to. And I could get home in the lunch hours and start—you know, newly married, I thought get home and get the vegetables ready, and all this rubbish [laughs]—that lasted for about three days, but that was the idea. I thought… I wouldn't be able to cope with running a house and going up to town… I wanted a nice local job, it was very close to the flat, so I could nip home at lunchtime and do the shopping, that was why I chose the job.'

Louise's first child was born three and a half years after her marriage. At first she found her pregnancy hard to accept.

> *Louise:* 'I asked, you know, if it was possible to terminate and (the doctor] wasn't very agreeable—but looking back, I probably wouldn't have done it, it was just that—I went to him because I hadn't come on, and he told me that I was pregnant. It was a bit of a shock I did ask, but he—he lied in fact—he told me that I was sixteen weeks gone, and I wasn't, I was nowhere near that, I was about ten[5]...looking back [my husband] would never have agreed to it anyway…to me, having a baby meant staying at home and washing nappies and things like that'
>
> *S.Y.: 'So you thought it was going to mean giving up work?'*
>
> *Louise:* 'End of my life, in fact—yes.'

Through discussing what she saw as her predicament with other people, Louise came to realize that having a child need not mean leaving her job.

> *Louise:* 'I thought about it before he was born. And weighed up lots of possibilities….I got talking to a girl who happened to take my place on maternity leave, and she told me her child

> was at a childminder's.... She said, do you want me to put you in touch with this girl? And I went round to see her, and it was very clean, she was registered, obviously... I was happy with her and she was happy with me....he went there before, in fact, he was six months. They were short-staffed at the office, because it was holiday time.'

Louise felt confident that her decision to stay at work and take maternity leave had been the right one for her. She found the period at home with her young baby difficult.

> *Louise:* 'I was not really very happy—my husband used to come home at night, we didn't seem to have anything to talk about...my mum still can't understand it, because she scraped and saved to, you know, bring us...up, and she feels that if she could do it—and they had no money at all—she doesn't see why I shouldn't.'

Since returning to work from her maternity leave, Louise has moved from London to Kent (because her husband has been promoted in his job). When this happened she was able to obtain a transfer within her firm, and had three weeks' leave of absence at the time of removal. During this time, she was able to make arrangements with another registered childminder for her son. Louise would like to work part-time, but her employers have a full-time only policy, and as she has been unable to find suitable alternative employment, she has chosen to reduce her workload by employing domestic help at home for four hours per week

These six women, whose attachment to the labour force has been virtually unbroken since they joined it on leaving full-time education, all showed evidence of an active commitment to paid employment. They had relatively few employers and most were currently well-satisfied with their pay, working conditions and with the nature of their jobs. Most had been able to take advantage of opportunities for promotion, and all planned to remain in employment until retirement. All referred to some difficulties in combining full-time paid jobs with raising children, but with the support of either husbands and other relatives, paid help, or the cooperation of friends and employers, these had not proved insuperable, and none suggested that she regretted the decision to remain in employment The choices they made might not always be ones which other women would select, but many might benefit from a genuine opportunity to consider remaining in paid work as an option.

ALTERNATIVES: SOME EFFECTS OF INDIVIDUAL BIOGRAPHY

Whilst most of the women interviewed had employment careers which followed the 'dominant' pattern described at the start of this chapter, and a minority' chose to remain in paid work despite changes in their family' lives, a further minority had employment careers which were quite clearly affected by the special circumstances of their personal lives. None of these ten women had conformed to the norms currently governing family formation behaviour and the conduct of personal relationships. Thus for them the social processes of marriage and childbearing had differed in important ways from those experienced by the majority of my respondents.[6] Whilst marital breakdown has become a commonplace of contemporary relationships between the sexes, and had been experienced by well over a third of the women interviewed, frequent breakdown of personal relationships (whether marital or extra-marital), the bearing of children outside of stable unions, and the failure of women to marry, continue to constitute behaviour which breaks with normative expectations. These are the characteristics of the women in this group. Disrupted private lives can have important effects upon women's employment careers. Some women seek stable, full-time employment as a 'constant' in their otherwise changeable lives. This enables them to escape dependence on either the state or men for their economic well-being, and gives them a sense of maintaining control over their own lives. Others find that the personal insecurities of unstable and unsatisfying relationships, often complicated by ill-health (mental or physical) and unplanned pregnancies, keep them from permanent or full-time employment

In four of the ten cases, attachment to the labour force had been strengthened. These women were all living alone with a child or children, and were, in effect, employed full-time.

Mavis was in her late twenties, had never married, and had an 18-month-old son. She was living in a small council flat, and gave every appearance of coping well with organizing her life and managing her responsibilities.

> *Mavis:* '[It's] not really [a strain]...because I've always sort of sailed through things, and sort of not worried. Well, I do worry a little bit, but it doesn't bother me what other people think... I do what I want to do, and I don't care what anybody says.

She had two paid jobs, working 40 hours per week for a food processing company, packing food, and 7 hours on Saturdays as a butcher's assistant. She had been doing this for nine months when I first met her, and was still doing so when contacted again a year later. In the week, her child went to a registered childminder; whom she paid £12.50 a week, and on Saturdays her neighbour looked after him. Her Saturday job was quite important to her, and she had worked for this employer. on.and off for eight years, going back there when the baby was 6 months old and she was living on supplementary benefit.

> *Mavis:* 'That was a great help...because, also, he said "You know you can help yourself off the counter, like." So, I mean, that was an even bigger help, that was...things like butter and cheese, and your meat, and it did save me a lot, and after...doing it about three or four weeks, I didn't honestly know how I could have gone back to just being on Social Security alone—I couldn't—well, to think about it now, I don't know how I really did manage.

Three months later she took the full-time factory job, and although she was toying with the idea of working shorter hours, she was aware of all the factors she needs to, weigh up.

> *Mavis:* 'Well, you see, you can gain and you can lose—at the moment, I can't claim for FIS,[7] because I am earning too much—but in November, they all go up again, so I can claim for them again.' (FIS = Family Income Supplement)

Kate and Cathy were both in their mid-thirties. Kate had four children, aged between 6 and 14 years, all living with her. She had been married three times, divorced twice, and said she was 'estranged' from her third husband. Cathy had been married and divorced twice, to the same man, and had three children. At the time of the interview she lived alone with the youngest child, a 7-year-old, while the elder two lived with their father. Neither woman was financially supported by a former husband, and both worked as hospital domestics. Kate worked a 40-hour week and did regular overtime of about 15 hours. Cathy worked part-time as a supervisor, but usually worked a 42-hour week including overtime:

Kate's first marriage had lasted two years, her second for twelve. She had one child from her first marriage and three from the Second. Her third marriage was breaking down after only a couple of years, when we met She described her estranged husband's attitude to her job.

> *Kate:* 'He doesn't like 'the idea—because of the independence side of it I suppose.... I was earning my own wage...so it gave me almost equal rights to him...and he didn't like the idea from.

She was bitter about her past.

> *Kate:* 'I've always done everything myself, anything to do with the home, cooking, looking after the children, everything. I've always been the one ye even taken on the responsibilities of bills, always have done.... I don't feel at all happy about it, mainly because it should be a shared thing between husband and wife. I don't know if it's me, or if it's just the type of people I've married—it just doesn't work out that way.

Her early experience of employment was in clerical work, which she found boring, and as a supermarket cashier. While her children were young, she worked for about seven years as an agricultural worker (working about nine months in every twelve), before having to 'give this up because of an injury, and taking a job as a hospital domestic. She planned to stay in this job 'quite a few years, I hope. All the time I'm able to, I will.'

Cathy's early employment career was inauspicious. In the first two years after leaving school at 15, she worked as a supermarket shelf-filler and counter assistant, in two jobs as a waitress, and as a factory operative. She was made redundant from one of these jobs, sacked—'for being mouthy'—from a second, and left the others of her own accord. Before taking a fifth job as a trainee laundry worker, she also spent some time caring for her sick grandmother. Cathy's employment career was broken again before she completed her training, when she became pregnant and had her first child. She married for the first time nine months later, and did not return to paid work (this time as a 'casual' agricultural worker) until three and a half years after this, by which time she had a second child. She continued in this work for about six years, although in the meantime she divorced, and three years later re-married, her husband. She then had to stop work to have a third child, but returned to agricultural work again soon afterwards.

> *Cathy:* 'I done one season of potato picking-up, after I'd had her....I've always suffered with my back, and that last spell of picking up potatoes just about finished me. I'd just about had enough. And then I decided that I would see if I could get a job inside.... I knew that there was one going (at the hospital) and I applied for it, and got it.'

Cathy's husband had no objection to her taking a more secure job.

> *Cathy:* 'He thought it was good that I was working...because then he could cut me housekeeping down, you see, no, it's the truth' He always told me to get to work anyway—I did as I was told.'

As this second marriage came to an end, things deteriorated further:

> *Cathy:* '[my wages] all went in the housekeeping... I mean, I kept them all, from last May—because he never gave me anything at all—I was having to keep him, 'n all.'

How long did Cathy plan to stay in her present job? 'Until they get rid of me, I should think'

Susan was in her mid-forties, and had been living alone with her three children for over twelve years. Prior to that, she had been twice married and divorced. Susan's employment career began when she was 15, with a period of clerical work which lasted six years. During this time she married for the first time, giving up the job when she was expecting her first child. In the next three or four years, before her marriage broke down, she had another child and engaged in periodic seasonal work on farms, taking her children with her. After her marriage ended, she took on various casual jobs, including part-time clerical work and washing cars, before forming a relationship with the man she was later to marry. At first she lived with him, unmarried, but when she was expecting his child, she succumbed to pressure from her family, and, against her better judgment, married him. A few years later she obtained a part-time clerical job in the firm where her husband worked. This lasted for two years, until the marriage began to break down and she felt compelled to leave. After her second divorce, Susan gradually became more fully integrated into the labour force. She worked for a while in the school meals service, and then moved to a full-time office job. Finally, she took the advice of her sister, who worked for a public sector employer.

> *Susan:* 'I applied for a job here—my sister is an Executive Officer here, and, she'd brought up her family on her own. She said you' needed to get into a secure job, because you want a pension—you'd got to think about, you know, bringing up your children on your own—and this obviously made sense.'

Susan had been in this job for ten years when we met. She had accepted modest promotions, and had become very involved in trade union work At the time of her interview she was branch secretary of her union, and was also actively involved in Labour party politics, thus making the kind of link between her working life and her private life which is characteristic of male trade unionists. As she put it: 'What I do for the trade union here fits in with what I do in my leisure time—it's hardly separated.'

She expected to stay with her employers.

> *Susan:* 'I hope until I retire...all the time I'm fit... I mean, I shall need a pension.... We have excellent conditions of service, and because the [employers] have always worked closely with the unions, we don't have the unfairness that you get where you don't have union representation...[we have] flexi-time...we have a good superannuation scheme, we've got a welfare officer, benevolent society—this sort of thing...it's very secure.'

In many respects, the four women described here conformed closely to the stereotype of a 'male' than of a 'female' employee. Working regular overtime, taking a second job, relying upon earnings as a sole means of support, and active involvement in trade union activities are all characteristics more commonly found among male than female employees. Of course these characteristics have nothing to do with biological sex. What these women's employment careers demonstrate is that where women find it necessary to think of themselves as breadwinners, and shoulder all responsibility for themselves and their families, they are likely also to follow what has often been thought of as a 'male' pattern of employment

Three other women in this group were in paid employment when interviewed, but were only marginally integrated into the labour force. All were living alone with their children, but were not economically self-supporting in the way the four, women already described were. Jackie was receiving supplementary benefit, as well as support from two men, her former husband and the father of her second child, while both Hilary and Jane were in receipt of Family Income Supplement as well as a small amount of maintenance from their former husbands. Jackie and Hilary were both employed part-time, while Jane worked a 40-hour week, and sometimes did 5 hours overtime as well. In what ways had their personal histories resulted in their marginal integration in the labour force?

Jackie's employment career had been severely disrupted by ill-health several mental breakdowns, anorexia nervosa, and alcoholism. During the first three years of her employment career, she had three different jobs in residential homes for the elderly and handicapped, working as a care or nursing assistant: She left two of these jobs on account of her health, and the third following her marriage (when she was 21). After her marriage she took a full-time college course and qualified as a medical secretary, subsequently finding employment as secretary to a hospital consultant. She left this job after a year when expecting her much• wanted first child.

She had not anticipated returning to employment for some years, but an opportunity to work 6 hours per week in the evenings as secretary to a general practitioner came up, and she took the job. After, just two months she had to be' re-admitted to hospital. Subsequently her marriage broke down and after a short spell living alone with the baby she lost custody of the child to her husband, 'because of my drinking'.

> *Jackie:* 'When I got her back [four months later] I still wasn't working, and I just lived here on my own with her for a while, and I didn't work until the following year, until I got sober.... I started that about nine months after I stopped drinking.'

Her next job was secretarial work for a charity on one day a week, and she was doing this when we met.

> *Jackie:* 'I don't claim my money from there—which is £6 per week—until my telephone bill comes in—so it's purely for the telephone.'

She explained that a telephone was vital to her because of her alcoholism. Shortly before we met, Jackie had a second child. She intends to stay on her own, and says that the baby's father now 'maintains him'.

Hilary, in her early thirties, with three children-aged between 8 and 14, was married for just two years, although she has subsequently lived with another man for about four years. After leaving school at 15, Hilary had a number of short-lived jobs, as a factory worker and as a cinema usherette, before joining her parents, both agricultural workers. As she put it 'I went on to the farm with Mum and Dad... I did quite a lot of farm work'

She stayed in this work until her first, unplanned, child was expected.

> *Hilary:* 'Well, it didn't upset my plans—because I never had any plans—I never plan things anyway, it's no good...it's just that I knew—this fella that I was going with—before I married him...it wouldn't work And I thought, you know, getting married, *it* might alter him...well, it didn't. And then, when I found that I was pregnant, I thought "Oh God, how are we going to manage?"...and this is what it was.'

Her husband was unemployed throughout the two years of their marriage. 'I was going to work to keep him.' After her marriage ended, and following a spell when she lived on supplementary benefit, she began living with the man who is the father of her second and third children, a self-employed builder and decorator. During the four years this relationship lasted, she was not in employment, and her involvement in a car accident meant that 'The very last year that he was with me, I couldn't walk.' Hilary felt that neither of the men with whom she had been involved had helped her to shoulder the responsibilities of raising a family: 'I've brought my three up on my own, really.... Really, I mean, because the two boys' father, we never used to hardly see him, anyway.'

When she had recovered from her accident, she took a part-time job as a hospital bed-maker.

> *Hilary:* 'I wanted to get out... I was just shut in, day after day, and I just couldn't take any more of it. It was either come to work or crack up in the end, I think.'[8]

With help from her family with childcare, she kept this part-time job for over eighteen months. However, 'The reason I didn't stay was...because of the children, you know the seven-week school holiday.' Her next return to employment was as a part-time hospital domestic, a job which she had held for over three years when interviewed, despite a long period of sick leave, and a period of working reduced hours so that she could visit her youngest child in hospital following his injury in a road accident. She was not at the time of the interview entirely satisfied with her situation at work.

> *Hilary:* 'I have been moved about, quite a bit, just lately...they shove me off somewhere else. I fell out quite a few times with [management].... If I could find another job tomorrow, I'd go to it.'

Hilary was not finding it easy to cope: her children were difficult to manage, and she has had to call upon social services for assistance.

> *Hilary:* 'My children get me down....you know, sometimes...they really do make me cry....to think that I'm trying as hard as I can, to keep that house going and keep it nice, and they just don't care.

In the light of her past history, Hilary's expectations about her employment future seemed rather unrealiztic: she thought she would stay 'until I find something else—or I get married—then I won't have to go to work'

Jane was a divorcee in her mid-thirties, with three children aged between 11 and 15. She had been married only once, for about seven years, and did not do so until after her three children were born. She was divorced five years before we met. After leaving school at 15, Jane was employed for five years in a variety of different jobs before having her first child. She worked as a shop assistant, in two factories, and as a bus conductress. She left the shop for better pay, was made redundant from one of the factory jobs, and left the other following an argument with the foreman. She left the bus company because of her pregnancy. There then followed a period of five years during which she did no paid work and had three children. How did she feel about being a single mother?

> *Jane:* 'Dunno... I just had to shoulder the responsibility, as with all three of them...it just happened....so that was that...'

At first she lived with her parents, but towards the end of the five years married and went to live with her husband. Her return to employment was prompted by the loss of her fourth child soon afterwards.

> *Jane:* 'I was getting a bit depressed, you know, with losing the baby and that, and I was sterilised—I had a Caesarean and sterilisation at the same time—so I took a job—that's about it.'

She took full-time work as a hospital domestic, but left after a year.

> *Jane:* 'I started having problems with the old man...whilst I was in hospital, he was carrying on with this woman....'

After two years without employment she started working again, as a barmaid in a pub.

> *Jane:* 'I started there a couple of dinner times, and then did three or four a week...and then several evenings a week. And then we split up completely...the marriage had really broken down, and then, obviously, you know, I needed extra money, because of being on my own with three kids, so I took a job here.'

This time her job was again as' a hospital domestic, working full-time. She had been in this job for four years when I interviewed her. Although previously her personal life had tended to limit her attachment to employment, she now recognized that she needed to continue earning a living. I asked how long she expected to stay in her job.

> *Jane:* 'Well, as long as possible.'
>
> *S.Y.: '[Until] you come to retire?'*
>
> *Jane:* 'What can I say?... There's not a lot you can say about it, is there? It's a job.... The chance is, I might have to be.'

For these women, then, participation in the labour force had been, reduced by the nature of their personal relations and health. Unlike the four women described earlier, Jackie, Hilary, and Jane had not used employment as a means of structuring uneven and disrupted personal lives, but found that their employment careers were limited and fragmented by them.

The remaining three women had personal histories which temporarily interrupted their employment careers.

Annette was gentle and softly spoken, a woman who looked younger than her 27 years. Although she was caring for two children aged 12 and 14, she had no natural children of her own and had never married. At the time of the interview she had been living for four years with Jim and his two children by his ex-wife. Jim's wife had 'walked out and left' the family some six months before Annette moved in. Annette worked full-time as a clerical assistant and had also taken on the role of mother to Jim's children, and wife to Jim. Her early employment career had been rather chequered. She left school at 15 and worked briefly in a factory, and then in a hairdresser's, finding both unsatisfactory. After this she took another factory job, this time wiring electrical goods. She stayed in this job for two and, a half years, before being made redundant After some weeks out of work, she obtained a job as an office junior.

> *Annette:* 'I learnt how to operate the switchboard, and went from being a junior to doing all the credit control and the wages.'

Meanwhile, she had applied for another clerical job.

> *Annette:* 'My sister worked there... I suppose that was really the reason I went there—plus it was more money.'

She was taken on, and stayed two years before starting to feel restless. She then gave in her notice, and took work for the summer at a holiday camp—'getting away from home for a couple of months'. Afterwards, she worked briefly as a barmaid, before obtaining clerical work again, in a small company. By the end of the year, however, she had been offered her old clerical job back, and this time she stayed for almost three years, only leaving after moving in with Jim. She was quite keen to stop working, and Jim was anxious for her to do so: 'He's a bit possessive and a bit selfish, and he just wanted me at home.' After three years out of employment, however, Annette was anxious to return to her old job:

> *Annette:* 'The frustrations of being at home all the time had set in by then... [he didn't want me to come to work at all—it was purely at my insistence—at which he is pleased now—but it did take quite a few months.'

She had been back a year when we met What were her plans for the future? She explained that she had decided not to have children of her own, but that was not all.

> *Annette:* '[I have] distant thoughts of having a little business of my own, perhaps a little shop.... I think I like working better knowing that it's not something that I'm going to have to do for another forty years or whatever...if I wanted to give up, I can give up.'

Alice was a 40-year old divorcee. She had left her husband and three children five years previously to live with another man, but the relationship did not last. She then spent some time living with her father, and, since his death, with another man and, more recently, her elder son. Like many of the women interviewed, Alice had several jobs between leaving school and having her first child, and married during this period. She left employment to have her first baby, and during the next six years her second and third children were born. At this stage she engaged in seasonal agricultural work and took on evening jobs—as a factory operative and as a cleaner. After the birth of her third child, she gradually began working more hours per week, at first as a cleaner but later as a laboratory assistant (at the same place of employment). She worked in this last job for about four years, and eventually left her family to set up home with her employer. She explained that she had been, unhappy about her marriage and her husband's attitudes to her employment

> *Alice:* 'It seemed to me that he would want me to work all day and all night, my money always went straight in the house—it was expected to go in there—it was never mine.... That's where I wrong... I felt like a slave. He liked to have his drink, and I was working for him to have his beer. I would come home after working from ten till six...and he admitted he'd been up since half past four, but he'd been asleep all afternoon, and he hadn't bothered—he hadn't made the bed, he hadn't washed up, he hadn't done anything...and before that anyway—he was never capable of looking after me.'

When her new relationship failed, Alice had a breakdown. Afterwards, in her own words, 'I pulled myself together, and went to work.' The work was in a paper mill, 'cutting holes in paper' and she found it hard: 'It was bonus work...you had to do so much...you had to keep going.' After two years, during which time she was also caring for her dying father, she gave the job up and took work as a full-time hospital domestic instead. Two years later, at the time of the interview, she was still working full-time, often doing 11 hours overtime each week She had no plans to leave: 'I think I shall be working here—well. I just think I shall always be here.' Alice's affair, divorce, and nervous breakdown had not severely disrupted her employment career, but had created a hiatus in its development

Penny's employment career had been interrupted in a way similar to Alice's, although the change in her personal life which caused' the interruption was different. Like Alice's, Penny's employment career followed a typical pattern for about twenty years. She took employment, married, and left to have her first child. She then did seasonal framework before moving into full-time permanent employment in sales after her child started school. She continued working full-time, although changing from sales to domestic work when her son was in his early teens. When he was 18, however, she found she was expecting another, unplanned, child. I asked her how she had felt

> *Penny:* 'I don't really know. I wasn't overjoyed, I wasn't bitter I always wanted another child.'

Having the child meant giving up her job, but also coincided with the breakdown of her marriage.

> *Penny:* 'It finished.... And then, the hard times hit.... I had two choices—either live on social security, and poverty, or come back to work, and get above—just a little bit above poverty.

She returned to her former job, again full-time, and was able to place her child in the workplace nursery. What of the future?

> *Penny:* 'I don't think I shall change [my job]... I don't think I'd like promotion... I think I've come to a standstill in my life—I think I just like being as I am. I don't think I could take on any more responsibilities because I already have enough... I'll keep continuing as long as can. I've got quite a lot of years left to continue work, and I still hope I can fulfil the years.'

As with Alice' and Annette, Penny's employment career was temporarily interrupted by developments in her personal life. Having a child unexpectedly late in her life had a similar effect on her employment career as moving in to be 'mother' to an existing family had for Annette, or leaving a family to establish a new relations hip had for Alice.

I have tried to show here that 'distinctive' personal histories such as those described do not have any simple effect upon women's employment patterns, but may influence them in a variety of ways. Some women use employment to structure their lives, while others may find changes and disruption in their personal lives spreading to their employment careers.

In this chapter, I have presented detailed discussion of the patterns of labour adopted by the women interviewed. Although most followed variants on a pattern usually regarded as typical (employment—childrearing—employment), two minority groups whose experience differed in important ways also emerged. In the first, women did not leave the labour force at all, but used maternity leave, or made other arrangements, to enable them to continue in their jobs. The second group consisted of a number of women 'whose personal histories deviated significantly from current norms governing personal relationships and family formation; in some cases this deviation had the effect of reinforcing integration into the labour force, in others of restricting it. It is important not to ignore the significance of the two minority groups. The former suggests a commitment to participation in the labour force with which women who are also mothers are not usually 'credited', while the latter tells us that there is no simple effect on employment careers which can be attributed to deviation from social norms concerning interpersonal behaviour.

The women in the main group (the 'dominant' pattern) had all left the labour market at least once to raise a child or children, and had returned to it at some subsequent point; none the less there were significant variations within this pattern.

Between leaving school and leaving the labour force to have a first child, most of the women in the group held more than one job; in many cases, changing jobs, even at this initial stage in the employment career, meant changing from one type of work to another, although this changing of occupation was uncommon amongst those (few) women who engaged in further education after school.

In establishing how women came to leave the labour force when expecting a first child; it was noteworthy that about half of first pregnancies were unplanned. These women thus had little opportunity to plan seriously for a future combination of domestic labour 'and wage-earning. These 'unplanned' first pregnancies reflect the fact that most young working-class women view marriage and a (first) baby as inevitable steps in the transition to adulthood. These steps are not usually subjected to rational economic planning, and often a 'the sooner, the better' approach is adopted. Once they are taken the individual can then get on with organizing her life around what are seen as its essential components husband and children. Such economically irrational behaviour (which contrasts clearly with the career-oriented approach characteristic of the middle class) can best be understood in terms of the constraints and restricted opportunities of working-class life. Even amongst those whose first child was planned, little thought had apparently been given to returning to employment in the future, although many women said that they had vague expectations about this at the time.

Most women were to return to paid work much more quickly than they had expected. The return to employment represented a new experience of work, and the next few years were mostly characterised by a succession of part-time, temporary, or seasonal jobs. Most were in low paid and insecure occupations, and many would have gone unrecorded in official statistics. For the minority of married women who had more than one child and who remained outside the labour force throughout the entire childbearing phase, the average length of time between leaving and returning to paid employment was about eight years. It was notable that these women tended to have stable marriages and relatively well-paid husbands. Most placed a high value on their mothering role, and many sought employment partly because of a sense of lost identity when their youngest child started school.

After returning to employment there was a tendency to engage in several part-time jobs over a period of some years before taking on full-time employment Some women chose to remain part-timers, whilst for others full-time work was an aim which could only be achieved when the youngest child reached a particular age. Almost without exception, the women intended to remain in employment until retirement For many this intention reflected the fact that they had finally found themselves an acceptable occupation, where they were treated with some respect, derived some enjoyment from their work or working environment, and were earning wages on which they had come to rely. An important minority of the women were more ambitious however, and they intended to seek-promotion, further training, or a higher grade occupation. Many of these were women who worked for employers offering training and a career structure to all able members of staff. They had been made aware of the contribution they could make at work, derived a sense of self-worth from this, and had gained the confidence to pursue a career. Others were not positively motivated in this way, but rather felt undervalued and discontented in their present jobs. They knew they could do more demanding work, and recognized that they would need to change their occupation if their skills and abilities were to be used.

The evidence from the analysis of employment careers suggests that women may not be such passive members of the labour force as has sometimes been claimed. They have an experience of paid work which is fragmented and variable, but they also return frequently to employment, and intend to stay. Indeed, many have relatively ambitious plans for the future, and desire to be further integrated into the labour force.

CODA: BARBARA'S STORY

Barbara is 35, has been married to Frank since she was 18, and has two sons, Mark aged 17 and Philip aged 14. Mark left school recently and is doing an apprenticeship. Slightly plump, Barbara has a kindly, almost matronly appearance, and punctuates her conversation with the phrase 'I've been very lucky.' Looking back, she says that if a girl 'had a life like mine she wouldn't have a lot to complain about', although she readily admits that 'we' have our ups and downs—but (that's) all part of life.'

Barbara's employment career has conformed to the traditional stereotype for married women: several years in full-time jobs between school and having children, then a complete break while her family were young, followed by a return to employment in part-time work

This pattern of employment reflects the traditional role which Barbara plays within her family. As she says herself, 'I'm not a great women's libber.' Of central importance in Barbara's life have been her responsibilities with regard to 'running her home', a phrase to which she returned frequently. She says proudly that she 'didn't start work *(sic)* until the children were both at school', and finds some contemporary attitudes towards raising children rather puzzling,

> 'I supposed I'm old-fashioned...if you're having a baby, then obviously my thought would be to stay at home and look after it—I wouldn't want to go and leave it...but if that is sort of what career women really want, then I don't understand it completely, but I would think...[the law is right to permit it].'

Although she has no wish to he at home all day now that her children are older, Barbara has always considered it important to plan her life around the demands of her husband and sons. She explained what having a job meant to her, and how she fitted it into her life.

> '[Having a job] makes me better-tempered in some ways... You're so small-minded when you're at home, you just live in your own little world.... If it suits people, I mean, it's entirely up to them of course...obviously we all come out for the money, but I mean it is the company and the outside attachments, the friendships that you make as well.... Even if I was well off—obviously if you were filthy rich you'd probably have other things to entertain you—but... I would have to have an awful lot of money not to, I think....otherwise I think you get a little bit stale ye always been lucky ye been able to find work where I can fit it in with family life ye more organized my jobs round the family than the family round the jobs.'

It may be useful to indicate just how Barbara has been able to do this. After the birth of her first child in 1963 (she gave up her job as a shop assistant at the beginning of that year) she was at home full-time until September 1970 when Philip started school. Only once in these eight years did she consider taking a job: when Mark was just a few months old she started work as an assistant in a children's nursery, leaving the baby with her mother who lived nearby. She found the separation from her child too hard to bear, however, and after two days abandoned the job. The years at home with the children were not entirely dedicated to caring for the needs of her own household however:

> 'I used to look after an uncle...we lived close by.... I looked liter him for seven years...he had his own place...and I used to just go along and do his cleaning. When he got beyond looking after at home...they put him into hospital...and then he died.'

Barbara took this additional responsibility quite for granted. As she saw it, caring for an elderly relative was simply another aspect of a married woman's duties towards her family.

When both her sons had started school Barbara started to look for a part-time job. She faced some opposition from her husband, and her mother was not enthusiastic. However, she persuaded her husband to 'let' her take a job by offering it as a means of achieving a specific objective:

> 'I told [him], if he wanted a car.... It was really to get extras... I mean, if we went out anywhere, it was either buses or we had to walk, and we thought it would be nice.'

This tactic was apparently successful; in any case, Barbara obtained Frank's consent, and made enquiries at a local college, where she started work as a part-time catering assistant: 'helping in the kitchens, clearing tables, serving meals, that sort of thing'. Barbara's mother had reservations about the idea of her daughter taking a job. She had never had a paid job herself, although as Barbara explained, 'she used to do little bits of needlework and that...she was able to make herself the little bit extra.' Nevertheless, she was soon persuaded that the arrangement could do no serious harm, since she recognized the financial pressures on Barbara and her young family. (Frank has worked for the past fifteen years as a warehouseman in a retail store. Prior to this, he worked as a bread roundsman and as a milkman.

None of these jobs is particularly well paid.) Indeed, Barbara acknowledged that her mother 'was prepared to help if she could', but added that 'I wouldn't have done it if I'd had to get her to look after the children a lot.' Rather she had 'helped out on odd occasions.'

The job at the college involved striking an individual bargain with management:[9] officially, working at the weekends 'was supposed to be compulsory'.

> 'When I went for the job, I said, "No, I can't take the job because you want weekends"—and he got me to work a couple of evenings [instead]...and I...used to have a young girl—she looked after the children for half an hour before my husband got home. She lived next door but one, and she just came in and looked after them.'

Later, this arrangement about weekend work was not allowed to stand, and, faced with what was for her an impossible choice, Barbara left the job in the following summer. Her comments about the incident are illuminating:

> 'They were insisting then that we work weekends—that was purely because some of them were being funny about it—and so they said, "You'll have to do weekends", and I said, "I can't do weekends because my husband's working every other Saturday." And I didn't feel it was fair to ask the family, so I gave that job up, and had the summer holidays off.'

This explanation reveals that there were other factors in the background influencing the choice which Barbara was forced to make. She had the summer holidays in prospect, and although she was not officially required to work during this time she knew she would be asked to do so (in connection with conferences at the college), and that she would have either to refuse, or to seek support from her mother. Her reluctance to call on her family for support was influenced by both her feeling that the children were essentially her own responsibility, and by her knowledge that her mother was already involved in helping her sister with childcare. Thus a variety of factors combined to produce her decision to resign the job.

As the summer holidays ended, Barbara started to look around for work again. She was experienced in shop work, but did not look in that area:

> 'I didn't think it was worth trying, because I knew I wouldn't get the school holidays... I had to sort of compromise...and I mean most shop work is Saturdays anyway.'

As the school term began again, she decided to try a different kind of work.

> 'I did two days as a crossing patrol person along by the school—but my nerves wouldn't let me do that. Oh dear, I couldn't put up with that. I did it for two days and I went home and cried my eyes out. I just said to my husband, "I just can't go up there and do it".... A policeman is supposed to stand with you the first week apparently, and he was with me for one day—plus the other lady had left to have a baby, and the thing said "Stop Children"—and the comments I used to get.... Anyway, my husband went up and saw the headmaster, and said, "It's no good, she can't do it". And I began to wonder what I was going to do then, I used to look at the papers on Friday morning...and then I saw this little job.'

This account reveals something of Barbara's relationship with her husband, as well as of the difficulties which undertaking a new and unfamiliar task can entail. The failure to provide Barbara with proper training and the vulnerability involved in performing a task in public, where there is no protection from the comments of passers-by, both contributed to her lack of confidence in a job which involves a serious responsibility for the safety of children. The involvement of her husband in communicating her decision to abandon the job Illustrates the dependent nature of her relationship with him. As we shall see, it is not a relationship in which she has no power, but it is one in which she defers to his authority and wishes, especially in matters which concern the world beyond their family household.

Her next job (whose significance for her is neatly summarised in her use of the adjective 'little') was a part-time office-cleaning job. She worked at this for three hours each morning, making a 15 hour week. This job did not conflict with any of her domestic responsibilities, but as she suggests below, in discussing why she left it after two years, it had other disadvantages.

> 'We Wanted to do improvements on the home which would mean taking up more on the mortgage.... It was only just three hours a morning, and it wasn't very well paid, and I looked for a part-time assistant job in the paper...and there was one [in] a wallpaper shop... I came for an interview...and they didn't want Saturday work... I used to work from 9 am till 1 pm—I was there about six years—and then I changed the hours to suit myself, as gradually the family were growing up.'

Barbara was to stay in this latter job until she knew the shop was about to be closed down. It offered a good arrangement for her because she was able to have the children in the shop with her (when necessary) during their school holidays, and had some flexibility in the hours she worked. It also gave her the opportunity to work on her own initiative and to take on responsibilities of which she had no previous experience. Although she had worked in shops before having her family, she had worked then as a counter assistant, mainly in two small shops, a grocer's and a baker's. Barbara enjoyed the challenge which this job represented for her, but found eventually that it began to impose rather too much upon her home life. She contrasted it with the duties of her current job, as a sales assistant in the retail store where her husband works:

> 'I had a lot of responsibility in there—management relief when management was off, responsibility as far as ordering goes, plus I mean, the nature of the work is completely

> different...you really are serving customers there...here, it's just a matter of they come and take what they want and come through the tills.'

Had she preferred the more responsible job?

> 'Yes, in a vain way...but no, not really, because it was beginning to...interfere with home life...we didn't get the staff, and the only...action...was that I gave more hours, which I did...then the manager....was off five weeks sick...and I had to take over for five weeks full-time, and you just hadn't got any home life...I enjoyed it, as I say, from a vain way...if I-was single and hadn't got any other responsibilities, then fine...but this job does work much better.'

Despite this assessment, Barbara finds some aspects of her current job unrewarding, and misses the control over her job which she had previously:

> 'Sometimes you feel if you were just left alone you could get on with the job as you would like to—it's like everything else, there are so many rules and regulations, because of the conditions that they expect—it sometimes gets a bit much—but you understand why it is.'

As I have suggested above, Barbara prefers to fit her job around the duties of 'running her home', and chooses part-time work as her strategy for employment rather than the alternative of enlisting the support of her family or of the immediate household. I asked her about her husband's role in the work at home:

> 'He's always willing to help...when I've been doing it full-time, or something like that—washing-up, he's always been one to give a hand...if he knows I'm really pushed he will help me do the cleaning—but I'm a bit independent that way... I get the extra time off, and it's nice to get work done then, so we can share the time together.'

Barbara's 'independence' with regard to the home is a measure of the extent to which she sees this as 'her' domain. She is confident of her abilities to keep it running smoothly, and, unlike her dealings with the outside world, she sees this as a place where she manages and organizes matters as of right. In addition, she enjoys her husband's company, as their decision to have the same weekends off work suggests. In general, Barbara does all the cleaning, washing, ironing, and cooking herself, and she has a clear routine, involving doing particular jobs on set days, and ensuring that tasks like ironing, for example, do not 'pile up'. She prepares her sons' lunch-boxes daily, and is willing to cook twice in an evening if it suits them to have meals at different times. In addition to these tasks, she also does sewing: 'I'm making men's pyjamas at the moment. That I usually fit in at weekends or on my days off.'

Barbara has given some thought to the changed social arrangements whereby increasing numbers of married women have taken on paid jobs. She is not entirely happy about this development:

> 'The thing is, these days, I think they've *got* to—this is the sad part about it.... If want...a home own...mortgages are so high...plus, they do take the wife's wages into consideration now, don't they? When we first started ours, they didn't—'in some ways it seemed cruel to us, but I mean if was a lot kinder because you can manage on one wage... I feel so sorry for them...they can't start a family when they want to, perhaps...we encourage our boys to save as much as they can, mainly with that thought.'

The child of older parents herself, Barbara is sure that having a family while young is the best arrangement:

> 'Had my mother been younger, we could have done different things... I was always told I'd led a sheltered life and... I feel it more *now*.... I look at different people and they've got a wider experience of things than I have... my parents were very sort of protective.'

In fact, Barbara's adolescence involved a very straight forward transition from dependence on her parents, and an acceptance of their authority 'I was the type who did what I was told. I mean, that's what I'd always been brought up to do, and I didn't rebel or anything'—to dependence on her husband and deference to him—'I was only 15 when I met my husband, I just (wanted to) leave school and...get married and have a baby.... I had no real ambitions to do anything.'

Her early experiences of employment tended only to reinforce her sense of herself as powerless and as needing the protection of her parents or a husband. Not only was she driven from her first job by the unwanted familiarities of her boss (see earlier in this chapter), but her second employer, a shopkeeper, also treated her with no respect: 'He made you look very small plenty of times.' Significantly, her departure from this job was at the prompting of her parents:

> 'They were putting on me rather a lot... I used to have to take a lot of writing work home, and the family thought it was getting a bit much.... He didn't really want me to leave—be made it very awkward and had me in tears, but... I wasn't staying.'

As Barbara's husband had worked for a large retail store which employs many married women on a part-lime basis throughout the past fifteen years, I was curious as to why she had not sought work there until so recently (she had been employed there for less thin a year when we met). She explained:

> 'I'd always said I wouldn't before. I think when I was younger, I was more possessive. I think we were both probably a bit possessive. I didn't think it would work... But then... one of the foremen suggested to me, "Why don't you apply in our place?"—and we'd always said we wouldn't, so I thought it over for a while, and eventually I said to my husband, "What do you think?"

In the end she decided to apply for the job, 'for the security really', her confidence that it would have this characteristic stemming from her husband's experience.

Barbara has had no hesitations about staying at home if either of her sons has been unwell or has needed her for any other reason. I asked her how she felt about doing this:

'It was just the natural thing to do. Luckily again, wherever I've worked, they've realized that the family came first.'

In Barbara's experience, the standard arrangements with her employers in such an event have been either that she loses pay for the hours not worked, or that she makes up the lost time. 'I've been lucky.... If I couldn't work certain hours, I could do it at some other time.'

Barbara's earnings represent a significant contribution to the family budget. When we met in early 1980, she was earning approximately £30 per week (basic), while her husband's basic wage was approximately £69 per week. Their weekly household income was thus about £100, subject to deductions for tax and national insurance, and supplemented by a small contribution from their elder son. Their wages 'all go into the same bank account'. I asked Barbara if they could manage without her earnings:

> 'At the moment we run two cars—my son is having one of them soon—so obviously the first thing to go would be *my* car. It would mainly be the family holidays and the car—we might perhaps go for a smaller car...and just sort of a normal cutback—sort of fizzy drinks and biscuits, all the little extras in that line...entertainment, probably—since I've been here we've been going out a little bit more.'

Barbara and Frank are buying their own home, so have a mortgage ('we don't have hardly anything to pay now') as well as the usual household bills to pay. Barbara says they have 'most of what we need we've been doing the home up now for a couple of years', but the house is less well-equipped with domestic appliances than many homes. It contains a washing-machine (twin-tub) and a fridge-freezer, but lacks items—tumble drier, automatic washing machine, a large food freezer—which other women find valuable. In general, their standard of living is modest, but it is difficult to see how they could maintain this level without Barbara's contribution. Barbara plans to remain in employment until she reaches retirement age. She thinks it likely she will stay with her present employer and she says she may seek a modest promotion (to Deputy Supervisor), when she has been in the job a little longer. She has no intention of working full-time in the job, however, a decision which in itself effectively bars her way to any further promotion. It seems probable that Barbara and Frank will now complete their employment careers in the service of their current employer.

9

Women Workers at Home

Family Incomes and Work Decisions

The women in the sample came from very poor families where the average income per family was about Rs. 250 per month. Whatever the contribution of the women to the family income, it was nevertheless crucial for the survival of the family. Following this, it would be logical to argue that the decisions of these women regarding any particular work or the total quantum of work done would significantly depend on the relative levels of their family incomes and responsibilities. While attempting to examine this hypothesis about the existence of a significant relation between the levels of family income and the quantum of work done, a difficulty arose—the available data showed only the actual ex-post amount of work done by workers at different levels of family income. This could not be used to formulate ex-ante aggregate supply schedules at different levels of family income because the existing position was the outcome of this as also of other determinants of supply and demand for such labour. There was a probability that not all the women in the group found as much work as they wanted, thus, the quantum to actual work done would appear to be less clastic in relation to changes in the family income than was the case.

In order to avoid this difficulty, one '912' category workers were considered. This was one category of work of which there was apparently no shortage at the going rates of wages. As the wage rates of later entrants to this occupational category were somewhat higher than the average for all such workers, there was reason to believe that demand was not a limiting factor. Another advantage observed in this labour market was the fact that the supply and demand for work was not in large indivisible units, it was fairly flexible and a worker could add or delete additional jobs to or from her existing work load. In other words, if necessary, she was free to take up or give up work for one of her several employers and thereby alter her work load.

There was a fairly steady negative relation between the workers' hours of work (the quantum of work) and the levels of monthly per capita income of their families. Over 70 per cent of the group with very low incomes worked for nearly nine hours or more per day. Very few worked part-time or less than 30 hours a week. The position of workers from families earning over Rs. 20 per capita monthly income was quite different, the majority worked for a normal length of time and a significant percentage even worked part-time.

The family incomes of workers were considered without the contributions of these workers because with the addition of the workers' contribution there was a tendency for most per capita family incomes to cluster round the modal value. In other words, it appeared that the women worked chiefly to raise the level of per capita family income close to the standard value. If the level was particularly low without their contribution, they worked harder. If not, the opposite was true. In any case the level of family income appeared to be a major determinant of the quantum of work done by each worker. This was presumably true of workers in other comparable occupations.

Contribution to the Family Income

Given the fact that women worked in order to raise the level of the family income as compared to the norm, the question arises how important was their contribution towards this end? Was it marginal or vital? It was observed that in almost all these families the woman's contribution was vital. In nearly half the cases, the woman earned over 40 per cent of the total income. In over a quarter o the cases, the woman's contribution was over 60 per cent. Surprisingly, the percentage of those earning more than 40 per cent of the family income was as high as 39 per cent for workers of 15 years or below. For those between 16 and 25 years, it was only 34 per cent, this figure was significantly below that for the younger group, probably because the young workers of 15 years or less came to the labour market only when the family situation was really desperate. Of those between 26 and 50 years of age, over 50 per cent earned more than 40 per cent of the family income and nearly 20 per cent earned over 80 per cent of it. For the oldest age group, this percentage was even higher.

Among the women who earned over 60 per cent of the family income, 82 per cent were in domestic services, and a large number of this group were resident servants. This figure was much higher than the weightage of domestic service in the general sample population, probably because it was easier to earn a higher income in domestic service with the terms of appointment being flexible which allowed a person longer hours if necessary. The rates were somewhat better in some of the cases. Looking from another angle, it could be said that women went in for domestic service jobs when they were more desperate than the average.

Secondary or Supplementary Earners. One of the standard arguments for the casual attitude towards discrimination against women in economic activities is that women are viewed as secondary or supplementary earners within a family. In all household activity analysis, the economic activity of only the head of the household is considered primary and all other earners are considered secondary for the household. In this study, the generalisation that women's work is secondary was not wholly supported by the evidence obtained from the sample. There were several widows, divorcees and unmarried women who claimed that they were the head of their household. In addition to these, there were several married or unmarried women from households where the head was unemployed and the woman was the principal earner. A large majority of this group had several dependents—unemployed husbands, fathers, children and siblings.

Of the 164 women, over 50 per cent were in the '912' occupational category as against only 36 per cent in the total sample. On the other hand, there were relatively few skilled workers. This could be explained in terms of the fact that the former type of work was relatively easy to get and was more steady. Skilled work on the other hand, was often in short supply and while supplementary earners could perhaps afford to wait for an opportunity to get skilled work, those on whom a family's living depended could not do so.

TABLE 1

Distribution of Occupation-wise Workers by Age and Share in Family Incomes

Percentage share in family income of the worker			*Age in years*			
	15	*16-25*	*26-35*	*36-50*	*50+*	*Total*
1	*2*	*3*	*4*	*5*	*6*	*7*
20.0						
'912' workers	1	1	7	5	2	16
Other domestic workers	—	2	1	5	2	10
Skilled workers	6	16	17	4	—	43
Unskilled workers	1	9	10	5	1	26
Total	8	28	35	19	5	95
20.1-40.0						
'912' workers	3	6	18	14	3	44
Other domestic workers	—	4	3	6	1	14
Skilled workers	3	17	8	3	—	31
Unskilled workers	1	13	4	7	—	25
Total	7	40	33	30	4	114
40.1-60.0						
'912' workers	6	8	9	11	3	37
Other domestic workers	—	1	4	12	3	20
Skilled workers	2	8	4	5	—	19
Unskilled workers	1	2	5	2	—	10
Total	9	19	22	30	6	86

1	*2*	*3*	*4*	*5*	*6*	*7*
60.1-80.0						
'912' workers	1	3	9	9	-	22
Other domestic workers	1	3	2	3	—	9
Skilled workers	—	3	3	1	—	7
Unskilled workers	—	1	—	2	—	3
Total	2	10	14	15		41
80.1						
'912' workers	1	1	8	10	4	24
Other domestic workers	1	1	9	14	4	29
Skilled workers	—	1	3	—	1	5
Unskilled workers	—	3	1	2	9	15
Total	2	6	21	26	18	73

Women's work is often dismissed as secondary in yet another way. Even when a woman earns a significant part of the family income, this amount is often used for purchasing non-essential commodities for the family. In other words, the wages raise the standard of living of the family above the basic minimum rather than ensure the basis minimum itself. This was not observed in the sample studied here. The earnings of the women in the sample were essential, not for ensuring extra comforts for the family, but for providing the bare necessities.

It is clearly evident from the table above that woman's work had not been adequate to ensure even the basic necessities for the family. More than half the families were unable to buy a full supply of cereals, pulses, sugar, cooking oil and kerosene to which they were entitled under the rationing system. Very few were able to buy anything extra for the family. It was seen that even women who had worked for five or more year failed to accumulate reserves to buy durables. Not more than 22 women in this group possessed a radio set. Another ten owned a watch or a clock. Only ten families owned all these three commodities. It was observed that in this group of women who had worked for five or more years, the higher a woman's contribution to the family income, the less were the family's chances of obtaining any extras. In other words, since a woman's total earning capacity was severely limited in these occupations and in this labour market, a family which was largely dependent on a woman earner was on the border of subsistence. This state of affairs reflected adversely on the labour market employing women. It did not detract from the importance of a woman's work for the family' survival.

TABLE 2

Women Who were Formal or Informal Head of Household

Civil status	*Total number*	*'912' workers*	*Skilled workers*
Widows and divorcees from house-hods with no other head			
(a) with dependents	88	52	14
(b) without dependents	27	13	3
Married women from households with unemployed head			
(a) with dependents	27	14	2
(b) without dependents	5	3	1
Unmarried women from single member households	2	1	1
Unmarried women from house-holds with unemployed head	15	2	6
Total	164	85	27
Percentage	(100.0)	(51.8)	(7.9)
Percentage in total sample population	41.00	35.75	26.25

Apart from this information regarding the expenditure on essentials and luxuries, information about their life style was also elicited. An important factor to be considered here was the amount of help they received in executing their double load of housework and other wage work. As seen earlier, most of these women had very long working hours without the relief of occasional paid leave or a weekly holiday. In addition to the long working hours, these women had a particularly heavy load of housework. To begin with, all but two of the families had to fetch water from a well, a public tap or a tubewell. Most of the women collected cowdung to make cakes for fuel and also went over garbage heaps to find any bits of paper, wood or half-burnt coal which could be used as fuel. The only readymade foods available were bread and *muri* (parched rice). Most of these women had large families with more than one minor children.

To ease their heavy load of housework, only three could afford paid help, while the others could not even afford the most elementary labour and time-saving gadgets. Only 356 women offered information on this issue—30 per cent had a kerosene stove for cooking, while the others relied wholly on coal stoves which require a tremendous amount of effort to light and keep going. None of the families had any cooking gas facilities, and only eight owned a pressure cooker. Although electricity was available in most areas, the majority used an oil lamp for lighting. Less than ten per cent of the houses had electrical fittings, and the ones who did have electricity in the house used it very sparingly and used only low watt bulbs.

Among their other possessions, nearly a quarter possessed one or two costs. These cots were often *charpais* which the adults took out at night to sleep on the pavements. The extremely poor families were also aware of the hazards of malaria and a common and essential commodity in these areas was a mosquito-net. Over half the families possessed at least one net. Others had more than one net including a separate one for children. These few gods generally completed the list of their entire possessions, though some owned a chair or a small table, and usually a trunk and a clothes horse. The men in the family frequently had a shirt or a pair of trousers made of synthetic material, but rarely did the women or the children possess such relatively expensive things except when they were given old clothes by others.

Health and Education of Children

Another way of effectively utilising the income of these women could be for giving their children a better start in life which would include lowering the incidence of infant and child mortality. In the sample, the rate of child mortality was quite high. Nearly 13 per cent of all children born alive had died before the age of one and over a quarter of the children born alive had died before the age of one and over a quarter of the children had died before reaching five years of age. In this sample there was considerable improvement over time—children born since 1970 had a much higher life expectancy than those born between 1960 and 1970 and a still higher expectancy than those born before 1960. The current estimate (at the time of the study) of infant mortality for the whole of West Bengal was only 8.07 deaths for 100 live births within one year of birth and the figures obtained from this sample were consistently higher than this figure.

It may be significantly that among the children born since 1970, the mortality rates for infants and children of unskilled workers mothers were significantly higher than among the rest. This may be partly due to the differences in family incomes and partly to the differences in cultural backgrounds.

A striking feature observed in this connection was the high incidence of miscarriage among skilled workers. It may be possible that following 1970, a significant percentage of miscarriages could have been induced as part of the family planning drive, though to a certain extent, it could have been a result of the long hours these skilled workers spent working on their sewing machines throughout the year.

Even if women could do little to improve either their own or their children's health or their surroundings, they could use their income to provide the children better education. But in this direction too, they achieved little. The West Bengal Government records indicate that by 1975-76 for male children in the age group 6 to 11 years, entry into primary schools was nearly universal whereas for female children, it was over 60 per cent. In this study however, not even half the male children and only about one-third of the female children between 6 to 11 years of age attended primary school. Those who did manage to attend school showed a lower rate of dropouts as compared to the total West Bengal average of 33 per cent or more. Official records for West Bengal reveal that nearly half of all the boys and a quarter of all the girls in the 11 to 15 years age group were in secondary school. The comparable figures in the sample weer 20.5 per cent for boys and 17.5 per cent for girls. On the whole, 55 per cent of all the living children of these women were illiterate. The percentage of illiteracy among children in the 6 to 10 years age group in 1976-77 was not significantly lower. Apparently, these children had not been able to take much advantage of the expanding educational facilities in the region. Added to this was the disturbing fact that several women had been compelled to send their children who were below 15 years of age to work.

Leisure Time Activities

With their limited income there was not much choice of entertainment open to these women. Though 40 per cent of them were literate, not more than 15 per cent read anything at all. Most of them owned no radio or transistor sets and only about 20 per cent ever listened to an occasional programme. Cinema was a very common form of entertainment, and over 75 per cent said that they managed to see a film occasionally. However, only the young unmarried girls had some leisure time and spare money to buy a film magazine or to see a film at least once a month. A common form of relaxation was a visit to one's relatives or to a religious place. The younger married women found it extremely difficult to find time for visiting their parents. Their '912' workers were the worst off in this respect because they did not get time off even during festivals.

To conclude one may say that the data indicated that women's decisions regarding the quantum of work they did in the labour marked depended not so much on the levels of wage rates as on their per capita family income. The poorer the family, the more the amount of work the women tried to undertake. Interestingly, there were substantial differences in the per capita family income levels exclusive of the earnings of these women workers, but inclusive of their earnings the per capita income in all worker families tended to cluster round the mean level. This mean level was in accordance with the prices prevailing at the time of the survey, very close to the margin of subsistence. It could be said that these workers' main motivation in seeking work was to raise the family per capita income level to a target level. This explains why these women put in extra work when marginal and average wage rates remained constant or even deteriorated. About 40 per cent of the women in the sample were the chief earners in the family and were the formal or informal head of their household. Regardless of the age group, over half the women earned more than 40 per cent of the family income and a quarter earned 60 per cent or more of it. Therefore, the tendency to regard women's work as secondary and less deserving of social consideration is not only unjust to them as workers but could seriously affect the welfare of their entire family they belong.

Women in the unorganized occupations belonged to families on the brink of subsistence. There was a close link between on the brink of subsistence. There was a close link between women's decisions regarding the amount of work done and the shortfall in the family income for the basic requirements to ensure the survival of the family. In spite of the substantial percentage-wise contribution they made, the families were hardly able to afford a regular and adequate supply of the bare necessities. Few of them could afford to build up a stock of any durables. Even though they worked for unusually long hours outside the home, few of them could afford either paid help or buy any gadgets to reduce drudgery of housework. Nor could it be said that their work enabled them to give their children a significantly better life. They could not ensure for their children a higher than average life expectancy or education level or even a childhood free of economic pressures. Children were often found helping their mothers regularly in order to enable the latter to carry on with their work both at home and outside, and were also compelled to take up regular paid work themselves.

10

Urban Working Women at Work Place

The problems and difficulties of working women are multi-dimensional, varying from woman to woman at personal level, and section to section at general level and hence need to be analyzed in depth. One may believe that there are two clear-cut sections—privileged and unprivileged among the urban working women. Women working in factories, mines, plantations or in electronics, garments or chemical units or banks, schools and hospitals appear to be the privileged sections among women.

The problems of working women at work places are multiple and differ from woman to woman according to the nature of the work and position. Ms. Aruna Broota, a phychologist of Delhi University, is categorical in stating that no girl is respected in the office if she is known to be a single woman. In fact, in India women are considered less of and individual than as an object of vice by men whether she is single or married. this is particularly true for the women who are working among the males. Working women of the present generation, in the opinion of Ms. Broota, are at the cross-roads. They are aware that they are being exploited and ill treated. Yet they consciously or unconsciously adopt their mother's roles of subservience to the male. So, women, in general, have to be taught to develop their self-confidence, as well as self-respect and not accept the apologetic and subservient role instilled in them since childhood.

Working Women and Colleagues

The efficiency of a working woman is always suspected. Especially in the upper class cadres, even though other qualifications are equal, men are preferred. the authorities are doubtful whether she would be able to handle male subordinates, take independent decisions, cope with crisis and manage her duties. Even though she has proved her efficiency, they think twice before promoting her. Even if she is given a chance, there is always a remark that she has been taken because she is a woman.

The male co-workers in the office cannot mentally accept the superiority of the woman's work. They take extra pains to ridicule her. The male colleagues get together and pass comments. As the woman is brought up in a protected atmosphere in the family, she is not mentally prepared to face this kind of situation. She feels helpless and often breaks down. This further leads to the misconception that women workers are not fit for outside work.

Office and Family

There is another type of problem which arise when she has to work over-time to complete her work. In certain government jobs the woman employee also face transfers, she finds it difficult to go, having the family behind. If she is married she can not go leaving her husband and children. In such a situation generally she has to give up the job. If she is unmarried the parents would not permit her to go alone. If she is married and working, she has to leave the job if her in laws do not approve of her working or if she is married in some other place then also she has to resign. Again if she wants to work at a new place, it becomes difficult for her to find a new job. In some cases women have to leave the job when the children are too young and there is nobody in the family to look after them. By the time children are grown up, women are out of touch with the field and are not able to find work again. Unfortunately, in our country the system of part-time jobs have not developed yet. Part-time jobs would have been more convenient to young married working women with children. But it has not been acceptable as they are poorly paid for and part-time jobs consume comparatively more time and require equally hard work from her.

Women as Managers

It is equally difficult a situation where the woman is a boss. The male subordinates do not like to accept the authority of a woman boss. If she demands work, efficiency and discipline, she is criticized as harsh and dictatorial. She is supposed to dominate only to hide her inefficiency and inferiority complex. If she is polite, mild and courteous, she would be labelled as inefficient, talkative and what not. In any way, they do not carry out her orders and instructions, neglect their duties and take advantage of her goodness. They try to harass her in many ways. In short they are not able to accept a woman as their head.

There is another problem; while working with men, a woman tends to develop close relations with any one of them owing to prolonged and constant association. This, in the case of a married woman, creates social and psychological problems and tensions in her relationships, while in the case of an unmarried girl, it can create all sorts of socio-psychological problems if she gets involved with a married man. Sengupta in her study (1964) points towards the emergence of similar problems. In this connection Rosenquiet observes, "certain social conditions, most of them connected with recent changes in economic life, provide an environment quite favourable to divorce. The arrangement of office work, as now generally found, may be mentioned as an example. The professional men of male office worker and his female secretary, stenographer, or assistant are likely to develop personal attachments which endanger the marriage tie. More especially, this is likely to be true of one of the partners in this business relationship, usually the woman, is unmarried."

Even if the woman who is working in the office with men makes only good friends with them and has no intimate relations with any one of them, she is still liable to be suspected and often accused of having intimate relations with them. This often humiliates and annoys her a lot and creates frictions in her married life.

Scanty Choice

Another notable problem for the woman worker is that they do not get jobs in the fields of their interest. They have to accept the work they get. But this problem is not confined only to women. Many male workers also have the same problem.

The professional women have their own problems. As she is professionally trained, she aspires to utilise her skills, to put up the best performance and to earn a proper income. But the in-laws do not accept her working. In this way many women doctors, engineers and technicians leave their profession after marriage or do work for limited hours for pleasure only. Even when they work the fellow professionals, especially the males have a negative attitude. Sometimes the work women get do not befit their qualifications. For example, it is often believed that teaching, medical practice etc. are the ones more suitable for women, and thereby they are forced to accept what is available and do not achieve the levels they are trained for.

The composition of staff at the work-place also create problems. Some traditional families in India, for example, would like their women to be posted exclusively in a girls college or school. These families are afraid that in a place where the majority is men, their women will be looked upon as sex objects. The liberal-minded families do not entertain such a baseless apprehension and do not stand in the way of their women working in a male-dominated office, or a boy's school, or a co-educational institution. Sex segregation in the offices and establishments is an unhealthy pattern either for the present or for the future. It is a negation of equality with men.

Transport Problem

The present transport system is far from satisfactory; generally women have to suffer the worst due to misconduct or eve-teasing by co-passengers. Sometimes they have to wait for hours on the bus-stop to board a bus. Even when the bus comes, due to it being over-crowded she is not able to catch it. Even in train the position is not good. At present there is only one ladies' compartment in local trains in cities like Bombay and Delhi, and that too, is often occupied by men. At the peak hours one can hardly entrain or detrain without difficulty. In some metro-cities there is a "ladies' special" during busy hours. But it is unsatisfactory and limited. So the authorities should provide for more than one ladies' compartment in local trains and more 'ladies' special' to solve problems of various type for the women workers.

Wage Discrimination

The issue of discrimination in wages throughout the world is a matter of vital importance. Mencher and Saradamoni noted that it was often taken for granted that women should be paid less than men for similar jobs. Throughout the world, women are concentrated in low paid job sectors according to an I.L.O. report. Apart from lower wave rates poor urban women were rarely given any access to training schemes and their promotional avenues were severely limited. At every level of work, they are paid lower wages, defeating the constitutional position of equal pay for equal work for both men and women.

There has been quite a few micro-studies that show that women workers in unorganized sector invariably get paid much less than men. G.D. Gambhir in his study on "Labour in Small-scale Industries in Madhya Pradesh with special reference to women and child labour in cotton ginning, bidi making and rice milling and shelloc manufacture" found that wages of unskilled women workers ranged between 65% to 75% that of the unskilled men-workers. Men coolies earn double that of women coolies. In Kerala, in cashew processing and coir industries women are paid less than men. Women construction workers are paid uniformly lower wages than their male counterparts in spite of the fact that she is doing equally, if not more hard work in comparison to men. In fact women in the unorganized sector as well as the organized sector are discriminated directly or indirectly. One can take a look at the wages in the organized sectors.

Only 11 per cent of the country's female work-force is employed in the organized sector. The organized sector comprises units registered under the Factories Act of 1948 and covers those using power and employing ten or more workers, as well as units not using power but employing 20 or more workers. In addition the organized sector is governed by legislation such as the Minimum Wages Act, Labour Welfare Regulations, and Contract Labour (Regulation and Abolition) Act. Strictly speaking violations of those Acts can be challenged in a Court of Law.

In the organized sectors of the economy, people are selected for job-positions and their rate of emoluments are fixed primarily in relation to the nature of the jobs concerned. There could therefore, be theoretically no sex-based differences in wages in the organized sectors. It is, however, possible that some establishments try to separate some jobs carrying less pay and it may so happen that only females get recruited to such jobs. This may not "technically amount to sex-based discrimination", though "such categorization of jobs' may also sometimes be done purposely."

Even in the public sector, where employment has gone up substantially, a large proportion of women are shunted into low-paid jobs. Official agencies admit that no assessment has been done as to what extent the equal pay principle has resulted in the displacement of women workers. After examining different industries the National Committee on Status of Women in 1976 came to be conclusion that the principle of equal pay has not been seriously applied in most of industries which continue to maintain wage differentials by direct or indirect methods. Evidence for this is available in occupational wage surveys conducted by the Ministry of Labour, indicating differences in the minimum, maximum and average earnings of women in most of industries. Though the survey reported that employees evade this principle by not employing men and women for the same jobs in the same establishments, such differentials were found even within the same establishments in some cases. A more successful method for evading this principle is by restricting women to certain jobs and prescribing lower wage rates for them. A study of 400 working women by Usha Talwar also reveals that lower pay for equal work is one of the most important issues faced by those working women.

Wage discrimination is a problem all over the world, especially in the third world countries, where the process of industrialization is still going on. A double standard on pay still plagues women workers everywhere according to ILO report. The average earning of women compared with men in non-agricultural activities in 1981 ranged from 44.8 per cent in South Korea to 86.2% in Australia. In the manufacture sector alone, these ranged from 43.4% in Japan to 90% in Sweden. According to I.L.O. Year Book the gap between women's and men's wages widened slightly between 1977 and 1981 in 7 countries—Czechoslovakia, Denmark, West Germany, Japan, Luxemburg, the Netherlands and Britain. the earnings of women compared to men went down from 55.8% to 53.5% in Japan and from 71.9% to 69.5% in Britain. On the contrary, there was some improvement in women's remuneration in six countries—Belgium, Cyprus, France, Ireland, Newzealand and Switzerland. The increase was highest in Ireland going up from 80.1% to 83.7%. However women working in the manufacturing sector in Japan experienced further erosion of their earning compared to those of men, as they dropped from 46.1% in 1977 to 43.4% in 1981.

In India the average earnings of women are highly depressed. The average earning of regular wage/salaried female employees is about three times higher than of the females casual labourers. If the men and women are working on the same post in Government's jobs, there is not so much discrimination. But in other institutions there is a disparity prevailing. There is another aspect of wage discrimination in India that is female workers "are exploited as a piece-rate worker doing manual labour for trader, middlemen, contractors and big companies in the corporate sector." "There is a variation in the wages for identical work and skills." "Self-employed workers accept wage rate which potently do not cover their cost. It is difficult to understand why and how the difference exists and why workers accept them."

Thus the wage-discrimination is a universal phenomenon and it needs a world-wide awakening and revolutionary movement to wipe out the basic discrimination at various levels of the economy and for this not only women but also men have to come under one-banner and fight against it.

Health Issue

Women anywhere in the world have to suffer from some in built disadvantages, compared to men, because of certain biological reasons. They have to put up with menstruation, pregnancy, child birth, lactation, child rearing and menopause and their various complications. Physically, they are less strong. they are also ore vulnerable to sexual aggression and abuse. The different cultural, social and economic situations in India have given different focus to these biological disadvantages of women. These situations also influence the way these biological disadvantages affect the health of the working women.

One may hence analyse the status and conditions of these working women in various industries. A study done by Shahnaz Anklesaria gives us a clear cut picture. She has pointed out the defects of Factory Act which seeks to ensure protection to millions of women covered by it. It applies to any premises where 10 or more workers are employed and where a manufacturing process is carried on with or without the aid of power. The Act is enforced by the State Governments through their factory inspectorates. It was amended in 1976 to include the three sections which deal specifically with health hazards that the workers face.

The Act outlines the principal health risks to factory workers, which arise from dangerous gases, acids and dust, harmful bacteria and micro-organizms, compressed and rarefied atmosphere, improper lighting, extremes of temperature, humidity and excessive strain. But it is silent on the impact of all these on women workers. The repercussions on women can be slightly different from those on men because of the additional physical and psychological factors and can be complicated by pregnancy, maternity and gynaecological issues. Further environmental factors like, heat, humidity, repetitive work, toxic substances also affect women. They can adversely condition pregnancy, child birth, lactation, child rearing and menopause and their various complications.

The law prohibits women's employment in dangerous and heavy operations in organized sector. At the same time in unorganized sector, as head-loader, handcraft puller, construction workers, women work more than men—for longer hours and sometimes for less wages.

What the Factories Act does say is that women must be prohibited from employment in dangerous and heavy operations. No women worker should be asked to clean or lubricate or adjust any machinery while it is in motion, if her work exposes her to the risk of injury from any moving part. No woman workers should be employed for pressing cotton in any part of a factory in which a cotton opener is at work. There are also specified limits on the amount of weight a woman worker can carry. This is limited to 65 lbs for an adolescent and 30 for a child. The State governments can, therefore, restrict or prohibit the employment of women in any operation which may expose them to serious risk of physical injury.

It is well spread belief that the physical structure and maternal functions of women place her at a disadvantage. But practices do not follow this. women have never shirked hard labour; whether it is farming, planting, transplanting, winowing, weeding, harvesting, grinding, pounding, nothing holds them back. It is has been seen that work which is physically very strenuous is done not by men but by by women like head-loaders, handcraft pullers, construction workers etc. Any "disadvantage" that women's maternal functions may cause is largely man-made. So these responsibilities have to be seen as vital functions to perform for which a woman must be adequately compensated. Male refusal to take on specific home and child-care responsibilities has also placed a dual responsibility of home as well as office on working women. These responsibilities cause mental as well as physical problem which ultimately leads to health hazards.

Further instead of outlining the kind of health hazards in modern industry for women, the law merely lays emphasis on the negative stereo-types of working women which restrict her access to certain kind of work.

The Act also says that there should be separate toilets and sanitary, dressing rooms for women workers. It specifies the need for keeping both clean. Besides the obvious health reasons. what is not so well known is that modern industrial processes subject employees not only to dangerous dust and vapours, but a variety of diseases—breeding organizms that can be transmitted by fellow workers to one another. Hence the need for eliminating unhygenic contacts between workers. In study after study we come across the women workers' complaint of the absence or shortage of separate toilets at their work place. The fact is that the Factories Acts which are enforced by the factory inspectors, are not implemented. Thus in different industries women workers are suffering from innumerable difficulties and nothing has been done to alleviate them. Both men and women can be working on the same jobs, but women can for a variety of reasons be affected more than their male-colleagues. A survey of the agate workers in Gujarat, revealed that lungs disease had affected 70.6% of women and 60.4% of the men. Pneumonia and T.B. affected 19.6% and 21.6% respectively of the women, compared to 17.9% and 12.9% of the males.

A study conducted by M. Vanamala on Public Sectors in Andhra Pradesh shows that except the maternity benefits, the other facilities are poor and inadequate. Only about 20% of the women employees are provided with transport facilities, 16 per cent housing facilities and 38 per cent child care facilities. This indicated that the public enterprises miserably neglected the women in providing employment opportunities and adequate status.

In the present situation maternity leave is being revised and improved. The provision for unpaid "special leave" of varying length in excess of the statutory maternity leave as is practised in France, may be followed. In fact health problem of under privileged working women are worst due to exploitation, oppression, denial of social and economic justice. Hunger, poor sanitation and housing, unhealthy source of drinking water, infesting of insects and parasites, lack of protection from various elements of nature, poor educational status and limited access to media of mass communication, are some of the major consequences of these conditions which affect the working pattern of the society. Under-nutrition and malnutrition are common phenomenon among the working women in India, particularly in the underprivileged section.

Besides the patriarchal discrimination, women in India suffer due to exploitation and oppression by the privileged sections. Such exploitation is also closely linked with extensive health problems that prevail among the women belonging to the underprivileged class. Because of this, they also have less access even to community financial health institutions. The struggle for health of women should therefore be a struggle for social, economic and political emancipation of the underprivileged as a class. With a platform of equal rights and status of women, women and men will have to fight together to attain emancipation of the underprivileged.

REFERENCES

Geetanjali Dash, *Status of Women Workers in Industrial Area in India,* (Unpublished M. Phi. thesis). Delhi University, p. 50.

K.P. Khanna and M. Mathew, *Women Workers in the Unorganized Sector of the Coir Industry in India,* ICSSR, 1979 (Unpublished thesis).

M. Vanamala, "Employment Status of Women in Andhra Pradesh State Public Enterprises" in K. Morali Manohar (ed.), *Women's Status and Development in India*, p. 87.

Promila Kapur, *The Changing Status of the Working Women in India,* p. 69.

Shahnaz Ankesaria, "Slow Death is their lot", *The Statesman,* January 4, 1984.

Urmila Patel, "Problems of Working Women in India" in T.M. Dak (ed.), *Women and Work in Indian Society*, p. 228.

Usha Talwar, *Social Profile of Working Women,* p. 51.

11

Informal Women Laborures in Indian States

Women Work in Ancient India

Women were employed to work as wine servers and as spies to get the secret of the drunkards without arising any doubts in their minds. Some reference in ancient literary works (particularly dramas) partly prove the existence of Dasis (female slaves) in those days. For instance, in Kalidas's *Mâlavikagnimitra, Parivrajita* testifies to the existence of Female spies, in *Mrichahakutika* of Sudrak. (a drama of Gupta age) the character of Madarika bears testimony of the existence of female slaves. Women in ancient India were also engaged as Gaṇikā. We find such Ganikas in Ṣudraka's *'Mṛichchakutika'* and in Dandin's *'Dasa-Kumăr-Charita.'* The system of employing women as Deva-Dàsis, which is still found in the South India temple, was widely prevalent in ancient India. References to the employment of such Deva-Dāsis at the temple of Mahăkăl in Ujjayani are found in Kălidas's Meghadoot, such Dasis were also kept in temple of Sun God when Hiuen Tsant visited India.

Women Work in Present Times

With the march of civilization, the impact of social changes and developmental efforts benefit the women much less than man. Social and religious reformers, enlightened public authorities, and women's organizations waged battles against the oppressive position of women through centuries. But scourges as illiteracy, ignorance, superstition still persist in some parts of the country resulting in unorganized low-paid exploited women workers. Through the centuries, women have been working for their families as long as sixteen hours or more right from day break till late into the night. They manage the household work on the farm, fetch water, look after the cattle, feed the children as well as the adults in the family, clothe and educate the children. In most rural households in India, the bulk of the energy consumed, specially in the domestic sector, comes from fire wood. In poor households this fuel is typically gathered by women and female children mainly from forest land and village common land. In recent years with depleting forest many of these households are facing a fuelwood crisis, the burden of which has fallen mainly on the women.

Women in Unorganized Sector

A high proportion of working women in India are employed in the unorganized sector mainly in agriculture, livestock, forestry, the percentage being 79 as per 1981 census. Working women are manifested in agricultural activities like land preparation, seed grading, sowing, dibbling, planting, irrigating, threshing, winnowing, storing crops, feeding cattle, looking after milch animal and poultry etc. The nature of works in agriculture which the women workers perform exposes them to particular health hazards. In various states, especially in South India, rich transplanting is done primarily by women workers.

Table 1 reveals that the percentage of the women workers in India in 1971 in the Primary, Secondary and tertiary sector were 83.06, 7.66 and 9.33 respectively and the corresponding percentage in 1981 are 79.80, 8.94 and 9.47. Thus, it is obvious that there has been shift of women workers from the primary sector to the secondary and tertiary sector during period under study. Again, out of total working women in 1971, the unorganized sector alone employed 94 per cent which has gone up to 96 per cent during 1981 per cent which has gone up to 96 per cent during 1981 census. Thus, it is observed that work participation in the unorganized sector has been an increasing trend. Immobility of labour is the greatest impediment of women work that keeps them confined to low paying, irregular and local avenues of employment in unorganized sector. Ignorance,

TABLE 1

Women Work in Different Sectors

	Industrial Categories	*Percentage distribution of female main workers*	
		1971	*1981*
	Primary Sector		
(i)	Cultivators	29.84	33.20
(ii)	Agricultural Labourers	50.86	45.18
(iii)	Livestock, forestry, fishing etc.	1.96	1.06
(iv)	Mining and quarrying	0.40	0.36
	Total	**83.06**	**79.80**
	Secondary Sector		
(v)	Manufacturing, Processing, servicing and repairs		
(a)	Household Industry	4.24	4.59
(b)	Other than Household Industry	2.77	3.55
(vi)	Construction	0.65	0.80
	Total	**7.6**	**8.94**
	Tertiary Sector		
(vii)	Trade and Commerce	1.78	2.04
(viii)	Transport, storage and communisation	0.47	0.38
(ix)	Other services	7.08	7.05
	Total	**9.33**	**9.37**
	Total main workers	***100.00***	***100.00***

Source: 1981 census (excludes Assam).

tradition-bound attitudes, lack of skill, seasonal nature of employment, heavy physical work of difficult types, lack of job security, long hours of work, lack of minimum facilities at the work place, ill-treatment and bondage are some of the features of the employment of women in unorganized sector. In the tribal districts of Orissa, because of deforestation, increased pressure on land, lack of irrigation and recurring drought conditions, tribal women have been migrating to outside their villages, district and state for periods ranging from 2 to 6 months for working in construction projects, brick-kilns and tea-estates.

A greater percentage of women are employed in the unorganized sector in our country. It is lamentable to note that there has been drastic decline in the proportion of women population to total population. It has decreased from 33.7 per cent in 1911 to 14 per cent in 1981, which can be seen from Table 2.

TABLE 2

Women Component in Total Working Force

Year	*Proportion of women population to total population*	*Percentage of women workers to total population*	*Percentage of women workers to total workers*
1911	49.1	33.7	34.5
1921	48.9	32.7	34.0
1931	48.9	27.6	31.2
1951	48.6	23.3	29.0
1961	48.5	28.0	31.5
1971	48.1	12.1	17.7
1981	48.3	14.0	16.5

Source: Government of India, Census reports.

It is apparent from the Table 3 that the ratio of women in unorganized sector has gone up during the decade 1971-81 from 94 per cent to 96 per cent. Thus, work participation in the unorganized sector has been on increasing phenomenon. Those unorganized has broad dimension like agriculture, animal husbandry, fisheries, home-based industries like handicrafts, handlooms, coir industry, agrabati industry, bidi industry, sericulture, construction industry and the like. A good deal of studies corroborate the fundamentally subordinate position of women in the unorganized (or which may also be termed as informal sector) sector and their easy exploitability. In this informal sector in India, millions of people earn living as the tailors, furniture makers, street vendors, taxi drivers are only a few members of this over-growing army of workers.

TABLE 3

Women Workers in India, (1971 and 1981)

	1971	*1981*
Female population as per cent of total population	48.2	48.3
Work participation (in millions)	31	48
Working women as per cent of total women	12.13	14.44
Total women in unorganized sector (in million)	29	46.24
Women in unorganized sector as per cent of total working women	94.00	96.33
Women in agriculture as per cent of working women	82.61	81.23

Source: Women work Force Trend and Pattern of Employment, by Atmanand, *Khadi Gramodyog,* March, 1990, p. 248.

In the tribal areas women contribute to the working in a more significant way than in the non-tribal society. While the ratio between the male and female labourers in the general population of the country is 5:1, it is 3:1 among the tribal among the non-tribal women 11.9 per cent are labourers whereas their tribal sisters have 20.75 per cent as labourers. The comparative picture of the participation rate of the non-tribal in the different sectors of economy have been represented in Table 4.

Women in Household Duties

Tribal economy being mainly confined to primary sector 90.6 per cent of the women workers are engaged in agriculture, as cultivators or as labourers, 2.67 per cent in livestock, forestry, fishing, hunting etc., and 0.6 per cent in mining. In recent years, because of various factors like industrialization, growth of road, transports facilities, provision of education, contact with outside world and social mobility-all combinedly resulted in increase participation of tribal women workers for economic gain and development.

TABLE 4

Participation Rate of Non-Tribal and Tribal Female Labourers in Different Sectors

Occupational categories	*Cultivation*	*Agricultural labourers*	*Mining*	*Livestock, forestry, fishing, hunting etc.*
		Primary Sector		
General women	29.8%	50.5%	0.4%	2.5%
Tribal women	42.7%	48.9%	0.6%	2.6%
		Secondary Sector		
	Household industry	*Manufact-uring etc.*	*Construction*	
General Women	4.3%	2.8%	0.7%	
Tribal women	1.3%	0.9%	0.3%	
		Tertiary Sector		
	Trade and commerce	*Transport etc.*	*Other services*	
General women	1.8%	0.5%	—	
Tribal Women	0.6%	0.2%	—	

Source: Challenges to the Fair Sex (pp. 72-73).

In addition to those women formally included as workers in the Census of national surveys, more than a quarter of the rural women and more than half of all women are engaged in these unrecorded activities.

Women Workers in Non-Agricultural Sector

The foregoing table which is the outcome of the economic census 1980 conducted by the Central Statistical Organization has revealed that at all India level (excluding Assam) there were 1841 million enterprises engaged in different economic activities other than crop production and plantation with 53.58 million persons working in them. Of these, 92 per cent were non-agricultural and 73 per cent of them didn't use hired labour. In other words, they were family enterprises, informal or self-employed units. In recent years, adequate attention has been focussed for the development of informal sector, which employs greater percentage of women work. In the wake of rapid industrialization and mechanization, women experience acute unemployment consequent upon the delay of traditional crafts and handloom sector. They are unable to face the new challenge and participate in the advanced modern industrialised sector due to lack of skill and technology which is obstructed by family obligations and conservative attitude of the people.

TABLE 5

Percentage of Women Reported as doing Household Duties Who Participated in Specified Activities for Family Benefits

		% W. in activity out of those engaged in house work	
		Rural	*Urban*
1.	Free collection of fish, game	6.24	0.80
2.	Free collection of firewood, dung etc.	14.34	3.11
3.	Maintenance of Kitchen garden	4.70	1.35
4.	Work in household poultry	11.06	3.11
5.	Sewing, tailoring, weaving	3.77	6.65
6.	Tutoring children	0.48	2.19
7.	Bringing water-from other villages	1.35	—
8.	Anyone of these specified activities	21.78	12.33

Source: NSS 32nd Round.

Male-Female Participation in India

The comparative position of men-women participation in India is represented in Table 7.

The table reveals that the women workers increased from around 90 million in 1973 to 117 million in 1983, (At a rate of 3 per cent average increase from 185 million to 231 million (At a rate of 2.4

per cent average increase per (annum). The women rural participation rate has also increased from 37.53 per cent to 38.74 per cent during 1973 to 1983. The participation rate of women in urban area is also higher compared to rural area during the period under review.

TABLE 6

Employment Status of Female Workers in Non-Agricultural Household Units

Economic Activity	*Employment in own account*			*Employment in establishments using wage labour*		
	Total No. (00)	*Female*	*F%*	*Total No. (00)*	*Female*	*F%*
1. Mining, Quarrying	2353	49	(2.0)	807	101	(12.5)
2. Manufacturing, Repair	22909	5512	(24.0)	73926	7249	(9.8)
3. Electricity, Gas, Water	21	1	(4.7)	2293	59	(2.6)
4. Construction	565	24	(3.6)	1588	268	(16.8)
5. Wholesale and Retail Trade	27618	2010	(7.2)	26421	1503	(5.6)
6. Restaurants and Hotels	2657	327	(12.3)	88.74	372	(4.2)
7. Transport	1759	33	(1.8)	7285	194	(2.6)
8. Storage, Ware-Housing	468	6	(1.2)	1816	115	(6.3)
9. Communication	5	—	—	2955	202	(6.8)
10. Financing, Insurance Real Estate and Business services	1157	23	(2.0)	10664	876	(8.2)
11. Community, Social and personal service	6173	803	(13.0)	63175	10221	(16.1)
12. Others	193	18	(9.3)	3898	270	(6.9)
	63664	***8769***	***(13.7)***	***203602***	***21430***	***(10.5)***

Source: Ec. Census 1980: Statement 6 (published in 1985).

TABLE 7

Comparative Position of Male Female Participation (1973-83)

	Population (in million)			*Work participation rate percentage to total persons above 5 years*			*Work participating Population (million)*		*Annual average increase P.C.*
	1973	*1978*	*1983*	*1973*	*1978*	*1983*	*1973*	*1983*	
(1)	*(2)*	*(3)*	*(4)*	*(5)*	*(6)*	*(7)*	*(8)*	*(9)*	*(10)*
Female Rural Area	210.3	241.0	264.1	37.53	38.48	38.74	79.0	102.3	3.0
Male Rural Area	226.6	259.2	284.1	63.84	64.06	63.23	114.6	179.5	2.4
Female Urban Area	66.0	76.0	15.53	15.53	17.0	17.31	10.4	14.0	4.0
Male Urban Area	71.6	81.8	57.09	57.09	57.48	57.71	40.9	51.7	2.6

Source: NSS enquiries on Employment and Unemployment, thirty eight round, January to December, 1983.

Work participation rates for main workers by age group, area and sex in India during 1971 and 1981 has been represented in Table 8.

A study undertaken by the National Institute of Urban Affairs has brought to light certain important conclusions which are specified below.

In urban areas, nearly 40 per cent of self-employed women are employed in services, followed by 30 per cent in trade, 15 per cent in manufacturing, 8 per cent in construction and 5 per cent in Primary activities. Substantial number of such enterprises consisted of individual enterprises mostly engaged in small business like dairying, pottery making, selling dolls, goldsmithy, pan-bidi selling, fruits and vegetables selling, laundry, cane and bamboo products in which the family members do also participates and cooperate as workers.

TABLE 8

Work Participation Rates for Main Workers by Age Group, Area and Sex in India, 1971 and 1981)

Age Group	*Area*	*Male*		*Female*	
		1971	*1981*	*1971*	*1981*
(1)	*(2)*	*(3)*	*(4)*	*(5)*	*(6)*
All ages	All	52.61	51.62	12.06	13.99
	Rural	53.62	52.62	13.36	16.00
	Urban	48.80	48.54	6.65	7.28
0-14	All	6.65	5.46	2.63	2.95
	Rural	7.56	6.30	3.05	3.53
	Urban	2.75	2.46	0.82	0.88
15-19	All	55.32	51.15	15.78	18.48
	Rural	62.31	58.19	18.80	22.27
	Urban	28.32	31.54	5.51	6.16
20-24	All	81.43	76.91	18.12	20.32
	Rural	86.56	82.71	20.58	24.29
	Urban	67.49	63.35	9.54	6.25
25-29	All	94.27	91.08	20.01	22.52
	Rural	95.45	92.79	22.16	26.14
	Urban	90.54	86.78	11.63	12.17
30-39	All	97.12	96.22	21.70	25.31
	Rural	97.61	96.71	23.78	28.45
	Urban	95.45	94.93	13.11	15.14
40-49	All	97.08	96.81	22.6	25.97
	Rural	97.62	97.25	24.4	28.90
	Urban	95.15	95.49	14.5	15.34
50-59	All	94.03	19.43	90.64	21.56
	Rural	95.50	94.08	21.08	23.94
	Urban	87.85	86.86	12.71	12.42
60+	All	73.82	63.71	10.64	10.19
	Rural	77.52	67.59	11.49	11.29
	Urban	55.35	47.49	6.46	5.75

Note: The data for 1971 have been adjusted to exclude that relating to Assam for comparability with the 1981 Census data.

Source: Census of India 1981, Series-1, Paper-2 of 1983; Key population Statistics based on 5 per cent sample Data.

A high percentage of the self-employed women work out-side the home (57 per cent) and only 43 per cent work within the home. Out of the outside women workers over 60 per cent are either mobile or operate them on pavements making vulnerable to the vagaries of weather which spells irregularity in work and income.

Table 9 represents workforce concentration both in rural and urban sectors. The largest concentration of labour for both men and women workers are manifested in agriculture and allied activity. Because of planned economic development programmes, there has been changes in the degree of occupational diversification and decline of labour in the agricultural sector. The rate of decline in the proportion of labourers in agriculture during the year 1973-83 is less in case of women workers (from 90 per cent to 87 per cent) than for male labourers (from 83.2 per cent to 76.8 per cent).

In the urban sector, the proportion of women workforce is about three times the proportion of male workers in the agriculture and allied activities.

Syndrome of Women work in Rural India

There has been substantial documenting of empirical evidence of women's work and their roles in rural India.

"There are a large number of women who primarily derive their livelihood from working in agriculture either as 'free' wage labourers, sometimes on a regular basis and after on a seasonal basis, or attached labourers being permanently bondaged to a particular landlord mostly alongwith their menfolk. These families possess no land of their own but sometimes may own a bullock or two or a female bullock to their credit. The income derived from these sources is nominal but women invariably spend a regular part of their time in rearing these animals. These women generally belong to illiterate scheduled caste, scheduled tribe and backward classes." Further, studies indicate that seasonal fluctuations in employment is higher in case of women in rural areas and women remain without gainfull employment of longer periods in the crop season.

TABLE 9

Occupational Conception of Work Force (1973-83) (Per Capita Distribution of Workers Sex-wise for Rural and Urban India)

Occupational Sector	*Rural*				*Urban*			
	Male		*Female*		*Male*		*Female*	
	1973	*1983*	*1973*	*1983*	*1973*	*1983*	*1973*	*1983*
(1)	*(2)*	*(3)*	*(4)*	*(5)*	*(6)*	*(7)*	*(8)*	*(9)*
Agriculture and allied activity	83.23	67.80	89.67	86.73	10.71	10.25	32.75	28.65
Manufacturing	55.73	7.21	4.65	6.91	26.86	27.39	25.02	27.39
Construction	1.56	2.57	1.06	0.87	4.26	5.05	3.26	3.64
Trade	3.06	4.43	1.46	2.06	20.17	21.10	9.39	1.54
Transport and Communication	1.00	1.78	0.04	0.05	9.04	10.17	0.94	1.54
Social and Personal Service	4.65	5.90	7.81	3.02	24.00	21.30	26.66	26.36
Self-employment	65.90	60.64	64.68	62.21	30.25	40.67	48.40	46.50
Regular Work Force	12.06	10.27	4.08	3.10	50.69	44.58	27.89	26.23
Casual Wage Labour	22.04	28.83	31.44	34.69	10.06	14.75	23.71	27.27

Source: Percentage distribution of all workers for males and females in rural and urban areas—NSSO, Journal, April, 1986, pp. 112-113.

Table 10 reveals that agriculture is the dominant sector which employs more women than other sectors.

"Almost 90 per cent rural landlords have expressed their preferential choices for those rural women workers whose husbands and their fore-fathers have been landless labourers for generations. Migrated labourers are preferred the least for farm activities. This may be one of the reasons that the landless age-old traditional labourers could not come up from their stark poverty and could not get rid of the landlord's clutches. They get easy access to farm employment with the landlord-elites who in turn have been exploiting them for generations. The exploiter exploitee ties are, very much strong in India agriculture even today."

TABLE 10

All India Workforce in Unorganized Sectors in 1981

Sectors	*(Number in Millions)*		
	Male	*Female*	*Total*
Agriculture	114.1 (75%)	37.56 (25%)	151.7 (100%)
Manufacturing	16.8 (81%)	4.3 (19%)	21.1 (100%)
Services	22.4 (84%)	4.4 (16%)	26.8 (100%)
Total	***153.4***	***46.2***	***199.6***

Sources: Women work force: Trend and pattern of employment by Atmanand, *Khadi Gramodyog,* Vol. XXXVI, No. 6, March, 1990.

"The scene may be different, the occupation different but the essentials of the story remain—be they cashew workers coir workers, fish graders, bidi workers or laee workers, cart pullers, or coolies, domestic servants—name any occupation, it is the same unvarying story of long hours of work, poorly remunerated with little prospect of upgrading. Women in the unorganized sector have in secure jobs, are kept on temporary or casual basis, with not even the barest of welfare facilities, under conditions that pose health hazards."

Various socio-economic, cultural psychological handicap continue women to a position, deterrent to their development.

Women work in Tea Plantations

The tribal population of Bihar, Madhya Pradesh, Orissa has been recruited in the tea gardens of Assam and West Bengal. There was heavy emigration of labour to the tea gardens in the middle of 19th Century. Recruitment was on family basis on men cold not be expected to leave their families behind. In addition to their domestic works women used to take important responsibilities in their homes.

The Table 11 indicates the employment position of women workers in tea plantation during 1981 and 1985.

TABLE 11

Employment of Women work in Tea Plantations

Year	*Employment in lakhs*	*Share in total percentage*
1981	3.66	45.37
1985	3.92	46.86

Sources: Labour Bureau.

Bonded Labour in Plantations

Women work have been abused and exploited like other sectors and therefore, to ameliorate their conditions Plantation Labour Act has been enacted and (subsequently amendments made to the original Act of 1951) brought into force with effect from 26th January, 1982. The Act makes provision for accommodation to their resident workmen and their families in all plantations. The planters adopted various methods of roraecruiting labour from all labour surplus area of India and brought them to the plantations. They were bonded labour brought under strict terms and conditions. It was a type of forced migration or slave trade under which labourers were made to sign a contract to serve tea gardens of Assam from 3 to 5 years. After the expiry of the contracted period the labourers were supposedly free to return home or get themselves re-employed for a fresh term, but in practice it was impossible on the part of the recruited labour to return home. However, many of them deserted tea gardens even before the expiry of the contracted term due to inhuman behaviour and bad working conditions.

Socio-economic Conditions of Women work

A research study conducted by the Madurai Institute of Social Work to go into the problems and living conditions of women workers in tea plantations of Kerala State. The study has manifested the followings.

Some women workers had been serving for more than 30 years and even were forced to engage their children in their work.

Most of the women were married in the age groups of 13 to 16 since early marriage relieved pressure on crowded families. The average income of the labourers being low, indebtedness and poverty were the sequal. The women toiling hard in plantations hardly go leisure time for extra carricullar activities or recreational activities, as they were otherwise busy at plantations or homes.

Another article throws light on the conditions of women workers in tea plantations of Assam reveals that most of women workers belong to backward tribal belts. Studies show that unmarried women workers and old women are more committed in plantations than the middle aged women, obviously because the latter are tied down by household work, child care, seasonal paddy transplantation in rainy season and paddy drying and husking in the winter. Surveys show that the entire North Eastern India has as much as 60 per cent women workers and in the case of Assam state alone 45 per cent women are employed in tea plantations. Nearly 70 per cent of the total industrial force in Assam is employed in tea gardens and industries and 40 per cent of the state's total income is fetched by tea industry. Assam has the largest area of tea cultivation in the world. It contributes about 18 per cent of the world's total tea production." Lack of education, poverty, backwardness, lack of consciousness, under-employment and other evils still haunt the women workers in Assam tea plantations.

Wage Discrimination to Women workers

There is widespread age and income discrimination in the realm of employed women work. Despite their non-stop work from early morning to dark in agriculture operations like transplanting rice, women workers are generally paid less than 60 per cent of the male wage. The inequality of women is generally due to greater concentration of poverty, backwardness and low level of literacy and technical know-how. As per 1981 Census, only 24.8 per cent of women are literate with higher rate of dropout of females than males in the school. It has been studied that the women workers in the unorganized sector suffer due to lack of education and about 33 per cent are illiterates and about 13.5 per cent are educated upto middle level.

This low level of literacy coupled with other physical, psychological and cultural handicaps results in employment of women workers in poverty paid primary sector. For women workers minimum wages and statutory working hours are alien words. The women as agricultural labourers are discriminated in wage payment throughout the country even in operations such as transplanting and weeding which are women intensive operations.

The wages paid to women workers is determined not by economic criteria but is a result of the cultural attitudes and practices and power structure in a society. Wage discrimination is due to the fact that there is a common accepted notions that men are more efficient than women and the income of a women is only a supplementary earning while men are considered as principal earners.

Women with lower level skills or no skills are exploited in their wage payments for monotonous and straineous work. Planners and policy makers generally remain insensitive to the position of women within the patriarchical power-structure in the family and unequal power relation between women and men in the community. Women put more hours of work than men and the earnings of men are invested mostly on menfolk on the terms of better food, clothing, health, education, leisure and recreation.

The inequality in receiving ages between rural male and female (women workers) can be perceived from Table 12.

In Orissa, labour force participation marginally increased from 31.22 per cent in 1971 to 32.75 per cent in 1981. Male workers participation rates were 55.32 per cent in 1971 and 54.38 per cent in 1981 and that of women workers were 6.84 per cent in 1971 and 10.71 per cent in 1981. The proportion of women workers in primary sector to total women work increased from 74.43 per cent in 1971 to 80.26 per cent in 1981 while the proportions of women workers engaged in secondary and tertiary sector declined during the period.

TABLE 12

Average Wage Salary Learning of Both Rural Male and Female Per Day in 1983

(in Rs.)

Age group	*Male*	*Female*
Regular wage/salaries employees		
15-59	16.09	10.85
60 +	9.21	4.30
All ages	15.04	10.11
Casual wage labourers		
15-59	10.53	5-11
60 +	9.35	3.77
All ages	10.27	4.89

Sources: National sample survey organization, 1987, pp. 337-338.

Women work in Tamilnadu

Women work in Salt Industry: A study has been made by Prof. Kamalraj regarding women workers in salt industry of Tamilnadu state. He has remarked that in India out of 2,19,190 crores of land utilised for producing 70 million tonnes of salt in Tamilnadu salt is cultivated in 34,772 acres for producing 15 million tonnes. Salt-industry being a labour intensive industry when salt is produced by solar evaporation technique 50 per cent of the cost in salt industry goes to the workers men, women and children. Men and women workers perform the same type of work, except scapping of salt. Men workers are paid Rs. 11 and women workers Rs. 9 as daily wage. The services of omen in the salt works are specially needed to supply drinking water for all the workers. Women have walk far off places for fetch pots of drinking water. Usually they carry the salt from the ridges to the plotform.'

Women work in Beedi Industry: A study made by Dr. Kanan and Ilango reveal about the health hazards of women workers in Beedi Industries of Tiruchinapalli in Tamilnadu state. The Beedi workers are more prone to allergic bronchitis and sinus problems, it may be probably due to the dust of the tobacco leaves which induces allergy. The girls are malnourished, about 60 per cent of them are anaemi-coupled with abject poverty. They also suffer from diseases of ulterus and other gynaec problems and even cancer.

Women work in Paddy Processing Industries: A study conducted by Dr. Sundari and Manimekhalai has brought to light that poverty illiteracy, ignorance, casual nature a employment, lack of skill to take up other work and absence of union have all resulted in the economic exploitation of women workers in the paddy processing units of Trichinapalli. Ninety per cent of women workers live below the poverty line. Added to the low income, the high level of expenditure and lack assets and indebtedness further ruins the economic life of these women workers. More than 80 per cent of the sample workers have debt ranging from Rs. 800 to Rs. 1200. In the absence of institutional facilities and lack of security, all loans have been borrowed from either professional moneylenders or neighbours at high rates of interest.

It is the economic compulsion more than any other factor which motivates women to seek employment in the paddy processing industries.

There is heavy concentration of widow workers in this industry. Women do not have regular employment and their unemployment losts about four to six months in a year. There is no job security and there is complete denial of welfare measures such as medical and maternity benefit, creche facilities etc.

Handloom Industry: Dr. Sundari and Manimekhalai has also studied the problems of women workers in unorganized handloom industries in Vengamedu village of Tamilnadu state.

Handloom is the unorganized sector charcterised with large number of women and child labourers alongwith male labourers who are engaged as a cheap source of labour power, the most common mode of wage payment is piece-rate wage under which the workers self-supervise their exploitation. The study reveals that 46 per cent of women workers were unmarried, 30 per cent were married and the rest were either widows or divorcees. Less than 50 per cent of the women workers were literate, 66 per cent of household income is spent for food items low income, high levels of expenditure, high rate of indebtedness are the characteristics of the women workers of this industry.

Informal Women workers of Bangalore

An attempt has been made by Thippaiah, on the basis of interviews with informal sector units of Bangalore metropolitan area which explodes some important findings. The study reveals that women workers are suffering from poverty, unemployment, under employment, insecure employment, exploitation, harassment, etc., Women workers are the most exploited group composed to their counterparts in rural areas. Most of the women workers in the urban informal sector are migrant families at different points of time because of drought, employment and marriages and wage differentials between urban and rural sector. Most of such labourers are in the age group of 18 to 32 years, with low level of literacy and live in slums and shanty towns which are devoid of basic amenities. The wage employed women workers are mostly skilled, semi-skilled, unskilled, casual and contract labourers in construction works, industrial and commercial enterprises.

The study reveals that the annual income of informal women workers was 1507 in waste collection activity as against the average income of informal male labourers, Rs. 2632. The informal sector women workers, are paid low wages and their wage are just around the subsistence level. Some women workers were asked to work 10 to 12 hours a day in addition to household work. Under insanitary and less healthier conditions women workers toil hard in order to make reasonable return. Proper medical facilities and safety measures are not provided for these women workers who are in contact with hazardous materials such as Chemicals in dyeing or cement dust in construction work. Consequently, most of these workers are suffering from ill-health and physical disabilities. The informal women workers of Bangalore are deprived of any social security benefits and as a result, children and dependents face a good deal of problems.

Women work in Rajasthan

An action research programme with motivational cum-educational camp was initiated by National Labour Institute (NLI), New Delhi in 1984 at Metholi village in Bharatpur district of Rajasthan.

The study has brought to light that the rate of growth of literacy among families in Rajasthan and particularly in the study area is significantly low. It demonstrates the neglect of women. The female literacy in Rajasthan in 11.42 per cent as per 1981 Census but in the rural areas it is only 5.46 per cent. The situation of the scheduled castes and scheduled tribes is bad, in their case, practically the entire population in the rural area is illiterate. It was noticed that the few literate women in these villages belonged to the upper castes. None of the women of marginal or landless families were literate.

Participant's Socio-economic Profile

Most of the participants were married (87.2 per cent), 5.1 per cent were unmarried and 7.7 per cent were widows. About 60 per cent of the participants did not possess any kind of agricultural land. Some of them did not have any land for house. The principal occupation of women workers was agricultural labour-cum-household work. Eighty two per cent of women agricultural labourers were found indebted. "Thus, they were young and middle aged, illiterate, married, agricultural labourers without much substantial work, with high incidence of indebtedness and no land to cultivate."

Lack of Employment Opportunities

In the absence of land, lack of employment opportunities was also identified as a persistent problem among the female participants. As the village economy is primarily agrarian, the only employment available within the village economy is in agriculture. However, agricultural employment available to women is only for two months in a year. Women do not get any other form of employment within the village and they cannot seek employment outside.

Study by Dr. Chandhoke

Dr. Neeva Chandhoke one analyst points out that women are triply subordinated—as housewives and mothers to men, as female in sex—segregated jobs with discriminatory wages and as workers, they are excluded from the higher levels of management in private and government enterprises.

The benefits of development have been mixed, benefitting men more than women, it has increased inequality of access to resources and opportunities. Development has little meaning if it continues the personal underdevelopment of women. There is a growing trend towards amelioration, but the concept of welfare improvement leads to little meaningful change. There will continue to be little change if women have to depend on men as decision-makers.

Women work in Orissa

Orissa is predominantly agricultural state, with agriculture contributing nearly 69 per cent of State's income. The working population contribute 32.8 per cent of the total state population of which 75 per cent are farmers and agricultural labourers. Rural women in the state constitute 88.98 per cent of the total female population and about 94.98 per cent of the total female population and about 94.69 per cent of the female labour force. Of the total female labourer force in the state 78.10 per cent are engaged in farm sector either as cultivators or as agricultural labourers. The literacy rate among females in rural areas of the state is 18.46 per cent as against 24.28 per cent for males.

The study demonstrates that improvement of economic status associated with relatively large holdings, rural women do not prefer to go out for wage employment. They spend more time on their own farm, attend household activities or engage themselves in other activities such as dairy, poultry bee-keeping, etc., which are mostly done within their own premises.

Female in our society, specially in rural areas are subject to several socio-economic constraints and discriminations. The incidence of poverty, unemployment and illiteracy are high among women. The study has brought to light that their low participation as recorded by official agencies do not necessarily reflect their low economic contribution. The study concludes with suggestions like "as women work contributes more in terms of time, output and income, they need a fair deal both in socio-economic planning and in decision-making. The wage for women security measures for women and legal protection should also be substantially expanded keeping in time with their role in the economy."

Women work in Balasore

A study made in the district of Balasore—a coastal district of Orissa, unfolds that women engaged in income-generating activities feel that they are inferior to the male-folk, as they earn less wages and perform unskilled labour. Women in this part of Orissa would prefer to remain undernourished and poor to undertake income-generating activities. Women play a wide variety of roles which are either preparatory or supportive to agriculture, animal husbandry, craft etc., but since most of their work is of informal nature devoid of wages, it does not satisfy employment criteria and hence not accounted for while estimating participation rates. It is seen that 60 per cent of the sample respondents work in farms like breaking clods of earth, manuring weeding, transplanting, harvesting, threshing and winnowing, while only 15 per cent of the sample respondents work in income generating activities like rope and basket-making, pottery, goat-rearing, handloom weaving etc., and these activities bring money to them. Low participation of women are because of low level of education, unpleasant work experience. They do not work because they are over tired and over-burdened with household work. They are being harassed by government officials for sanction of loans, and in the identification list of beneficiaries.

Women work in Ganjam

Another study conducted in Ganjam district of Orissa pertaining to role of women in agricultural sector reveals that the tribal women are taking up the hard task of cultivation in contrast to the women of plain and coastal areas. In tribal areas men share with women in all the operations except land preparation and irrigation. Knowledge and use of fertiliser is more widespread among the farm women in plain and coastal area and less in tribal areas. About 70 per cent of the respondents have reported about the application of fertiliser in their field. Use of chemical fertiliser in crops is considered to be harmful by the tribals. It is observed from the survey that in coastal and plain areas women have better knowledge about the use of high-yielding seeds, fertiliser and pesticides compared to tribal women. The rich and higher caste women do not work in the field but only supervise the work. There are different agro-climatic zones and consequently variations in agricultural practices and cropping pattern in the state of Orissa. Women population is about the same as that of males and they play a significant role in performing different agricultural activities.

Women work in the Tribal District of Koraput

An attempt has been made in a study conducted in Koraput, one of the backward districts of Orissa to assess the contribution of women to the development of rural economy. The study revealed that agriculture was the main occupation of the study area. The level of education among workers in the region under study was low. The position was still worse among women workers. The women workers do not have even access to new skills imparted through th extension an community development programmes.

In addition to agriculture, the female labourers were also found to be engaged in other economic activities like collection of minor forest products, construction of road and buildings, quarrying household industries etc. The low standard of living in the area makes it necessary for women folk to cooperate in other economic pursuits to some extent.

It was revealed that the contribution of men workers in crop production is 60.80 per cent and that of women workers 39.20 per cent.

The authors conclude that "it is high time that an integrated approach was formulated for the over all development of women folk to enable them to participate in the socio-cultural and economic development of our country. The problem of women's development should constitute an important segment of planning process. Any further neglect in this important issue would stand in the way of economic development of the country.

The Indian Council of Social Science Research, New Delhi has made several studies in a wide range of occupations in the unorganized sector on women, focussing new lights on different respects of women.

Studies, which were conducted in various parts of the country reveals the 'auful conditions' of the women workers in unorganized sector. It has been observed that a significant percentage of, the jobs in this sector are managed by women drawn from lower caste and lower class women. Ignorance, tradition bound attitudes, illiteracy, lack of skills, seasonal nature of employment, heavy physical work of different types, long hours of work with limited payment, discrimination in wage structures of men and women, lack of guarantee of minimum wage, lack of job security, lack of comprehensive legislation to cover these labourers in unorganized informal sector, lack of minimum facilities at the work-site, ill-treatment, migration and disintegration of families, bondage and alienation etc., are the characteristics of the employment of women in this sector.

All this boils down to a conclusion that women workers constitute an important segment of the total work-force in our country. More than 90 per cent of the working women are engaged as wage labourers in informal sector in our country. Compared with men, most of women workers are in the grip of poverty, backwardness, landlessness, under-employment and destitution. They are also subject to various types of exploitation like economic, cultural, sexual, political, psychological etc.

Informal Construction Women workers

Available data demonstrate that construction is one of the largest sectors of economic activity, second largest to agriculture in underdeveloped countries. Construction sector provides most of the economic infra-structure for the manufacturing sector and infact, provides greater employment opportunities to a large number of unskilled labourers. The construction sector, generally developed on traditional production lines, is considered as an important spectrum of informal sector. The complexity of the construction operation necessitates a host of skills, carpenters, masses, concrete workers, unskilled labourers etc.

Employment of Women workers in Construction Sector

As revealed from 1981 census, there were about 222.5 lakh persons in the labour force in our country. The available figures reveal that about 50 per cent of construction workers really lived in urban settlements while a large segments of labour force work in their villages and construction project site.

As an employment generator, the role of construction sector is significant as revealed from the Table 13. It is noteworthy that in the informal sector, on the fringes of monetary benefits considerable proportion of labourers, including women workers are employed.

Construction women workers are mostly exploited in the public works, development projects and relief works. To repeat, though the informal construction women workers are hired on a casual basis (daily or piece-rate), many of them have a long career of years, mostly migrating to distant and far off places. They suffer from temporary and shifting nature of work and undergo enormous physical strain, toiling hard in all seasons. They are mostly exploited by the contractors and middlemen, suffer from insecurity of job and poorly paid. 'Frequent changes in their worksites and the uncertain nature of their work deprive them and their children of the basic needs like health, education and even such a common thing as a ration card. Accidents and death at worksites are common and they hardly get any compensation." The frequency of accidents in the construction industry is on the increase.

TABLE 13

Employment of Labour in Construction Sector in 1981

(in lakhs)

Labour force	*In rural areas*	*In urban areas*	*Total*
Total number of workers in the country	176.4	46.1	222.5
Workers in the construction sector (including dams, bridges, roads etc.)	1.5	1.6	3.1
Workers in the building (industry alone)	0.9	1.2	2.1

Source: Census 1981, Govt. of India.

Studies on Construction Women workers

The Committee on Status of Women (1975) initiated two important studies on women construction labourers, one in Patna (Bihar State) covering three major projects, and the other in Delhi, covering nine construction sites. Finding of these studies unfolds the conditions of women in the construction sector.

A study made by DK Lal Das highlights sex discrimination against female workers in unorganized construction sector of Andhra Pradesh. The study observes that development has improved the standard of living but increased economic and social disparities. Women have been displaced from employment because of new technologies. Similar views have been expressed by the Report of the National Committee on Self-employment in Women as it remarked that technological changes have adversely affected the employment of women in Industries.

Prof. R.N. Mathur has studied the problems of construction women workers and especially the quality of life basing upon both primary and secondary sources. The study has highlighted various socio-economic aspects of Delhi. Women construction workers and has been illustrated through Census data and theoretical frameworks.

National Building Organization sponsored five studies (1977-78) in Delhi, Ahmedabad, Poona, Madras, KAVAL (Kanpur, Agra, Varanasi and Allahabad Lucknow) and surveyed 3425 workers for reviewing the living conditions of both male and female labourers. The findings of the study revealed that there was constant problems of instability and insecurity of employment for the workers. "The migration workers was because of unemployment at home, insufficient income and indebtedness, expectation of better prospects in the city was found as the main reason of migration to city. Ninty-six per cent workers in Delhi, 69 per cent in Ahmedabad, 78 per cent in Poona, 70 per cent in Madras and 59 per cent in KAVAL towns were migrants from rural to other urban areas. The proportion of women workers was 5.2 per cent in Delhi, 25.5 per cent in Ahmedabad, 19.8 per cent in Poona, 25.4 per cent in Madras and 2.3 per cent in KAVAL towns, and almost all of them were employed on unskilled jobs. The women workers generally remain unskilled inspite of their continuous employment in construction for a number of years. The contractors also find the employment of women workers beneficial because they perform the same type of task as men and are sometimes paid wages at a lesser rate.

The earnings of the construction workers fluctuate on account of discontinuity of employment which generally occur due to rains, non-availability of building materials and change of sites. Ninety per cent of the skilled labourers were getting more than Rs. 200 per month where as the unskilled were getting less."

Study on Socio Economic Conditions of Women workers in Building and Construction Industry

A recent study on socio-economic conditions of women workers in building and construction industry has brought to light several important facts and findings. The study revealed that women workers engaged in the unorganized segment suffer from disabilities and exploitation of much higher magnitude than those employed in the organized sector. Although the conditions of work in the unorganized sector are not satisfactory both for men and women, yet the problems confronted by the latter are generally more acute because they are more vulnerable to various forms of exploitation.

There is also absence of reliable statistical and other data relating to the working and socio-economic conditions of women workers engaged in the unorganized sector.

Construction works being scattered over all parts of the country and resources for covering the entire country being limited, the study was confined to four metropolitan cities of Delhi, Bombay, Madras and Calcutta.

Selection of Sample Projects

Only those construction projects which belonged to government, semi-government and public sector agencies and were employing five or more women workers at the time of the conduct of field study comprised the overall sampling frame for the study. In Calcutta City, where the proportion of women construction labourers was fund to be very low, only a few construction projects engaged five or more women workers. Thus, the coverage of the study was virtually reduced to three metropolitan cities of Delhi, Madras and Bombay.

Selection of sample projects for the study was made from the list of construction works which were collected personally at the time of the conduct of field study from the various construction agencies like central and state public works Departments, City corporations and Development Authorities, the Housing Boards etc. In total, 29 work-sites in Delhi, 14 in Bombay and 13 in Madras city were covered for the study. The total women employment, 503, 155 and 167 respectively as on the dates of visit to the work-sites of the cities under study.

Characteristics of Women Employment

Although many types of building and construction activities, viz. construction of building roads, railway lines, sewerage, etc., were being undertaken by various construction agencies, women workers were mainly engaged in the construction of buildings. In some cases, they were also engaged in road operations. Their employment in works like electrical installations, underground sewerage, rail works, etc., was either very low or quite negligible. This was so, as they were mainly engaged in carrying earth, mortar, bricks, etc., and these jobs mainly available in the construction of building. Though the Building and construction industry provides employment to all categories of workers, viz., highly skilled and skilled, semi-skilled and unskilled person, yet women constituted nearly 25.5 per cent of the total persons employed in the sampled construction projects covered in Delhi, 15.0 per cent in Bombay and 29.3 per cent in Madras and all of them were unskilled persons. No women workers engaged in any construction project studied in the three cities was engaged in skilled or semi-skilled occupations. Further, as high as 37.9 per cent of the unskilled labourers in Delhi, 22.0 per cent in Bombay and 51.2 per cent in Madras were women. The unskilled women workers were mostly designated as 'coolies,' whereas their male counter-parts were called as 'beldavs.' In some construction projects, male and female labourers were both categorised as 'Mazdoors' or labourers.

A staggering 95 per cent of the unskilled labour engaged in various construction projects covered in Delhi were those who had migrated from the rural areas of other states like Rajasthan, Madhya Pradesh, Uttar Pradesh, Bihar etc. The states of Madhya Pradesh and Rajasthan taken together contributed slightly more than two-thirds of the total unskilled labour employed in various sampled construction projects. The interesting feature of migration from Rajasthan and Madhya Pradesh states was that generally both male and female members of a household migrated. However, in the case of Bihar State, mostly male members migrated to the construction sites and the female members generally stayed back in their villages.

Wages and Earnings

In the case of highly skilled, skilled and semi-skilled jobs in which only males were employed, not a single case could be detected where the wage Act was violated. It was only the skilled category that the prevailing wage rates actually being paid were labour than those remained under the minimum wage rates of the workers, particularly of women workers, were in many cases below the minimum wages fixed under the Act.

The daily wages being paid to unskilled women workers were less than the statutory wages in as many as nine of the 14 construction projects studied in Bombay and 5 of the 13 projects studied in Madras. In some cases, women workers' daily wages were even less than half or three-fourth of the minimum wages.

The women workers were not entitled for any leave with wages and were paid only for the days they actually worked. The labourers were also not getting any social security benefit under any Act. They were not benefitted by the Employee's Provident Funds and Miscellaneous Provisions Act, 1952 even though some of them had been continuously employed at the same work-sites for long periods.

Working Conditions and Welfare Provisions

The work at the selected construction sites were carried on mostly during day time in a single shift. However, the work continued till late night when roofs of the building were to be laid. In such cases, women workers also worked during night hours. There is at present no legislative provisions which could prevent women construction labourers from working during night hours.

Women workers employed in the sampled construction projects were found carrying heavy loads of cement bags, mortar, bricks etc., which in some cases weighted more than 30 Kg. At present there is no legislative provision which would prevent the women construction labourers from carrying heavy loads. No women worker at any selected work-site was found to have been provided with handgloves or any other protective equipment for handling the hard and rough building and construction materials. Thus, their hands and feet in most of the cases were fond in pitiable condition having many scratches. At present there is no legislation providing safety provision for the labourers engaged at the worksites. The employees had not made any special arrangements for providing drinking water to their workers. Whatever water was being used for construction purposes was also available to the labourers for drinking. Latrine provision was not there in most of the work-sites. Urinal facilities and washing facilities were also not available. The maternity Benefit Act is not applicable to the women workers working at the construction sites. The living accommodation provided by the employers consisted of make-shift huts mostly without any ancillary facilities like Kitchen, Bath, etc. There were no drainage, sanitary, and ventilation facilities in these labour huts. No recreational amenities nor any canteen did exist at any of the construction sites. The working conditions of women workers were worse than those of male workers. There is, infact, need of a separate comprehensive legislation for the workers engaged in the building and construction industry which may take into account all the peculiar characteristics of the Industry. There was widespread illiteracy among the women construction labourers. As many as 68 of the total 79 children of the women workers in Delhi and 39 of the total 45 children in Bombay i.e., 86 and 86.6 per cent respectively were not attending schools. No male or female labourers engaged at the construction sites studied in the three cities was reported to be a member of any trade union. There was lack of consciousness among the women construction labourers as almost all the women workers were not even aware of the beneficial provisions contained in the important labour Acts like the Minimum Wages Act, 1948, the Equal Remuneration Act, 1976, etc.

Dadan Construction Women workers

In the state of Orissa women workers migrating to different parts of the country through contractors or Sardars known as dadan labourers. Several economic factors are responsible for such an exploitative dadan construction women workers. Being landless and burdened with the heavy weight of maintaining a large Family, and being deprived of job opportunities, the labourers do not dare avoiding the offer that would bring them some income. But it is deplorable to note that they are made to work pretty long hours in excess of the statutory workhours, not being provided with medical benefits, proper food and shelter. They are, quite often, not paid the wages that had been promised to them. In many cases, they are paid less than the agreed wages. Deprived of their wages, they are sometimes forced to board trains without the needed tickets and are cought and thrown into jails.

Reports in the news papers reveals that each year about two lakhs of dadan labour of Orissa which also includes women workers for construction industry, are going to the other states to seek employment. The recruitment of dadan labourers in Orissa is made mostly from the rural and tribal areas of Keonjhar, Mayurbhanj, Sambalpur, Sundargarh, Puri and Ganjam districts. However, it is not possible to estimate the exact size of the inter-state migration of workmen. According to 1981 Census, out of a total of 35 lakh construction workers, 10 per cent are women. Although the construction labourers are covered under various Acts like the Minimum Wages Act, the Contract Labour Act and the interstate migrants Act, these laws are more observed in their breach than in their genuine enforcement. Thus, a paramount feature of construction sector is its heavy dependence on migrant labour. This sector employs a large number of casual workers who are outside the purview of protective labour laws which apply to organized labour in other fields. The peculiar nature of employment in the construction sector has created enormous problems of construction labourers, specially, the unskilled and women workers.

REFERENCES

Saran, K.M. *Labour in Ancient India,* Vora and Co. Publishers Pvt. Ltd., Bombay 1957, pp. 64-65.

Nair, G. Ravindran, Women Workers—The lingering Paradoyes' *Social Welfare,* May, 1988, p. 5.

Mencher, Joan and K Saradamani, Muddy feet and dirty hands; rice production and female agricultural labourers, *Economic and Political Weekly,* December, 25, 1983.

Kaptan, S.S., The income, wages and working conditions of women in the inorganized sector, *Social Welfare,* May, 1989, p. 29.

Prasad, Sushama, Sahay, Economic and Physical Exploitation of tribal female labourers, p. 73, in Gupta J.L., *Challenges to the Fair Sex: Indian*

Women Problems, Plight and Progresses, Delhi Giani Publ. House, 1988, XXIV p. 132.

Desai Neera, Maithreyi, Krishnaraj, *Women an Society in India,* Ajanta Publication, New Delhi, 1987, p. 84.

Dr. K. Murali Manohar, *Rural Women, Class Formation and Development,* Kakatiya University, Warangal (Andhra Pradesh).

Saikia, Anuva, Seasonal variation of female participation in farm work, *Kurukshetra,* Vol. XXXI, No. 19, July 1-15, 1983 p. 17.

Sunita and others, Rural Women work: Differential treatment by land lord-elites, *Journal of Extension System,* 3(2) Dec., 1987, p. 80.

Desai Neera Maithreyi, Krishnaraj, *Women and Society in India, op. cit.,* p. 94.

Gupta, Vishwa Nath, Women work in tea plantations, *Social Welfare,* Vol. XXXVII, No. 2, May 1990, p. 3.

Badruddin, Women Workers in Assam tea plantations, *Social Welfare,* Vl, XXXVII, No. 2, May 1990, p. 29.

Mathur, R.N., *Quality of Working Life of Women Construction workers.* Commonwealth Publishers, New Delhi, p. 45.

Sharma, Narayan Prasad (Dr.) Wage differentials for women agricultural labourers, *Yojana,* July 1-15, 1989, 33(12), p. 8.

Pushpa Sunder, Characteristics of Female Employment—Implications of research and policy. *Economic and Political Weekly,* May, 1981.

Rojas, Isabela. "Factors in womens' labour force participation' quoted in "Women work Force. Trend and Pattern of Employment" by Atmanand, *op. cit.*

Mathur, R.N., Quality of working life of women construction workers, *op. cit.,* p. 35-36.

Sahool, B. (Dr.), Changing pattern of women employment in Orissa—Problems and prospects *Vision,* Vol VIII, No. 384, January-June, 1989, p. 38.

Kamalraj, M., Women in Salt Industry, *Khadi Gramodyog,* Vol. XXXVI, No. 10, July 1990, p. 411.

Kannon Jayam (Dr.) and Ilango P., Health Hazards of women working in Beedi Industries, *Social Welfare,* Vol. XXXVI, No. 12, March, 1990, p. 10.

Sundari, S. (Dr.) and Marunekhalai, N.—Women Workers in the paddy processing Industries, *Social Welfare,* Vol. XXXVI, No. 10-11, January-February, 1990, p. 14.

Sundari, S. (Dr.) and Marinekalal, N. Problems of women workers in Handloom Industry at Vengamedu, *Khadi Gramodyog,* Vol. XXXV, No. 6, March, 1989, p. 286.

P. Thippaiah, Women Workers in Urban unorganized sector, *Social Welfare,* Vol. XXXVI, No. 2, May, 1989, p. 21-22.

Jain, Mahaveer, *Metholi Revisited: An account of camp processes of Agricultural women workers,* National Labour Institute, New Delhi, November, 1985.

Patnaik, S.C and Debi, Sailabala, An assessment of Womens' Economic Contribution to the Farm Sector: A micro level study, *Journal of Rural Development,* National Institute of Rural Development, Rajendranagar, Hyderabad, Vol. 5, July, 1986.

12

Women Labourers and Government Policy

India Constitution promises to secure all its citizens, justice, liberty, equality and to promote fraternity among them all. To realise the goals the Constitution guarantees certain fundamental rights. Alongwith these, certain negative rights, prohibiting discrimination or denial of equal protection of law are also guaranteed. The Constitution recognised the unequal social position of women and a special clause empowers the state to make special provisions for women and children even in violation of the obligation not to discriminate among citizens. *[Article 15(3), Constitution of India.]*

Article 1(1) and 16(2) of the Constitution grant the right of equal opportunities in regard to employment to men and women without any distinction. The Directive Principles of State Policy which has a bearing on this point is 39 (a). Article 43 of the Constitution says, "The State shall endeavour to secure by suitable legislation or economic organisation or any otherway to all workers, agricultural, industrial or otherwise, work, a living wage, ensuring a decent standard of life, and full enjoyment of leisure and social, cultural opportunities.

Special laws have been enacted for the protection of women workers in factories, mines, and plantation, and to provide maternity relief to women workers in organised sector. There is a plethora of laws for the protection of benefits of working women which regulate the hours of work, provide measures for safety and well-being of female labourers especially in organised sector. The unorganised sector has not been concerned effectively by any of these laws. The legislative measures are framed from time to time in order to ensure that women are not discriminated and exploited. These are the special marriage and Divorce Act, 1954 Suppression of Immoral Traffic in Women and Girls Act, 1956. Hindu Adoption and Maintenance Act, 1956, Hindu Succession Act, 1956, Maternity Benefit Act, 1961. The Dowry Prohibition Act, 1961, Indecent Representation of Women (Prohibition) Act, 1986. The Commission of Sati (Prevention) Act, 1987. All these legal measures and Acts aimed at ameliorating the condition of women labourers and safeguarding women from the tyrannies of age-old social customs, superstitious values and exploitation.

Hindu Marriage Act, 1955

The Hindu Marriage Act applies to all the Hindus by religion which includes Vaishnavas, Lingayats and members of the Brahmo, Prarthana, Arya Samaj. It also applies to the Buddhists, Sikhs and Jains and to legitimate and illegitimate, children of parents who belong to the above religions and sects. All 'Hindu's who do not marry under the special Marriage Act are governed by this Act. Under Hindu Marriage Act the conditions for marriage are:

(i) Either spouse should not have an earlier living spouse.
(ii) Should not have mental problem, mental illness.
(iii) Men should be 21 years complete and girls 18 years complete.
(vi) The parties should not be sapinda to each other unless the custom or usage governing them permits such marriage.

A Hindu cannot contract a second marriage with another till the first marriage is dissolved by divorce or decree. If this is done he/she can be prosecuted by law. A report given to the police by the near relative is entertained. If such a second marriage is proved he/she can be imprisoned and also find. Under the Act, certain types of marriages are void and fraudulent.

When the spouses find it difficult to continue to live with each other, either of the spouse can apply for divorce under the law.

For the dissolution of the marriage, the law has provided certain conditions only on which a decree for divorce can be granted by the court. However, the dissolution of a marriage can be applied for not before the expiry of one year of marriage or of passing of the decree of judicial separation unless permitted by the court under special circumstances. The grounds on which the dissolution of the marriage can be granted by the court are cruelty, adultery, unsoundness of mind, desertion, not being alive, suffering from disease and mutual consent.

The Special Marriage Act, 1954

The Act permits marriage of people from different religious faiths without changing their religion.

The Hindu Marriage Act, 1955 and the Special Marriage Act, 1954 were amended in 1976 to provide for the right of a girl to repudiate before attaining maturity, marrying as child whether the marriage has been consumated or not. Cruelty and desertion were added as grounds for divorce and mutual consent were recognised.

Hindu Succession Act, 1956

The act confers the rights of absolute ownership over property and the women can make 'will' leaving her share of property to the heirs. Section 10 of the Act provides for the property of an intestate being divided among the heirs in accordance with certain prescribed rules.

Hindu Adoption and Maintenance Act, 1956

Any Hindu man of sound mind can take a son or daughter in adoption provided that if he has a living wife and he gets the consent of his wife to do so, unless the wife has completely renounced the world, is of unsound mind and has ceased to be a Hindu.

A Hindu woman can take a child in adoption if she is unmarried or is a widow, her marriage has been dissolved, her husband has renounced the world, has changed his religion and he is declared to be of unsound mind.

Under Section 9, the consent of father and mother is necessary for giving the child in adoption unless (i) they or one of them is dead or (ii) the father or mother has completely and finally renounced the world or (iii) has ceased to be Hindu or (iv) has been declared by a court of competent jurisdiction to be of unsound mind.

The Child Marriage Restraint (Amendment) Act, 1976

The Act raises the age of marriage for girls from 15 to 18 years and boys 18 years to 21 years. The offences under this Act have been made cognizable.

The Factories Act, 1948, Mines Act, 1952 and Plantation Labour Act, 1951

These Acts prohibit the employment of women between 7 p.m. and 6. a.m. in factories, mines and plantations, regulate the working hours and contain provision for their safety and welfare. The Government is authorised to fix the maximum load that may be lifted by women and to open creches etc.

The Employees' State Insurance Act, 1948

The benefits provided under this Act include sickness benefit, maternity benefit, disablement benefit, dependent benefit, medical and funeral benefit.

The Maternity Benefits Act, 1961

This Act is applicable to every establishment, plantation, mine or factory and provides for payment of maternity benefit at the rate of average daily wage for the period of women's actual absence. It has been amended in April, 1976 to cover women, who do not fall within the purview of the Employees State Insurance Act, 1948. A proposal to further amend the Act is under consideration of the Labour Ministry.

The Factories (Amendment) Act, 1976

The Act provides for establishment of creches where 30 women are employed (including casual labourers or contact labourers) as against one for every 50 hitherto.

The Equal Remuneration Act, 1976

The Act provides for (a) the payment of equal remuneration to men and women workers and (b) prevention of discrimination on the ground of sex against women in the matter of employment and for matter connected therewith or indentical thereto. There is a proposal under consideration of Labour Ministry for amendment of the Act with a view to further liberalising its provisions in favour of women.

The Contract Labour (Regulation and Abolition) Act, 1978

The Act regulates the working conditions of contract labour (which includes women), payment of wages and provides for welfare facilities and creches for the children of working women engaged in construction work.

The Medical Termination of Pregnancy Act, 1971

The Act legalises induced abortion by qualified doctor on humanitarian and medical grounds. This is primarily a welfare measure to protect the health of women though it has also a family planing aspect. Women can now have induced abortion through qualified people. The service is free in public hospitals. All the documents are kept confidential. Before undergoing surgery, if the patient is a minor or of unsound mind, written consent of the guardian is necessary. Since the inception of the programme in April, 1972, 223 million terminations were done upto September, 1981.

The Dowry Prohibition Act, 1961

The Dowry Prohibition was first legislated in 1961. The Act was amended in 1984 to make the offence cognisable, to enhance the penalty both fine and imprisonment and to widen the scope of the Act to make it more effective. The Act was further amended in 1986 to make the penal provisions more effective and stringent. The minimum punishment for taking or abetting taking of dowry has been raised to 5 years and a fine of Rs. 15,000. The advertisements in newspapers, periodicals etc., offering a share of property as consideration for marriage is punishable. The amendment proposes appointment of Dowry Prohibition Officers by the State Governments.

Offences under the Act have been made non-bailable. A new Offence of Dowry Death has been included in the Indian Penal Code consequential to the amendment in the Act.

The Suppression of Immoral Traffic in Women and Girls Act, 1956

The Suppression of Immoral Traffic Act prohibits trafficking in women and girls for purposes of prostitution as an organised means of living. The Act which was amended in 1978 was further amended in September, 1986 with the objective of making the penal provisions in the Act more stringent and effective. The amendment Act is retitled as "the Immoral Traffic (Prevention) Act, 1986" and the salient features are—widening the scope of the Act to cover all persons, whether male or female who are sexually exploited for commercial purposes; enhancement of the period of imprisonment where offences are committed against minors and children; appointment of Trafficking Police Officers, who will have the powers to investigate inter-state offences; prescribing punishment as laid down for rape under the Indian Penal Code or the seduction of victims of trafficking while in custody; interrogations of women and girls removed from the brothels to be held by women police officers or in their absence in the presence of women social workers and setting up of Special Courts for setting offences, which have inter-state ramifications.

Amendment to the Criminal Laws

The Indian Evidence Act, the Indian Penal Code and the Criminal Procedure Code were amended in 1983 to make the offence of rape and such crimes against women much more stringent and effective and also to make a new provision to the Indian Penal Code to make cruelty against women by the husband and other relations punishable. The onus of proof of innocence would rest on the accused of such offences.

Family Courts

An Act was passed in 1984 for the setting up of Family Courts in the country with a view to promoting reconciliation in, and securing speedy settlement of disputes relating to marriage and family affairs and for matters connected therewith.

Indecent Representation of Women (Prohibition) Act, 1986

The Indecent Representation of Women (Prohibition) Act, 1986 was passed in Parliament in December, 1986 with the objective of having separate legislation to effectively prohibit the indecent representation of women through advertisements, books, pamphlets etc. The indecent representation of women has been defined to mean the depiction of the figure of a women in such a way as to have the effect of being indecent or of being derogatory to women or is likely to deprive, corrupt or injure the public morality; to prohibit all advertisements; publications etc., which contain indecent representation of women in any form; to prohibit selling, distribution circulation of any books, pamphlets etc., containing indecent representation of women. Offences under this act are made punishable with imprisonment of either description for a term extending to two years and fine extending to two thousand rupees on first conviction.

The Commission of Sati (Prevention) Act, 1987

The Commission of Sati (Prevention) Act, 1987 was passed by the Parliament in December, 1987 to provide for more effective prevention of the commission of Sati and its glorification and matters connected therewith or incidental thereto. The Act defines Sati comprehensively to include not only the burning or burial alive of a wife widow with a deceased husband but also of a widow or women with the body of any other relative or any article associated with the husband or relative; anyone who abets the commitment of Sati by inducement, encouragement, participation in processions, preventing the widow from saving herself etc. would be punishable by the maximum penalty, i.e., death or imprisonment for life; the abetment of an attempt to commit Sati would be punishable with imprisonment for life; in the case of persons prosecuted under these offences, the burden of proof that he had not committed the offence shall be on him; those convicted for such offences shall be disqualified from inheriting the property of the persons committing Sati; persons convicted under such offences shall be disqualified under the Representation of People's Act, 1951 from the date of such conviction and shall continue to be disqualified for a further period of five years after release; glorification of Sati has been defined in details. The Act of glorification includes observance of ceremonies, collection of funds and construction of temples; punishment by imprisonment which may extend to seven years for the glorification of Sati has been prescribed; while the provisions of the Act necessarily have to be prospective, acts of glorification carried out in further would be covered; the propagation of the practice of the commission of sati or its glorification by a candidate or his agent shall be deemed a corrupt practice under the Representation of People's Act; powers have been specifically provided to the Collector/State Government that, if satisfied that in any temple or structure any ceremony is carried out with a view to prepetuating the multilated concept as dealt with in this Act, the state Government in the case of structures and the collector in other cases, can direct the removal of such temple or structure and the Collector can also seize, properties collected for the glorification of Sati.

Women belonging to small farmers, landless labourers, lower middle classes' (lower petty bourgeoisie) and the industrial working class fall under the severe yoke of oppression than their counterparts. By far to this section of women sexests, sati and even dowry hardly matter for their very survival is at stake in this class-ridden and patriarchal society who are in majority.

However, law has accorded special protection to the women ever since the time of Manu. This is because of their physical structure, social status and conditions of the Hindu Society. Most of the Hindu women are illiterate and ignorant of their legal rights and duties, economically dependent on men, socially backward, politically un-informed. Accordingly, the framers of the Indian penal code and the criminal procedure code provided special provisions for women, including Hindu women.

Some important offences relating to women under Indian Penal Code (IPC) are:

However, despite these legislative measures, the economic and physical exploitation of unorganised labour force in general and female labour force in particular, continue unabated. Central and State Governments though framed several rules and enacted legislations to combat the exploitative forces but the irony of the fact is that there has been a staggering gulf between the framing rules, enacting legislations and their effective implementation. The women labours and tribal women in particular, have been drawn into the unorganised labour force for about past three decades are in process of striking a balance between their economic problems, which force them to accept the drudgeries of unorganised labour employment, and the exploitative both economic and physical forces. Women have always been the victims of aggressive male sexuality. Among bonded labour households it has been observed that women have to provide sexual favours to the landlords creditors to whom the household is indebted. Further, it is pointed that the widespread use of sexual violence and exploitation is not the exclusive prerogative of men in the government, the police and the military. Women are raped at work, on the streets, in the fields, in their houses by men who are their employers, their neighbours, their relatives.

Indeed, in one study (Gupta, 1985) relating to the Jaunsar-Bawar region of Uttar Pradesh, women from bonded labour households were routinely sent into prostitution to repay the debts incurred by the husbands, typically for subsistence. The brothel owner pays the husband an advance which the latter uses for debt payment, while the wife puts in several years as a prostitute. Dr. G.K. Kamble has narrated causes where masters of bonded labour families as they have full control over family members and could compel their women for immoral acts. In certain regions, wife of a bonded labourer was mortgaged with the landlord to clear off debt. During mortgage period, the landlords could use her as a congubine. Such women were often ill-treated by the masters and forced to be the victims of brothel houses in urban areas. Sexual exploitation of migrant women is fairly common.

Forms of abuse range from humiliation and economic blackmail to physical brutality. The wounds sear the mental and physical health of many victims for life. Yet those victims often refrain from seeking help because they fear further violence, lack economic security or wish to shield their personal lives from public scrutiny.

A summery by the Family Planning Association of India show that 68 per cent of women admitted to some kind of sexual abuse by relatives or friends of the family. Women are commodities, objects of pleasure, objects to be used and discarded. Prostitutes, rape victims, victims of harassment in buses, in gardens, in factories and in offices, and even in temples.

Thus, the forgoing analysis demonstrate that unless the various labour laws and Acts are made leak-proof, the unorganised labour, including the tribal female labourers in particular and women labour in general, would continue to be economically and physically exploited.

Development-oriented Measures

In recent years government has undertaken various policy measures for the development of women which have been enumerated below:

DWCRA

Women from nearly half the population of India, and it is they who raise children to muturity. As such it is in their hands that the future of our country rests. Development of Women and Children in Rural Areas Programme (DWCRA) therefore, has been planned to make women economically productive and confident members of society and equal partners with men in bettering the living conditions of families.

Role of Gram Sevika

In the implementation process of DWCRA Gram Sevikas play the paramount role. Gram Sevika has been assisted by Mukhya Sevika and Project Office in a particular locality. To maintain the records of project implementation, to identify different ways of improving the capacity of women for income generation among the members of society etc., are the duties of the Gram Sevika. Gram

Sevika helps women in analysing their socio-economic situation and assists them in finding solutions for their problems. Gram Sevika should also be in a position to give ideas, information and assistance regarding any possible income generation activities that women of a group can undertake. She can help them to get information from banks, District Rural Development Agency (DRDA) and other Government programmes and thereby, forms a link between women of group and outside agencies.

Women who come under the purview DWCRA programme are devided into various categories like those who follow the traditional occupations like weaving, basket making, daily wage earners, miscellaneous occupations like flower selling, fire wood selling and those who are absolutely unemployed. Besides trainign in income generating activities, organisation of women labourers, provision of easy and low interest based credit, learning of skills etc., are also provided with the women workers through the DWCRA.

Selection Criteria

Criteria for selecting an income generating activity under the programme are: (i) raw material required is available locally can be transported to the working place at reasonable cost. (ii) ready marketing facilities. (iii) Small investment (iv) simple skills that can be learnt quickly (v) those that can be pursued at home or in the village, (vi) short gestation period and (vii) easy availability of training facilities and other technical inputs. Training, monitoring and evaluation of the programme is ultimately the test of success and hence has to be given the priority consideration. Involvement of women in DWCRA programme is of great significance for effective and proper implementation of DWCRA programme. The training of DWCRA functionaries is arranged by the National Institutes of Rural Development, Hyderabad. The traditional skills of rural women are being supplemented by training imparted under Training of Rural youth for Self-employment (TRYSEM) programme.

Women and Education

The sixth five year plan (1980-85) remarked 'a low rate of

literacy and low economic status stress the need for greater attention to the economic advancement of women." And that improvement in the socio-economic status of women would depend to a large extent on the social change in the values, attitudes and social structure prevailing in the country. Education has to be recognised as the basis on which health care of the children, the mother herself and the realisation that frequent pregnancies are a source of great danger to the women and her family can be safely built. Education enables women to be aware of their rights and responsibilities for the development of the nation as well as the region in which they live. Education adds to one's earning capacity, widens the scope of employment.

The National Perspective Plan for Women

The National Perspective Plan for Women (1988) has recommended the following measures for effective improvement of women at the grass roof level in the democratic institutions:

(i) Reservation should be made of 30 per cent seats at Panchayat to Zilla Parishad level and local municipal bodies for women. Whenever possible, higher representation of dalit/tribal women of weaker sections should be ensured.

(ii) Thirty per cent of executive heads of all bodies from village Panchayat to district level and a certain percentage of chief executive of panchayati Raj bodies at lower, middle and higher levels must be reserved for women.

(iii) A more effective step would be to declare a certain percentage of constituencies in the lower tier of Panchayati Raj as exclusively women's constituencies and all executive positions in a certain number of territorial jurisdiction reserved for women candidates.

Thus, the National Perspective Plan for Women aims at not only integrating women aims at not only integrating women into the mainstream if economic development but also ensuring equity and social justice for them.

An Evaluation

The position on women is closely associated with their economic standards which in turn, depends on opportunities for participation in economic activities. Development of women is considered as an index of society's stage of development and therefore, effective use of human resources of which women constitute an integral part is indispensable. "The opposition to increasing opportunities for women's participation in economic activities springs firstly from a conservative view regarding women's proper role in society. It also arises due to situations of chronic unemployment and under-development where the prospects of large-scale entry of women in the labour market is regarded as a potential cause of economic disorganisation. Technological changes have adversely affected the employment of women in industries as also noted by the Report of the National Committee on self-employment of women." Because women's Traditional economic contribution to the survival of their families in being eroded by Technology as the control and profit of technologies flow largely to men.

The attitude of employers has also been rather lukewarm towards the employment of women on account of protective legislative enacted for women labourers. The enforcement of Equal pay principle for men and women, the increased financial burden to be incurred by the employers because of maintenance of creches, the payment of maternity benefits etc., appear to have adversely affected women's employment in organised sectors. In industrial organised sector, stumbling-blocks are created because of the limitation on hours of work, prohibition of women employment in night shifts and restrictions on load carrying etc.

So long as gender is an important indicator of economic, social and political roles, here will be a need for special policies targeted to rural women for education, trainign technology transfer and credit. The inequality of women every where origionates to a very large extent from mass poverty and general backwardness of the majority of the population caused by under development. The causes of the inequalities between women and men are directly associated with a complex historical process. The inequality also derives from political, economic, social and cultural factors. It is obvious that poverty and under development have sharpened and continue to sharpen these inequalities which is strikingly apparent in the present world profile of women: while women represent half.

The Central Social Welfare Board (C.S.W.B.)

The CSWB extends financial assistance to voluntary organisations for setting up income generating units under the 'Socio-economic programme' by introducing technical and marketing support with focus on diversified occupation for women. Educational and vocational training courses are being organised by the aided agencies to improve their employment prospects and for rehabilitation of women in distress. In order to develop leadership qualities among rural women and to involve them in developmental activities, the Awareness Generation Project for Rural Women has been evolved. A National Plan of Action was formulated by the Ministry of social welfare which suggested a series of measures for the betterment of women including those unemployed.

A new scheme, namely, Women's Development Corporation would be taken up for promoting employment generating activities by supporting schemes for women groups and women from poorer section of society. A Women Development Planning and monitoring cell will be set up for collection of data and monitoring of plan programmes.

National Commission of Women

The Planning Commission in 1990 has focussed its attention on women workforce in the unorganised sector where they are exploited, underemployed, paid low wages by middlemen and exploited by anti-social elements. A national commission on women would set up to "monitor and accelerate the process of equal representation for women to enforce all legislation for women's rights including labour laws and to check discrimination in all spheres." The commission will also look into specific problems arising out of discrimination and atrocities against women, identity the constraints and recommend strategies for their removal.

Planned Measures

During the sixth plan, the government launched a good deal of schemes and programmes in order to ameliorate the working conditions of women. A special cell was established in 1976 to look after the employment of women and monitor the implementation of the Equal Remuneration Act. The Equal Remuneration Act was to provide for wages equal to those of men for work of similar nature. The Directorate General of Employment and Training (DGE and T) established three regional vocational trainign centres at Bombay, Bangalore and Trivandrum, and a National Vocational Training Institute at New Delhi, with the total absorbing capacity of 600 women trainees. Exclusively for women about 144 Industrial Training Institutes have been established in different states with the intake capacity of 11,200 women per annum by the end of sixth plan period. As an integral part of IRDP, the National Scheme of Training of Rural Youth for Self-Employment covered 3.27 lakh women during the plan period. It is aptly remarked that "added impetus was given to the training of women in instrumentation technology for repair and maintenance of electronic equipment in offices and hospitals. In certain areas of West Bengal, tribal women were trained in making blocks from stone chips, in bambo craft and rope making. Tribal women were also trained as rural health workers in Maharashtra. For creating increasing awareness of the role of women in development and the need for improvement of their status, various media units under the Ministry of Information and Broadcasting presented an appealing programme on social and economic problems and other related issues faced by women."

Financial Allocations

An outlay of Rs, 2,487.47 crores (Rs. 1,250.81 crores central and Rs. 1,236.66 crores State share) was provided for the seventh plan for the National Rural Employment Programme. The total Central provision made 1985-86, 1986-87 and 1987-88 comes to Rs. 1,492.27 crores for implementation of NREP. It has been reported that the employment generated during 1986-87 was 395.39 million mandays which has substantially exceeded the plan target of 290 million mandays per annum. During this period the Government set up the women's Development corporations in all the states and Union Territories for providing better employment opportunities for women in order to enable them economically self-relient and independent. These corporations were entrusted with the responsibility of identifying women entrepreneurs, supply of credit through financial institutions, facilities of training through the institutions etc. Under the scheme of Development of women and Children in Rural Areas (DWCRA), 50 districts have been brought under this programme during 1986-87 and 1987-88.

Syndrome of Observations

In spite of planned endeavours, enactment of Plethora of laws for the regulation of hours of work safety and welfare provisions for informal women labourers, their effective enforcement is far from satisfactory. In practice, wage discrimination continue unabated. "Many studies have indicated that the nature of economic development, agricultural mechanisation, commercialisation etc., have their adverse impact on women's employments. Women are treated as a source of cheap, unskilled secondary labour that can be hired to suit the requirements of the employer. Conditions of 95 per cent of the working women in the fields, mines and construction sites cottage and household industries are even worse. They have to do monotonus strenous back-breaking work at very low wages, in unhealthy and inhuman working conditions without facilities, permanency of jobs, creches, maternity benefits and protection of unions."

Despite equal turn over of work, discrimination and disparities and inbalances exist as an ever ending factor. The existing disparity has been, inter-alia, because of a combined complex factors like the absence of bargaining capacity of labourers, lack of special machinery to implement the relevant Acts, lack of extension of credit facilities and absence of strong unions.

A perusal of the foregoing paragraphs makes it obvious that women population of our country though constitute half of the total population, yet their socio-economic condition is distressing. They are exploited and their contribution is invisible in the planning process in the Surveys, studies and census reports. There is yet an effect national policy to emerge. New paradigms are to be evolved for mitigating their basic problems. The unorganised sector or what we call informal sector, has not been covered very effectively by adequate legislative provisions in ameliorating their socio-economic conditions.

REFERENCES

Shastri, Madhu, 'Status of the special protective provisions of penal and criminal codes under the constitution of India" In Sushila Agrawal (Ed.) *Status of Women.* Printwell Publishers, Jaipur, 198, pp. 23-24.

Pathy, Suguna, Of women and society, *Frontier,* Oct. 28, 1989, p. 10.

Devi, Mahesweta and Ghos, Nirmal, *Bonded Labour in India* (In Hindi) Radhakrishna Publishers, New Delhi, 1981.

Ghadially, Rechana (Ed.), *Women in Indian Society—A Reader,* Sage Publications, New Delhi, 1988, p. 203.

Gupta, Jyoti, 'Himalayan Polyandry: bondage among women in Jaunswer-Bawar' pp. 258-281 in Utsa Patnaik, and Manjari Dig-Waney (Ed.) *Chains of Servitude: Bondage and slavery in India,* Sangam Books India Pvt. Ltd., Madras, 1985.

Tripathy, S.N. (Dr.), *Bonded Labour in India,* Discovery Publishing House, New Delhi, 1989, p. 17.

Bhasin, Kamla, Girl child or fish among crocodiles. *Kurukshetra,* Vol. XXXVIII No. 12, September, 1990, p. 31.

Roy Edmond, Development of Rural Women, *Orissa Review,* December, 1988, p. 32.

Joshi, Uma, 'Improving the Status of Rural Women,' *Social Welfare,* Vol. XXXVI. No. 3-4, June-July, 1989, p. 14.

Rajuladevi, A.K., Technological Choice and their Impact on Eomen. *Kurukshetra,* Vol. XXXVI, No. 2, Nov. 1987, p. 7.

Sinha, Ajit Kumar, Improving the Lot of Rural Women. *Yojana,* Vol. 32, No. 9, May 16-31, 1988, p. 28.

Gupta Ashoka, Let men change their attitude *Kurukshetra* Vol. XXXVIII, No. 12, September, 1990, p. 11.

13

Women Scavengers

The scavenging (sweeping public and private places) profession in India is strictly circumscribed by concepts of purity and pollution. As untouchables (officially classified as the Scheduled Castes) scavengers and sweepers are at the very bottom of the Hindu caste system. Divided into subcastes, their traditional work in rural India consisted of removing human excreta and refuse, often in basket-loads carried on their hands, and cleaning village roads. Despite adaptations, the basic nature of the job has not changed. Though the flush system is increasingly replacing the dry latrine, sweepers are needed to keep the sanitation system of India's cities and towns going. As no other caste will perform such defiling yet essential tasks, men and women of these castes retain a virtual monopoly over their traditional occupation.

It is an occupation in which both sexes participate. At the same time, job mobility chances for men are substantially greater than for women. Looking at data from studies conducted over the past twenty-five years, it becomes clear that the position of the female sweeper has changed little. Again, within the occupation as well, women tend to do the more defiling, arduous and less paid tasks. A 1952 study in Madhya Pradesh found that twice as many women as men were sweeping roads; men got promoted to supervisory posts, became watchmen, or were trained for driving refuse trucks, while women remained scavengers. Male Bhangis in Bhiwani and Mathura are increasingly becoming labourers, rickshaw pullers and tonga drivers. Of those in the profession, most were in government employment, while their womenfolk remained in private scavenging jobs. Unpublished data collected for a sample study in the rural and urban areas of post-green Revolution Haryana showed that more than a third of Balmiki men had left the profession for better paid higher status jobs.

Working Conditions

In 1977, we conducted a small study in a West Delhi Tenement colony among 80 Balmiki women, a sub-caste of the scavenging Bhangi caste of North India. The aim was to determine male-female patterns of mobility and authority structures. Traditionally the Balmikis claim descent from Valmiki, the author of the *Ramayana:* this was substantiated in the Census of 1881. Delhi's Balmikis, most of whom are migrants from the neighbouring state of Uttar Pradesh, live dispersed throughout the city, living in slums and tenement colonies.

The migrant agricultural labourer or small farmer in India often has to leave behind his wife when he moves to the city; on the other hand, in North India the scavenger or construction worker brings his wife with him because he is sure of employment for her. Statistics on migration indicate that when the female participation rate is high in occupations which can be profitably continued in the urban milieu, there is a greater degree of equality in the sex (migration) ratio. Further evidence shows that in essential, caste-bound occupations such as scavenging and laundering, women are invaluable participants in the system. In her study of slums, Singh found that washing of clothes was done only by women of the Dhobi caste, while ironing was shared between the men and women. Similarly, though the Delhi Municipal Corporation reserves 75 per cent of scavenging jobs for men and 25 per cent for women, the ratio is almost 50:50. A senior official commented that with more men moving out of the traditional caste occupation, the Corporation—the largest employer of scavengers in Delhi-had to engage women in excess of the stipulated quota. While male Balmikis still dominate the profession, the official felt it was significant that an increasing number were attracted by jobs in shops, commercial establishments and factories. On the other hand, this was rarely the case with women.

One of the most pressing problems for lower-class migrants is finding living accommodation in the city. Though the colony in which we did my field work was specially built for Municipal Corporation sweepers, at the time of interview, it was peopled mainly by illegal occupants. Shortage of urban living space means that migrants take shelter wherever they can. In the present situation relatives and co-villagers of the original tenants arrived several years ago in search of jobs. Even after the death or moving away of the rightful occupants they stayed on, resisting all attempts at eviction. This soon led to overcrowding, insanitary conditions and illegal constructions. In the colony under study only about half the families who had someone employed with the Corporation were legal tenants. The rest were illegal occupants.

Most of the women interviewed were between 21 and 35 years of age, and 60 per cent had migrated to the city, primarily at marriage. Half the sample had started working between the ages of 10 and 15 years, and late employment was the exception rather than the rule. The average number of children was 5.3, and the nuclear family appeared to be the dominant norm. Poverty was the chief reason which took Balmiki women out to work. All were in the traditional caste occupation, and a few said that they washed clothes in addition to their duties of cleaning latrines and throwing away garbage. Though some complained of the dirty nature of their work, no respondent spoke of a likelihood of leaving the profession. A fear of untouchability and a lack of training for any other occupation inhibited women from thinking of a change.

While the older sweepers appeared more resigned to caste discrimination, some of the younger women were assertive in their reactions. A typical example was Kamla, who had been put to sweeping by her mother at the age of 11 years. At the time of interview she was cleaning five homes, as well as looking after her four children between the ages of twelve and five. She accepted that she would have to work for many years to come; but she felt humiliated at being treated as an untouchable:

> "Who says that there is no untouchability? There is plenty of it. Even after all these years we are not allowed to go anywhere near the kitchen. We work for Baniyas who are very fussy. There is one relative of theirs—she says she is a school teacher—she lifts up her sari if she has to pass me. When she does that we feel like throwing acid on her face. Don't we have hearts and bodies just like you all? I'm sure your shudder to clean your baby's behind. What about us—foraging for generations in excreta and muck and carrying dung on our heads? It was only a man called Mahatma Gandhi who tried to change things for us; nobody else has done anything ever since. We life with the same stench with which we started."

While a third of the husbands of those interviewed were in non-scavenging jobs, women sweepers appeared more concerned with getting ahead within the profession. There was a substantial difference in the job requirements, remuneration and perquisites of women working in the municipal corporation, government institutions and hospitals, and those employed in private homes. Those working for the Municipal Corporation, its schools, government dispensaries and hospitals enjoyed in addition to a higher salary, maternity and other paid leave, uniform, and security of tenure. Hospital and school sweepers had to clean latrines, while the main function of Corporation sweepers was to sweep public roads.

In contrast, private sweepers often worked in several homes and were not entitled to any fringe benefits. Many complained of being tried after climbing several flights of stairs during the day and carrying garbage tins to and from the refuse heap. Maternity leave was unknown; it was common for most women in private service to work almost to the day their child was born, as well as provide substitutes—often a kinswoman—for their period of absence. The incumbent's salary during childbirth and subsequent isolation was claimed by the substitute. It was not surprising that 70 per cent of the present sample who were in private employment aspired for government or quasi-government employment, rather than a movement out of the profession.

In addition to harder working conditions, private sweepers were paid much less; sixty per cent of the present sample said that they earned less than Rs. 100 a month. Four women said that for working in about thirty houses they earned Rs. 50. This works out to Rs. 1.66 a month per house, or 0.05 paise a day for cleaning a latrine and throwing away garbage. The degree of exploitation is evident, where a minimum bus fare costs 0.30 paise and a cup of tea, 0.25 paise at a wayside stall. While there is no sex-based wage discrimination in public employment, no respondent had a husband who earned as little as these four women. Nor is mobility into permanent and better jobs easy; only five of the present respondents said that they had been taken into the Corporation after many years of private employment. Three admitted that the influence of kinsmen employed in the Corporation was instrumental in their being absorbed. Two widows had filled their husbands' posts.

Profiles

Disparities in life-style are vividly brought out if we look at the histories of Bimla and Rajbatti. Bimla, private sweeper, lived with her husband and four children in a one-room mud-walled tenement, while Bimla, her husband Hari and the youngest daughter of four months slept on a string cot, the other three children slept on the floor. The wooden front door was the only source of ventilation; a few gleaming cooking vessels were stacked in a corner near the bucket-stove. While children's clothes lay on the cot and a broken chair, a well-used suitcase contained two term winter quilts and Hari's woolen uniforms. An open drain abutted on the entrance, and we often saw the younger children defecating into it. In summer, the family slept out of doors, as did most other residents of the colony.

Bimla's father had retired as a senior sweeper in the railways and lived with his wife and other five children in old Delhi. Though the three sons had been to school, all the daughters were illiterate. Bimla was married to Hari, a *farash* in a government office at the age of 14 years. A couple of years later, her first child, a daughter, was born and subsequently three more children followed in quick succession. After the last child, she insisted on having a tubectomy operation. Though Hari earned Rs. 395 a month, Bimla felt that she should work because she wanted a better life for her children. Besides, Hari had taken to hard drinking soon after the birth of the third child.

A slim twenty-six-year-old with sharp features against a dark complexion, Bimla worked in fifteen houses and earned seventy-five rupees a month. It was a twenty-minutes walk to the colony where she worked. She left at ten in the morning and was back home by two in the afternoon. In the evenings, she spread out a piece of jute matting on the pavement parallel to the main road running past the colony and sold vegetables which Hari had brought at the retail market earlier in the day. During the two years that we observed her, Bimla's life underwent certain major changes. When we spoke to her first, she had a matter-of-fact approach to life:

> "In our community there is no choice for a woman with regard to working: we don't ask questions. At the age of ten we are handed a broom. It's true that my parents did not put me to work before we were married, but we used to wander around with my mother and occasionally help. We never went to school—my father said that it was a waste of time. But we don't agree. My three older children are all in primary school, though the elder girl helps me with the cooking and cleaning.
>
> We do the day's cooking before we leave for work. My husband's duty hours are such that he is back by 10 a.m. and then goes back again at 4. p.m. He sometimes does the cooking. Usually he buys the rations and the kerosene oil. We have to take the baby with me. What is the option? We only own a bicycle, though in my father's house we were used to radio. We do not even have a water line. We have to pay something monthly to our neighbour Rani for taking water from her tap. They made it clear to us that they are doing us a great favour,

and others may be willing to pay more. But because we are neighbours, Rani is prepared to give the water to us rather than to anyone else. The world is a cruel place. People don't even give water to other free of charge.

For the birth of the first two children, we went to my *maike* (mother's house). My husband made arrangements for someone to relieve me at my place of work a month in advance each time. But this was no longer possible when the third child was on the way. We worked till the day on which my last two children were born. We nearly lost my job, because though my husband used to stand-in, he was very erratic. This was mainly because he thought it demeaning to clean latrines. On the last two occasions we had to stay at home for forty days because we had got so weak. When we joined work, we started taking the baby with me and nursing it whenever it cried. In winter and in the height of summer it was not easy: The baby used to cry the minute we took her out of this room. She used to get ill every month. Anyway, now we have had enough of children. We had myself operated after the last child was born. Most of my employers address me as 'jamadarni.' There is no personal relationship. We clean the latrines, throw away the garbage, sweep the stairs and driveways. We are not supposed to sweep any of the other rooms, though sometimes when the servant who does that is absent, we are asked to stand-in. We get very tried, carrying dustbins and bending over the stairs fifteen times in the day. We get a cup of tea in three houses, but no gifts at festival time. One lady gave my baby some old clothes when she was born.

We give my salary to my husband. He then hands me a sum of money with which to buy the daily vegetables. He buys clothes for children and for me. But lately, he has started drinking and abusing me. We don't know the reason for this. He rarely used to beat the children. Now he thinks nothing of raising his hand."

When we saw Bimla again after some months, she had lost weight and was untidily dressed. Earlier, she had been particular about her clothes. Her neighbour told me in a whisper that her husband had become a drunkard and used to beat her up regularly. His excuse was that she had illicit relations with a man who used to buy vegetables from her. Bimla had a different story to tell:

> "My husband thinks that one can do business with a sour look on one's face. Just because we smile at my customers, he thinks that we are behaving badly. Some months ago, my sari had accidentally slipped off my shoulder, at a time when one of my regular customers was buying vegetables from me. Hari saw me talking to this *chaprasi.* Since then, he is convinced that we have been having an affair with him. Though my neighbours have tried to explain to him that this is not the case, he gets drunk and beats me up regularly.
>
> He has also stopped giving me any money for the household. How can we manage on Rs. 75? So now we have taught my little daughter of two years to get money out of his pocket. She climbs on to his stomach when he is asleep, and puts her hand into his pocket. The following morning he misses the money and starts shouting. But when we shout back and ask whether he expects us to starve, he keeps quiet. It is only when he is drunk that he gets violent.
>
> Apart from drinking, there is something else he has started. His parents owned a plot of land in his village, which he has inherited. He applied for a house-building advance loan a couple of years ago. The loan came through about eight months ago, and he takes casual leave every few weeks and goes to the village. He says that he is building a house. Two months ago, a relative of his visited me and said that he was building a house; but he had also started living with his dead brother's widow, a woman with married children. When we accused him of this, he beat me up and said 'Does a respectable man misbehave with his *bhabhi?* She is like a mother to me.' But we know he is lying. He does things with her because she

is supervising the construction of his house. He even brought her to my home last month. We lost my temper and slapped her face. Hari was enraged and hit me with a big stone. See, you can see the scar on my face."

Bimla's life is a striking example of the unequal status of the Balmiki women at work and in the home; her husband had left the profession and had joined the ranks of the ubiquitous government servant. When his wife was unable to go to work, he was reluctant to stand-in because it meant cleaning latrines. His work consisted mainly of dusting office rooms and furniture. In his own words. "We have hardly any work to do. Who bothers in a government office?" On the other hand, Bimla had to combine domestic chores with an arduous day's work. Leave was known and Bimla complained that her salary had been cut twice when she had been absent for a couple of days because of a child's illness.

At home, when it came to suspicion over extramarital relations, Bimla's husband beat her up regularly, Though she too had her doubts about her husband's fidelity, Bimla had no way of getting even with Hari. In addition, his frequent bouts of drunkenness and consequent refusal to support the family meant that Bimla had to look for more employment. There was substantial disparity between the social position of husband and wife.

In contrast, Rajbatti, a Corporation sweeper, had the same employment status as her husband who worked in a government school. Out of their combined earnings they had built an additional rook above the original tenement allotted to Rajbatti. The walls were freshly white-washed and a light bulb hung outside the front door where her son had recently put up a pained name plate. At forty, Rajbatti had nineteen years of permanent service behind her. The youngest of her six children was studying in class V, and the second son was a motor car mechanic. The total family income was about Rs. 800 a month. At the time of interview, Rajbatti's family owned two cycles, a radio and a sewing machine. Her eldest daughter who had taken classes in sewing, made small garments for people in the colony. Ram Swarup, Rajbatti's husband and her children shared in domestic chores. Rajbatti's working hours were longer than those of her husband. She commented:

> "We were married at the age of twelve years, but did not go to my husband's home till we were fifteen. After a month of fusing over me, my mother-in-law told me, `New, daughter, like all of us, you must take up a job.' We started working in a few private homes until my eldest son was born. After his birth, they did not force me to go back to work. But when he was two years old, my father-in-law, a Corporation sweeper, asked me whether we would like to try for a Municipal job. My husband was already employed in a Corporation school. We said that we didn't mind. We went through some kind of interview, and was quite surprised when we got the job. In the beginning, it was difficult. We had to help my mother-in-law with the coking when we came back from my 6 a.m. to 10 a.m. shift. Then once we started having children every year, we wanted to give up my job. Everyone thought we were mad. No one gives up a permanent government job. Besides we used to get three months' paid maternity leave each time. So we decided to stay on. As we lived with my husband's family, looking after the children was never a major problem.
>
> Now that it is all behind me, we are very glad we did not leave. It is true that we are out of the house for over eight hours in the day, but compared with women in private service, we are very fortunate. In the early mornings we sweep the roads, along with men sweepers. We have been given brooms with long handles so that we don't have to bend. We get home by 11 a.m., in time to see to the mid-day meal which my elder daughter has already prepared. We leave at 1.30 p.m. and am back home by 6.30 p.m. in the evening. In the second shift we clean the rooms of the local Corporation office as well as the bathrooms.
>
> My work is little different from that of my husband, We are entitled to the same benefits and earn about the same salary. It is because we decided to stick on to my job that we were

able to educate our children. After we retire, we shall get a person. Had we left my job, we would have been hard up. Besides, there is so much more demanded in private service. My neighbour, Santi, is expecting her third child. Poor thing, she is only eighteen years old. Though the baby is due in a few days' time, she is still working. Her employers have told her that if she cannot provide a suitable substitute she will lose her job. We have never faced any such problem.

None of my children are sweepers; it is true that the eldest boy is unemployed. But though he could easily get a sweeper's job, we want him to try for at least a *chaprasi's* post. Next year, we hope to buy some land in my husband's village. We look after the family finances. My husband and children hand over their earnings to me after retaining a certain amount for their own expenses. My old man gets drunk once in a while, particularly at festivals. We know my son smokes, and he certainly likes good clothes; but as he is contributing to the family funds, why should we grudge him his luxuries? My husband makes all the major decisions about how we should spend our money. Though we earn as much as he does, we do not expect to boss over him on financial matters. At one time, he was briefly out of a job. Even then, he was all-in-all; after all he is my lord and master."

The contrasting situations of Bimla and Rajbatti are examples of the internal stratification system within the scavenging profession. But though Rajbatti was more privileged than Bimla, her chances of a movement out of the profession were far less than for a man. A third of the husbands of women in the sample were in non-traditional jobs. In addition, a majority of those who were in the profession were in higher-status government or Corporation employment. Seventeen husbands were drivers, peons, night watchmen and mechanics, while seven were labourers. Two were office clerks.

Problems of Balmiki Women Today

Talking to Corporation officials in Delhi revealed that the number of Balmiki women seeking jobs did not seem to be decreasing. In addition to their own limited aspirations, most women in the present sample said that husbands would resist the attempts of wives to move out of the occupation. A case system which gives Balmikis a job monopoly is fully exploited by the community; assured of a secure income from the female members of the family, the menfolk often take time off to learn a trade, or look around for better jobs. Nine women—more than 10 per cent of the present sample—supported unemployed husbands or those who earned less than themselves. Another three women whose husbands were drivers and mechanics said that they had been the main provides while their husbands had been under training.

Boserup has pointed out that though more urban men are joining the modern sector, women persist with traditional occupations. This is corroborated by 1961 Census data on Delhi Balmikis which shows that while a quarter of the scavengers were women, only one woman out of thirty was likely to be in trade and commerce or manufacturing. A lack of training opportunities, large families and hindered physical mobility are important factors which keep Balmiki women in the occupation. In addition it is advantageous for men to have wives in easily obtainable jobs which require no outlay or training. Again, when women provide the cushioning between starvation and subsistence, men are set free to seek their fortunes in other occupations.

Taking a linear view, Boserup points out that the female's displacement through mechanization and industrialization means more than a loss of income; her position in the market and the home steadily deteriorates. Without adequate training facilities, women continue in traditional occupations. Ultimately, however, with the progress of the modern economic system, it is possible that they will be pushed out of the productive sphere altogether. Industrialization introduces the "polarisztion and hierarohization of men's and women's work roles" which affects relationships within the family. Boserup further adds that in societies where there are legal provisions for divorce, separation and maintenance, and employed divorcee or widow will be treated better by her male relatives because she can support herself. The overall cross-cultural impression therefore appears to be that irrespective of class position, and employed woman has substantially more status than one who does not have a job.

Domestic Circumstances

Balmiki women perform a vital function in the city's life. If they chose to stay away from work, civic amenities would be substantially affected. Consequently, monopoly over a caste-bound occupation gives them an important bargaining position at their place of work. Using a few variables such as control over income, domestic workload, free-time activities and decision-making, we shall see whether the position of the Balmiki women in the home is affected by her being employed. Though Balmiki women did not question the need to work, a majority specified that the initial decision was taken by someone else. While a third said that their husbands had decided that they should work, 15 per cent of the women indicated that mother-in-law had taken the initiative. Most of those who had been employed before they were married said that their mothers had sent them out to work.

Three-fourths of those whose husbands were the heads of households said that all salaries earned were deposited with the women. It was culturally accepted that husbands should retain a certain amount for buying *bidis,* cigarettes, drink and clothes. On the other hand, no woman said that she kept apart some money to spend on herself. Fieldwork showed that women kept family earnings with them because it was convenient. Husbands appeared unwilling to take the responsibility of deciding how to make ends meet on a shoe-string budget. Nearly all the women said that they had to give accounts of the broad categories of expenditure to their husbands. All major financial decisions such as taking a loan, buying a bicycle or a radio were taken by the men.

Most Balmiki women in the sample combined the arduous task of scavenging with a full load of domestic duties. Men rarely participated in the daily routine of housework and child raring activities. The only major functions they appeared to perform were fetching fuel for the family hearth, occasionally queing up for rations, or taking a sick child to the dispensary. Almost half the sample said that they managed the housework single-handed, and this included twelve women who were out of their homes for over eight hours in the day. For the rest, helpers consisted of female kin or in-laws. If sons helped, they did so only until the age of about their peers while their sisters minded younger children or helped with the housework.

A third of sample scoffed at my question on free time. Outings to the cinema, distant market places and fairs were unknown, except during the festival season in October and November. Gossiping at the doorstep while the evening *chapattis* were being made appeared to be the most common from of relaxation. On the other hand, it was expected that men would have their drinking sprees, buy new clothes and go to the cinema. While we had not asked any specific questions on alcoholism, we were told by the local social worker that both drunkenness and wife-beating were common. Bimla's life was a case in point. Only three women—one whose husband was a clerk, and two others whose husbands were away from home often—aid that they went out and bought clothes for themselves and their children. For the rest, they had to depend on the largesse of their husbands, relatives or employers.

A Balmiki woman's earning ability led neither to economic independence, nor change in the traditional structure of male-female relationships within the family. An earning wife had no right to spend her alary on herself; all earning went into the common kitty for running the home. A man, on the other hand, invariably kept back some money for his personal expenses Again, wife beating continued to be a common offence. Those subjected to such excesses were pointed out to me with a certain degree of vicarious shame and included a middle-aged woman who supported her unemployed husband. Women took day-to-day decisions on what to cook or indicated when rations and kerosene oil were needed; on major issues, men decided where a woman should work, whether a loan should be taken or if a visit to the natal village was due. The expenses of travelling meant that women rarely visited their natal homes many of which were in rural Uttar Pradesh. Even when women managed to get away for a family wedding or for Diwali, their husbands or father-in-law had the final say on the length their stay.

Though Balmiki women are indispensable to Delhi's civic life, their men often decide the circumstances under which they shall go to work. An important feature of Balmiki economic organization is the system of "buying up" houses among private employees. By paying a certain sum of money to a Balmiki who is about to leave the area in which he or she has been working, another Balmiki "buys" up the right to clean in a fixed number of houses which constitutes the beat. No other sweeper can enter the area to work, nor can employers terminate the services of the incumbent and hope to get a replacement. Normally, a Balmiki who wishes to dispose of this right negotiates with kinsmen and friends. There is usually no difficulty in finding person who are interested in bargaining. While a widowed women will usually do the talking herself, a married woman's chief negotiator is her husband or a male in-law. In case the seller is a woman, transactions may be carried on directly by the woman, through in cases where there is difficulty in reaching an accord, menfolk may step in. When the seller is a man and the buyer a woman, or vice versa, men often take a major role in deciding the sum. Sometimes, a show of muscle power clinches the issue. While in all-male transactions women do not play any role, men usually had a decisive say in determining the area and number of houses in which their wives should work.

Other studies have shown that high-caste women play an important role in marriage negotiations. While we had not asked specific questions on the role of women in this sphere, observations indicated that that men were instrumental in initiating discussions. Wives may have been asked their opinion, but except in the case of widows or some older women, they were rarely given a formal role in talks. Field work in Taiwan and tribal Africa indicated that wives often exercised substantial covert influence either by withholding sexual service or organizing themselves with other women in informal groups. Though this was not an area that we had investigated, the incidence of wife-beating provided ample testimony of male reactions to recalcitrant or obstinate wives. A Balmiki woman may occasionally cook bodly, neglect her children or sham illness. Such expression of fratration can rarely be sustained over a long period of time and are no indications of wife's power.

Public Private Power

We can now draw some distinctions between power in the public and private domains. Balmiki women occupy a pivotal position in Delhi's civic life. The threat of a strike causes intense consternation among public authorities, as does a high rate of absenteeism. At work, sweeper women interact freely with male colleagues and employers. On buses, or walking along the roads to work, they spar loudly with men in the profession or other acquaintances. But public roles and behaviour patterns rarely affect male-female relations with the family unit. The Balmiki woman's power in Delhi city is not carried over to the home. One of the chief reasons for a female's lack of familial status is the absence of control over the product of labour, which in this case is the Balmiki woman's salary. This factor is also what often distinguishes an upper-middle-class working woman from a working-class of lower-middle-class empioyed Indian woman. The ability to decide how one's earnings are to be spent gives a woman a bargaining position within the family. While Balmiki women may have administered the family earnings, they did not have the liberty either theoretically or actually to isolate their salary from the rest of the income, or plan how to use it. When the majority of families lived at the subsistence level all income went to provide food and shelter for the family. In addition, an unemployed husband expected his wife to provide him with food and money.

Not only do mot Indian working women have little authority in deciding how to spend their salaries, but also their work is rarely socially valued. Among middle-class professions the dominantly female occupations of nursing and teaching are accorded a low social status. Though women perform vital functions in agriculture, men own land and capital in most parts of India, and take all the major decisions. Women's income is regarded only as "contribution towards the salt," while the man's income is essential for the staple crop. This attitude is reinforced when men go to the cities, and start earning more in non-traditional occupations. It was the duty of the Balmiki wife to work; an unemployed woman was regarded as a liability. While a man's desire to move away from a demeaning occupation was legitimate, a Balmiki woman who thought of leaving the profession was duly chastised.

Impact of Development

A working-class woman's position within the family is rarely enhanced by virtue of her being employed. She combines the roles of an additional earner with that of unpaid domestic help. A woman who stays at home may be shunned by her family or ostracised by the community. She avoids the dual roles of working long hours and cooking, cleaning and tending to children. In terms of physical fatigue, an unemployed woman has a distinct advantage over her employed neighbour. However, in a situation where women rarely have a choice in the matter, such observations are, by and large, pointless. What they do establish, however, is that unless attitudes towards women change, a shift, for instance, in the nature of work, from the traditional to the modern economy will rarely affect status. A woman's work is economically productive; it has to be socially valued as well. Further, without rights over their products and an independent identity, women will continue to be governed by male authority structures. For example, a *dhobi* (washer caste) woman who becomes a seamstress will have to depend on her husband's network for a loan to set up a shop; it would not be unreasonable than to expect the husband to have a decisive say in how her earnings are to be spent.

The argument is not against the absorption of women in the modern economy; it is only to point out that though a woman's work may become less onerous, it may be some time before her status within the family and society undergoes a commensurate change.

There appears to be a universal dilemma facing industrialized as well as industrialising nations. The change in the means of production becomes primarily a source of power and authority; a rationalization of values does not always keep pace with changed life-styles. Srinivas has commented on the ambivalence in the minds of those castes exposed to urbanization and Westernization. In other words, in a highly industrialized system old prejudices and active discrimination still persist; modernization *per se* does not lead to a change in value systems. Both men and women who are caught up in the process of development face certain problems. A man's mobility and limited domestic participation make the solution of these problems easier; a woman on the other hand has to make far greater adjustments in her style of life. A semi-skilled job in a factory may mean a substantial change in the working conditions of a Balmiki woman. At the same time, for the migrant peasant woman who was economically productive at her own time and pace in the village, the shift to an urban milieu may result is considerable anomie.

In a caste-based occupational system like India, the process of modernization has to contend with certain unique factors. As we have seen, important among these is the continued retention of women in traditional jobs. This case study of Balmiki women shows that most women in the agricultural economy, as well as those in low-status service occupations, are subjected to cumulative inequality. *Together* with their menfolk, they rank at the bottom of the caste hierarchy; *in relation* to their menfolk, they occupy inferior positions socially as well as occupationally. The more arduous as well as defiling tasks are performed by women. The immediate developmental problem then is not of women being pushed out of the economic system because of mechanization, but that of remaining behind in low status, strenuous occupations. Singh found that slum women in urban India have far fewer occupational choices than their menfolk. Most of them were employed in menial jobs. So long as the country's size and ecology serve to slow down the universal mechanization of agriculture and civic facilities, low-caste women will continue to find jobs in essential occupations. On the other hand, their men will be progressively involved in "passing" in caste society by changing their names, learning a trade and dressing in the latest style. The status of women is thus further depressed in relation to their mobile menfolk. Working-class women in a modernising face a loss of status not so much because of unemployment but in relation to their upwardly mobile menfolk. It is likely that when men move into more prestigious jobs, attitudes towards their wives may become more arbitrary. Some men prefer to take their wives out of paid employment, as at certain levels the fact that one's wife can sit at home is a sign of high status. There are also other reactions; the wives of two clerks in the sample were full of shame and self-recrimination. They felt that it was humiliating for their husbands to have wives in a demeaning occupation like scavenging.

Empirical evidence amply substantiates the developmental theorists' point of view that *men are the chief beneficiaries of the modern economy.* However, country to established notions, there is no imminent threat of unemployment for the bulk of rural women and those in certain caste-based occupations. In fact, modernization is helped by the continuation of women in traditional jobs which releases men for the new technology. In India where certain caste groups have control over some low-status occupations, it is not unusual for men to restrict female employment to traditional jobs. A change from one kind of occupation to another often involves some measure of uncertainty. For working-class men in particular, the risk of an unknown future is more worth taking when they are assured financial support from their women-folk than when both partners are on the job market or the wife does not work. We may generalise then that the increasing participation of Indian men at certain levels of the economy is facilitated by wives in traditional employment.

Education as a Means to Upward Mobility

What do such trends tell us about the future of social change among the underprivileged in India? Will things be different for the next generation of Balmikis? At independence in 1947 the newly elected representatives of the people were well aware of the need to help backward groups. Working on the premise that education helps social and occupational mobility, mass literacy drives and school expansion were stressed. In addition to free tuition and text-book aid, a certain percentage of seats were reserved in educational institutions for the Scheduled Castes and Scheduled Tribes. It was hoped that such positive discrimination would help a child overcome his background. But thirty years of experience have shown that education by and large reinforces the social system; the higher castes monopolise access to education. Yet, the discriminatory policy has not been a total failure. There is a growing elite among the Scheduled Castes whose success is due largely to being able to stay on in the educational system. It would be interesting then, to see how an illiterate group of the urban poor views education as a means of providing a better future for their children.

To start with, only three women were aware of the existence of freeships and reserved places for their children in school. As there was a distinct bias in favour of educating boys rather than girls, separate questions were asked on sex distribution of education. On the whole, it appeared that younger mothers were more optimistic and enthusiastic than those whose children had been exposed to the educational system. Fifteen mothers specified that their sons had dropped out of school and five had no sons. Of the dropouts, seven were employed as sweepers, mechanics and drivers while the rest were employed. Two sons had finished school and two were college students. All except one of the remaining 56 women wanted their sons to finish school. This desire for schooling, however, had to contend with two harsh facts of life: first of all, the respondents were not sure whether they would be able to se their children through school. This apprehension was based not only on the lack of ability to bear the expenses but also on the economic opportunity cost argument. Beyond a certain age it did not pay to have children going to school when they could either work in the home or outside and help supplement the family income; secondly, many respondents said that discrimination and prejudice in school worked against their children.

We were an observer to a protracted argument which developed between Mayavati, a Corporation sweeper, and a male colleague of hers. We were talking to Mayavati as she smoked a *bidi* after a day's work. Her responses were spirited and lengthy, When we came to the question of education, her co-worker, who had so far been puffing away pensively at his *bidi,* interrupted and said that in education lay the path to salvation. mayavati looked hard at him, took her *bidi* out of her mouth and hawked noisily into the nearby drain. She made it clear that she did not agree with Natho. All her four children were in school, but she felt that they were wasting their time. Attacking Natho directly she asked him what his "Class X pass" son had achieved five years after leaving school. Besides what about untouchability? She answered herself:

> "What do these schools teach anyway? Of what use is it to our children? Today they want books, tomorrow pencils and day after tomorrow something else. And in government schools it is all supposed to be free.
>
> The other day we happened to pass by the boys' school. We saw my ten-year old son playing marbles in the dust. We shouted out, 'Ohe Ramu, it is your free period?' He shook his head and said no. Some teacher was standing by and we heard her tell another one, 'Oh these Bhangis, they expect us to teach their dirty children.' We kept quiet and did not say anything but walked on. When Ramu came home we asked him what he did in school. He said. 'This and that, sometimes studies when Bahenji feels like it.' So, that's what school means for our children"

Natho did not make any comment during Mayavatis' monologue. When she stopped and looked questioningly at him, he asked her that if she felt so negatively about education, why did she continue to send her children to school. Mayavati paused for a bit, and shrugging her shoulders said, if they left school, "they would be on the streets." There were no jobs for them; yet she would resist their taking to the traditional occupation. School was a way of keeping children occupied temporarily.

Mayavati's comments were indicative of the general attitude towards schooling for boys. Its benefits as a way of keeping children out of mischief were far greater than its role in occupational mobility. Most mothers felt that it would have been more useful if their sons were able to have access to some from of job-oriented training rather than waste their time in schools. If most mothers were somewhat motivated to keep their sons in schools far fewer were so inclined for their daughters. This discrepancy in attitude towards education of boys and girls is borne out by other slum studies. Desai and Pillai found that illiteracy was three times higher among slum women than among the men. In her recent study of slum dwellers, Singh observed that while "parents tended to have unrealistic educational and employment aspirations for their sons' They did "not consider education very important for their daughters."

From the present sample, while ten did not respond or did not have daughters, thirty-six out of seventy—a little over fifty per cent — said that their daughters had not gone beyond the first few classes in school. Of these eleven had got married before they were fifteen and another six were employed as sweeper girls in early adolescence. Thirteen mothers out of the thirty-six specified that they positively did not want their daughters to be educated as they would anyway be married and employed as sweepers.

Phoolbatti, the mother of three daughters who had put her eldest daughter to work as a sweeper after five years of schooling exemlified the reasoning of many Balmiki mothers with daughters:

> "Nearly all our girls go to work as sweepers. Why should we waste time and money on sending a daughter to school where she will learn nothing of use? What does the Hindi alphabet mean to her? Will it help her to get any other kind of jobs? So why not put her to work so that when she is married she will know something of our work as well as be able to light the stove?
>
> We repeat, why waste time in sending my daughters to school? Do they learn anything here? Anyway, they will be married soon and their mother-in-law will put them to cleaning latrines somewhere. If they go to school they will get big ideas and

then be beaten up by their husbands or abused by their mothers-in-law."

Of the mothers who were sending their daughters to school, most were pessimistic about the use of education. Its role in job mobility was wholly discounted.

Further, the opportunity-cost argument was more applicable to girls of the school-going age tan to boys. This was in keeping with the role image of Balmiki women as maintained by the community. Six mothers admitted that their sons were in school while their female siblings had been taken out of the educational system and put to work as sweepers. Close questioning of these mothers showed that they did not feel that they had done anything unusual or unfair. School was a waste of time in a situation of extreme poverty; if daughters could help either by looking after younger children and thereby releasing mothers for extra work, or worked themselves, the family unit stood to gain more.

Out of the entire sample there were only four girls in class VIII and above, and, significantly, two of them were the daughters of clerks. In general the attitude was one of skepticism towards of clerks. In general the attitude was one of skepticism towards the benefits from formal schooling. Education was regarded more as a liability than an asset for adolescent girls. Thus, while there was some motivation for keeping sons in schools, it was non-existent for girls. With a third of fathers mobile out of the traditional occupation, sons had more chances than their female siblings of moving out of the system. Similarly, despite criticism of the educational system it was significant that Balmiki girls were in schools in greater numbers than their mothers. While ultimately the years in schooling were regarded as wasted, as girls made their way to their scavenging and their *susrals,* for the sociologist they have joined the ranks of the educationally mobile. For instance, though mothers were scornful of schools several admitted on closer questioning that being able to read and write would enable a girl to correspond with her *maike* (mother) after her marriage. To many who had been confined to a life of daudgery and exploitation it was important to be able to convey to one's natal home the situation after marriage.

We find them that modernization has not helped the status of the urban poor woman. On the other hand, by keeping the hearth going, she helps her husband to move ahead. The present analysis of attitudes towards education shows that even for the next generation, Balmiki women tend to react positively more often a son's schooling. For a daughter, school is a waste of time. In other words, conventional notions of the female role are so well internalized that women can visualise little change in the status of their daughters. In light of the empirical evidence examined so far it is difficult to be anything but pessimistic about the future of the poor women in India's cities. Nor is it possible to advise panaceas or solutions. Employment, we find, is not a variable which determines the power and status of the bulk of Indian working women. This may be true of men as well; but, the chances of a man in the city being able to lead a better life are far greater than the chances of a woman in a similar position.

REFERENCES

Andrea M. Singh and Alfred de Souza, *The Position of Women in Migrant Bastis in Delhi* (New Delhi, 1976), p. 55.

Samuel Jayakar, *Rural Sweepers in the City* (Mysore, 1952), p. 26.

Government of India, *Census of India, 1961* (Delhi, 1966), p. 422.

Esther Boserup, *Women's Role in Economic Development* (Chicago, 1970), pp. 139-140; 1976, xii.

Veena Das, "Indian Women: Work, Power and Status," in B.R. Nanda, (ed.), *Indian Women* (New Delhi, 1976), pp. 132-139.

Veena Das, *Indian Women's Work, Power and Status*, p. 193.

T.N. Madan, "The Hindu Woman at Home," p. 72.

A.R. Desai and S.D. Pillai, *Profile of an Indian Slum* (Bombay, 1972).

Andrea M. Singh, *Slum and Pavement Dwellers in the Major Cities of India* (New Delhi, 1976, mimeo.), p. 74.

14

Women Construction Workers

In terms of employment, the building industry is one of the largest in India, employing millions of workers. The total investment in the industry is made up of (1) the input of materials, (2) the input of labour of all types, and (3) the overhead costs. However, the industry relies essentially on unskilled labour; the use of mass production technology is practically absent. The industry is suitable to Indian conditions as it is primarily labour-intensive. Except in the urban areas, even machinery such as concrete mixers, power-cranes, reinforced concrete structures or pre-fabricated structures are not available. The employers have no real incentive for introducing better techniques as they are afraid of raising costs. The labourers, therefore, suffer from locational immobility as well. While construction work is considered unskilled, it is back-breaking. Workers cut soil, carry cement, stones, bricks, mortar, and water on their heads, crush bricks, and mix concrete.

According to the 1971 census there were 204,000 women construction workers in India (down from 290,000 in 1951); women comprised 10 per cent of the rural and 9 per cent of the urban workers in construction.[2] There is great regional variation in the proportion of construction workers who are female. Harijans or scheduled caste members make up the majority of construction workers in India. Among Harijans, the proportion of women construction workers is highest in the Western States and lowest in the Northern states.[3] Women in this field are drawn primarily from the rural poor and suffer discrimination on the basis of class, caste, and sex.

The methods and means by which labour is brought into various industries such as the building industry are not always straight forward and direct. Therefore, the labour often find himself/herself in a disadvantageous position. Language, caste, and class barriers inhibit direct communication between employer and worker. As ordinary villagers looking for jobs are not conversant with the intricacies of the employment process, a number of intermediaries or jobbers—known variously as *sardar, mistry, mukaddam, chowdhury, jamadar,* etc. —reap a substantial part of the benefit actually due to the workers. The jobbers understand the problems of the workers as they are able to communicate with them in their own language. Therefore they enjoy the confidence of the workers. When a group of workers are new to an environment, they look upon these jobbers as custodians of their interests and rights. Often the jobber thus becomes the supervisor or the labour contractor. Since the employers rarely want to take the trouble of dealing with the workers directly, the jobbers help in the day-to-day administration as well; for example, in granting leave or in providing substitute labour whenever needed. In return jobbers claim a share from the daily earnings of the workers. This is known as *peshgi* and involves (a) the *jamadar's* commission, and (b) interest on any loan which the labourer may have taken when he was looking for a job. Incidents have been reported in which the intermediaries secure unjust dismissals of workers and extract from them fresh commissions by providing them with reinstatements.

India has progressive labour laws on the books which are not enforced; most laws do not even cover the vast majority of Indian workers, those in the "unorganised" sector. As contract or casual labour, women construction workers are part of the unorganised sector. A 1971 law (Abolition of Contract Labour Act) sought to eliminate the practice of contract labour and provide some benefits such as maternity leave to women labourers in this field. It, however, is often violated. In some states construction workers are covered by minimum wage law; in other states they are not.

The government itself is a culprit in this regard. Many construction projects-buildings, roads, bridges, railway lines, etc.—are in the public sector. The government is the largest employer in construction contractors solicit the services of labour contractors for supplying labour in order to complete the work on time. Because the construction contracts are short-term, based on tenders, scattered at different places, and because. The work is temporary, contractors cannot possibly maintain labourers on a permanent basis. Moreover, construction labour being casual and migratory, it cannot be organised on a permanent basis. Government regulations provide for amenities such as creches, sanitary services, and holidays as well as specified maximum hours and minimum wage rats for workers in construction projects of the Central Public Works Department. These conditions are not met. In some cases construction workers are attached to a labour contractor on a long-term basis and work whenever he sends them. Often construction workers are migrant labour. Contractors bring whole families from depressed areas to work on large-scale projects in other districts or states. The practice of using migrant labour depresses the local wage rates. In other cases construction workers are hired on a daily basis and have no security of employment whatsoever.

There are ways—legal, illegal, and non-legal—through which employers circumvent labour laws; employees do not realise the potential of labour laws, which otherwise would help the workers. In this pattern, women employees are the most affected for reasons of ignorance and lack of organised strength. They have neither the support of militant unions nor the wherewithal to fight in courts. They are also handicapped in this regard because of both domestic obligations and the economic imperative of earning wages. The denial of equality in work and wages and the deprivation of basic amenities and minimum standards are particularly blatant in the case of women workers.

In spite of the fact that women carry as much load men do, contractors pay them at a lower rate. While a man is paid typically Rs. 7-8 per day in the late 1970s, women are paid the rate of Rs. 4.50-5 per day. Women are paid less on the grounds that they work on small jobs which do not require the specialised skills of the bricklayer or cement mixer. The following was the wage schedule in road construction and the building industry in certain states for the year 1969-70.[4]

State	*Year*	*Daily Wage Rates*	
		Men	*Women*
Kerala	1969	2.69	2.00
Madhya Pradesh	1970	2.50	2.15
Himachal Pradesh	1970	2.50	2.20
West Bengal	1970	3.00	2.00
Tamilnadu	1970	1.80	1.50

Wages have risen since these rates were established, but the male/female differentials remain. Worse still, labour contractors receive a payment in bulk at a flat rate from the construction contractors or the government contractors, for the total number of labourers supplied. Labour contractors get the signature or thumbprint of these illiterate labourers in the register book, though often paying them less than the fixed rate. The possibility of payment at the fixed minimum daily wage of Rs. 7 or Rs. 4.50 does not even arise. Thus not only is the provision of the Abolition of Contract Labour Law not observed, but the recruits are subject to exploitation by contractors.

As per the Model Rules of the Central Public Works Department of the Government of India there should be at least two huts with the *ayahs* (attendants) for children where there are more than fifty women working on a site. It is nevertheless rare to find such facilities. Canteens for workers are not always provided, so the women either have to take their meals with them for themselves and their families, if they are at the same site, or buy cheap food from the *chai-wallahs* (roadside tea shops). The contractors have no obligation to provide the workers with adequate housing, so small *jhuggies* or squatter settlements become the homes of these people. They live in dirt, squalor and constant want. Washing, bathing, and other daily hygienic needs have to be done in unfiltered filthy water, often in scant supply.

The desultory state of labour organisation and mobilisation has its effects on the problems of earnings in the construction industry. Increased wages and improvement of facilities are rigorously resisted by employers with much stronger bargaining power than employees. The wage rates in the building industry are conspicuously low, and the "sweating" of labour is still prevalent. The transitory nature of both work and workers in this industry prevents workers from forcing the issue with the authorities. Unfortunately the Minimum Wages Act of 1948 is not uniformly applicable to all workers, as they do not fulfill the requisite qualifications throughout the country. The rates and qualifications vary from state to state. Since these workers are not unionised, they have little recourse.

Women construction workers are special targets for wage discrimination. The Indian Constitution, in the Directive Principles of State Policy, has recommended equal pay for equal work. This Article (39D) of the Constitution—equal pay for equal work—is only a policy statement at present. It requires legislative sanction from all states and only when incorporated in the Minimum Wages Act will it take effect.

In this industry, to reiterate, women workers are in a disadvantageous position. In recent years, a steady decline in employment of women seems to be the trend, because of mechanisation and rationalisation. But many women are employed enlarge river valley projects or on large construction sites, like that of the Metropolitan Tube Railway of Calcutta. However, they mainly carry loads on their heads. They are employed by the contractors, who are under no obligation to provide these women with adequate shelter or other facilities. They are often found at sites with their children, as there are no creches or any other places where children can be left. They are not provided with any maternity or sickness benefits because they are essentially seasonal labour. Very often they are even denied accident benefits as well. These women workers are ignorant as well of the rights to which they are entitled; hence the status quo persists. For who among them, for example, would know of the ILO Convention of Equal Remuneration for Equal Work? They are almost mostly unskilled, illiterate, and have no capacity to improve their condition. The extreme elasticity of supply of female labour is another factor which keeps their wages from becoming equal to that of their male counterparts.

Demographic Characteristics

Based on three surveys of women construction workers (in Delhi, Bihar and Andhra Pradesh) a picture (not necessarily representative) emerges of these women and their social context.[5] Harijans and tribals are the largest groups represented, although they comprise only 15 per cent and 5 per cent of the Indian population respectively. Ninety-six per cent of the Delhi construction workers are Harijan migrant labourers from Rajasthan; Harijans and tribals together comprised 90 per cent of the Bihar sample and 67 per cent of the Andhra sample. As construction work is extremely physically taxing, most of the women are young (average age 25) having joined the workforce before they reached their teens. Almost all are illiterate. The Harijan women in Delhi and Bihar were married early and their marriages were arranged. The tribal women in Bihar tend to marry later. In Andhra the local (as opposed to migrant) women workers are mostly unmarried, as their parents depend on their earnings, and it is difficult for poor families with meager dowries to find husbands for their daughters.

Most of the women work to the day of delivery and resume work three to four weeks after the birth of a child, as they cannot afford not to work. Infant mortality is high and access to medical facilities is minimal. The women often take their small children to the construction sites, as no creches are provided. Few of the children of these women go to school and most work if there is any work available.

For most of the women, construction work does not provide a steady income throughout the year. For example, little work is available during the monsoon when many of the women must seek work as agricultural workers or as casual labour in other industries. Most of the women are in debt and they may pay between 25 to 160 per cent in interest a year. Contract workers tend to be in debt to their contractors and for that reason are not allowed to leave. Although many of these women are the major income earners in their families, they face the double burden of wage work and housework and defer to husbands or in-laws in terms of household decision making. Most of their income is spent on food for the family while their husbands' earnings are often spent on liquor. Approximately 30 per cent of the Andhra women reported that their husbands beat them when they were drunk. According to the researchers, "The [Andhra] women for the most part agreed that they were born to be subservient to man."

A CASE STUDY

Little Swarna had to crawl out of the hole which they now call home; it is not even a hut like the one where they had once lived in their village of Swargahata in the Midnapore District of West Bengal. But both mother and child are resigned to their fate. Dusk was falling as Surabala took her daughter Swarna with her to the "coolie lines" of the workers employed by the Tube Railway Authorities in Calcutta. Rows of tarpaulin, precariously balanced on rickety poles over small square areas of space partitioned off between families by torn *bora* or gunny sacks form the huts where squatters live. They have been living here for nearly three years now, just off Chowringhee Road and Park Street, the most fashionable, sophisticated part of the city. Prior to coming here they were working on the same project at Belgatchia, further north, and have been shifted to this new site by the contractor under whose employment they work. About 112 families—men, women, and children—live here working at this site. Women are earning Rs. 3.50 per day, while men get Rs. 4, primarily for carrying loads from one place to another. They live and work under the same conditions year after year.

Surabala says that the only work assigned to them is carrying earth, mortar, or bricks or crushing bricks, and the work is much more strenuous than in any other industry. She gets up when the cock crows and feeds the family breakfast of tea and *chappatis* prepared the night before. Before she can go to work she cooks rice and *dal* (lentils) for the family for the day. The women work three-hours shifts, sometimes as many as three shifts per day, depending on the work at the site. The short stay at one place and frequent movement from one site to another make it difficult for them to have a settled life. They seem to have lost interest in their households. Meager utensils are scattered here and there, and all they have to sleep on are either *charpoys* (string cots) on gunny sacks. There are not even proper ovens to cook on. They are too poor to buy coal. Children gather firewood scraps to light the fire to cook a scanty meal of rice and *dal* for the family once a day when the women are at home. The age of these women is surprisingly low. Most of them are between twenty-six and thirty. When asked about their youth they smiled and said, "How would one be able to carry load up and down if they are too old?" In most cases the work life of these women comes to an end when they are about forty. Most of them already have three or four children, having been married young. They have their children with them most of the time. "Who else would look after them?" The children while away their time doing nothing. None of them can read or write, and none have any will to learn. They are often sick from malnutrition and hunger, without any medial help. There are no toilets, so the air around is foul with order; the children have no idea of cleanliness or hygiene.

In West Bengal, construction workers generally come from the Kaibartas. Surabala is a Mahato. Both are lower-caste groups. Some of them are of Santhal (tribal) origin also. Even when they were living in their own home in the village they had to live segregated from the upper castes. We asked Surabala why they came away. Most of them originally had been peasant-farmers working either in the paddy fields or cultivating jute. "They thought they would be able to earn a better living in the city," she says. "Don't they want to go back?" We asked. "A number of us go back during the harvesting season when there is work to do in the fields, for there also we work as day labourers. None of us own any land., At other times there is no work in our native place and if we stay there we would have to go hungry." So they flock to the city. Most of them, that say to taken up this job out of poverty, and of their own accord. Surabala had to earn a living somehow after her husband's death to feed herself and her four children. A few of them have been persuaded by their husbands. A small percentage of women were forced out of their homes, either by landlords or by parents in-low upon being widowed. Nearly all felt that they would have to continue as day-wage labourers, but would like to change for a job where the strain would be less. Wages are paid on a weekly basis by the *jamadar* (labour supervisor) and occasionally deductions are made from the salary in payment for firewood or for guarding the *jhuggies* when they are out for work. There is also no specific system for sharing their earnings, they say. There are no holidays, so if they do not work, they do not earn. None of them owns land, but none seem badly in debt as is usually the case with day-labourers in the villages. Neither has any accumulation of savings been possible. Surabala says that some women get preferential treatment on the job, "may be because of their looks." She says women in the city don't pay as much attention to *pujas* (worship) as they did in the village. *Pujas* in the village are observed especially at harvest time and during the monsoon, but in the city women forget these customs, Surabala relates.

We found a woman in the same compound in an advanced state of pregnancy. She was still continuing her work but would shortly go home to her parents, she told me shyly. She looked about twenty-six or -seven, was the mother of three, expecting her fourth. Asked her whether she had heard about family planning, she nodded in the affirmative and looked furtively towards her husband. "Where did you hear about it?" We queried. "From the Block Development Office at her village," was the answer. But we had a feeling that she hardly realised what it meant.

We found that three considerations were working behind employing women labourers in this industry. Firstly, they were cheaper, since many come to the city with their husbands, and they were also readily available. Secondly, being naturally docile in nature, they were less troublesome, and thirdly, men were reluctant to do the job which they were doing ungrudgingly.

The women in general appear to be conservative in outlook. They themselves are women and are working; they are happier to have a boy child than a girl. Surabala hopes her son can get into some other occupation, or if he stays in construction that he can learn a craft. She hopes her daughter Swarna will marry, settle down, and have a home of her own.

Despite the back-breaking jobs of these women, their husbands or other menfolk staying with the family do not share the household chores. The men, in their free time, sit around, chat, smoke *biri* (indigenous cigarettes), or chew *pan* (betel leaves) while the women cook. Daughters too young to work on the job stay home looking after younger children, fetching water, and cleaning utensils. These women have traditional ideas about marriage, and they feel that dowry is an essential part in such an arrangement. This is one of the main causes of their indebtedness, but it is accepted as natural.

REFERENCES

1. *Ekalavya, the Mobile Creches Annual,* 1977, Bombay: Tata, 1977, pp. 57-63.
2. Committee on the Status of Women in India (CSWI), *Towards Equality,* New Delhi: Ministry of Education and Social Welfare, 1975, pp. 155, 172.
3. *Census of India 1961,* Part V-A, Statewise, cited in Harshad R. Trivedi, *Scheduled Caste Women: Studies in Exploitation,* Delhi: Concept Publishing Company, 1976, pp. 206-207.
4. Labour Bureau, Government of India, *Women in Industry,* New Delhi, 1970.
5. CSWI, pp. 172-173; K. Murali Manohar, *et al,* "Labour: Women Construction Workers of Warangal," *Economic and Political Weekly,* Vol. XVI, No. 4, January, 24, 1981, pp. 97-99.

15

Development Process and Working Women

The devastating consequences of the world economic crisis have exacerbated the problem of women, as a component part of the general problems of developing countries. They have demonstrated that the position of women highlights the major problems of developing countries today.

Since its inception, the Movement of the Non-Aligned countries, which encourage passes and represents the values and aspirations of an overwhelming majority of mankind, has been striving for the self-determination and emancipation of nations for equality among them, for a better life for each of our peoples, and for the improvement of the quality of the lives of men and women of all races and creeds, as was stressed by Shrimati Indira Gandhi in her address to the Inaugural Session of the Seventh Conference of Heads of State or Government of the Non-Aligned Countries—Parallel to its struggle for political independence, self-determination and the sovereignty of all nations and for peace and co-operation on a basis of equality, the Movement has taken strong and consistent stand in favour of the kind of development which would benefit all countries, developing and developed alike. Today, more than ever before, the world needs fundamental changes so that stable global development, as well as peace and security may be ensured. Ways out of the present crisis must be sought in a genuine democration of international relations. This implies, *inter alia* the elimination of all forms of the policy of force, domination, hegemony, discrimination, exploitation and inequality, of colonialism and neo-colonialism, the eradication of the abhorrent system of apartheid, racism, foreign domination and aggression, intervention, interference in the internal affairs of states, occupation and pressures. It also involves the acceleration of the process of self-determination of peoples under colonial and alien domination, the consolidation of national independence, sovereignty and territorial integrity of states, as well as the halting of the arms race in order to enable the enormous material and human resources wasted by the arms race to be used for the economic and social development of all countries, particularly of developing ones.

The role of women in development is most intimately related to the goal of comprehensive socio-economic development, and is a strategic question for the development of all societies. Any development strategy which neglects the need for enhancing the role of women cannot lead to comprehensive socio-economic development. The point of departure is to 'recognize the role of women as a dynamic factor and a valuable asset for the overall process of development—it is not a burden or cost nor a mere humanitarian concession to a disadvantaged group.

The scattered, piecemeal or curative approaches to the advancement of women view women as passive subjects of protection or as recipients of marginal welfare and social services, unrelated to policies and strategies for economic development or to structural changes in societies that result form economic changes. Such approaches have failed to prevent the growing marginalisation of women in the economy and in the political process in most developing, and even developed countries. In the absence of an integrated approach to development, a fragmentary approach to the position of women in development has been perpetuated and has led to the unsatisfactory option of promoting the advancement of women by social welfare, humanitarian and demographic approaches, without due attention to the transformations needed to create conditions in which women can unfold their full potential as a factor of development. These approaches should now be replaced by an integrated and participatory approach which relates the role of women in development, their aspirations and needs to the critical areas, issues and choices in the developmental strategy for economic growth, a more humane use of material and human resources, and for equity in power relations at the national and international levels.

Defined in its complexity and interaction among all dimensions of human life—political, economic, social, cultural, etc.—development has been conceived as an integral process of economic growth and social progress. This position represents a collective articulation of the desire of the majority of mankind to humanise the condition of peoples lives through the process of development.

The position of women and their role in this context are particularly important, not only because women constitute half of the human resources in developing countries, but also because they have to bear the brunt of the daily struggle for survival in developing countries. Although women are not a homogenous social group, and their position varies between and within countries, there are some features which are common to all societies. Historically their role in biological reproduction has generally restricted women's participation in the mainstream of social, economic and political processes.

Processes of change in women's position depend primarily on the interrelations between transformative factors and forces, spontaneous of consciously directed, and the inherited matrix of social and cultural institutions, values, norms and practices, forms of prod action and distribution. These are manifested in the division of resources, labour and power. In most developing societies, colonialism brought about major structural changes affecting people's access to and control over resources and power relations within and outside the communities and also the distribution of the roles and responsibilities of both men and women. After the attainment of independendence, wherever narrow economic growth-oriented models were adopted, the distortions and imbalances prevailing under the colonial regimes tended to continue. As a result, substantial sections of the population, which were already under 'various pressures and handicaps, became even more marginalised.

The request for equality for women received a considerable boost from two sources. First, in the struggle against colonialism and in the national liberation wars men and women had joined hands on terms of equality as members of one human family. Secondly, as a result of the Second World War, the concept of the equality of the sexes as one of the basic principles on which a community should be based was incorporated in the UN Charter, and with this first received global recognition.

The Movement of the Non-Aligned Countries—as a global factor in the contemporary world, has recognized that the equal participation of both men and women in all spheres of life is an important precondition for the attainment of meaningful development and the well-being of all peoples. The nonaligned and other developing countries have strongly supported the recommendations of the World Conference on the International Women's Year in Mexico in 1975, and the World Conference of the UN Decade for Women in Copenhagen in 1980, on the role of women in development, and further elaborated the common strategy to spend up their economic and social progress and promote the efforts towards the establishment of the New International Economic Order.

Experience acquired during the UN Decade for Women; Equality, Development and Peace (1976-1985) has indicated how the process of development can be promoted or constrained by the integration or non-integration of the productive, reproductive and household functions of women into development processes. The Decade has increased the general awareness of the continued violations of the basic rights and needs of women. It has also contributed to the knowledge of the role of women in development, reflecting the developmental dimension of the problem and stimulating farther along those lines at the national and internationals.

The review and evaluation of the progress in this field particularly at the mid-point of the Third UN Development Decade and at the end of the UN Decade for Women, indicate—that some positive changes have been achieved, particularly in providing some basic preconditions for the integration of women into development processes.

Almost all countries have improved their legislative systems and have taken measures towards eliminating *dejure* discrimination against women; the educational level—including that of women— has risen, health conditions have improved, as indicated, for example, by the life expectancy statistics, expansion of industry and services have created more employment opportunities, there has been some improvement in rural areas, social services and infrastructure have expanded, etc.

However, available data indicate that these improvements have been of only relative value in some countries improvements have been slow and the recent economic crisis has slowed down the positive trends in many countries or even reversed them. An aggregate analysis of the most characteristic indicators in the fields defined as the sub-themes of the World Conference on the UN Decade for Women—employment, health and education—shows mixed picture of achievement in the past which does not live up to the expectations, both in terms of decreasing the disparities between men and women in the group of developing countries, on the one hand, and the disparities between the developed and developing countries, on the other. In the last few years, not only has the position of the developing countries in world economic relations considerably deteriorated but the solution of the problems of the world economy is being attempted at the expense of these countries, particularly of the most depressed strata of their societies, including women. There is also evidence to suggest that, despite legislative steps, prejudices, traditional attitudes and practices continue to perpetuate discrimination against women.

Evidence shows that the process of marginalisation of women in development has been intensified by the current processes of economic change and may continue in the future.

The marginal position of a large section of society, and specifically women, can no longer be justified. The structural changes in the economies of developing countries which are likely to follow future developments in science and technology must be based on increased and genuine participation of all members to society, if they are not to result in still greater imbalances or even lead to disaster.

The role of women in overall development has not been fully understood, nor has it been given its full weight in the struggle to eliminate poverty, hunger, inequality and injustice at the national as well as the international level. The continued assumption that the responsibility for childrearing and for family needs lies with women alone, as well as the persistence of intra-household inequalities, place severe strains on women's health, limit their capacity to participate efficiently in the production process and further jeopardize their chances for a fair share in the benefits of society.

It is thus becoming overwhelmingly clear that in searching for solutions to these contradictions the inequalities between men and women have to be examined from a developmental perspective. On the one hand, the concerns of relevance to women cannot be resolved automatically through economic growth alone. On the other hand, egalitarian processes and policy action to improve women's position within developing countries are only a necessary but not a sufficient condition to increase the quality of life of the women in these countries, particularly in view of the grave consequences of the world economic crisis. Simultaneous and concerted action is necessary to improve the conditions for growth and development by appropriate domestic and international policies, articulating within that developmental framework measures to enhance the role and position of women as a factor of development.

In spite of the fact that women in developing countries are massively involved in key areas of production, such as agriculture, food production, trade, etc., their work is not fully recognized and valued. The activities of women as producers are usually not adequately included in statistics, thus making their contribution invisible. They usually do not have adequate access to the factors of production, to land, credit and other tools io raise their productivity—i.e., appropriate scientific and technical information, training and other policy support.

Contrary to expections that legal measures would systematically eliminate the division of labour on the basis of sex, many processes oriented towards economic modernization are actually perpetuating this division and introducing new divisions or reinforcing the old patterns of subordination. The discrimination against women has thus contributed to increasing poverty of all people, overpopulation, and over- dependency, particularly on external resources.

If the crucial problems of the contemporary world are viewed in their relationship and interdependence, the questions related to the role of women in development opportunities for the growing population, to solve the demographic problems, to secure basic needs and services, such as food, education, health housing, to establish the role of the informal sector of the economy, to approach and solve migration problems, to equip and prepare the human resources of tomorrow to face the challenges to the 21st century, to ascertain the impact of the frontier technologies, such as communications, microelectronics bioengineering, biotechnology, and to protect the environment. The research undertaken during the UN Decade for Women has articulated the critical connections between these developmental issues and the role and status of women— as beneficiaries or victims, active agents or passive sufferers, and demonstrates the necessity of the full integration of women into development efforts in both developing and developed countries.

The two facets of the role of women—in production and reproduction should be conceived as complementary and interactive. In order to release women's potentials for fuller participation in the productive and decision-making processes, there is a need not only for a sharing of parental responsibilities but also for institutional provisions which would benefit children and families. Women should have the right, the requisite knowledge and the resources to regulate their reproductive capacity. However, without economic independence women cannot achieve equality. Therefore, measures to expand satisfactory employment opportunities, to improve their economic status and the provision of the necessary infrastructure should be treated as an important and integral part of national and international development strategies.

The short term policies and emergency measures introduced for the management of the economy in the context of the present crisis should not distort the long-term objectives of development and prevent the social transformation, of which the integration of women in development is an indispensable clement.

The non-aligned and other developing countries have emphasised that development can be achieved only through maximum participation of both men and women, in all spheres and at all levels of life, work and decision making—in the priority-setting, design and implementation of measures for change. Such active participation constitutes the basic ingredient of the strategy for individual and collective self-reliance of developing countries.

The policy of individual and collective self-reliance provides an appropriate framework for the search for such development approaches, since it is based on the sovereign rights of states to control and develop their natural and human resources, and promote international co-operation, on the basis of equality and mutual assistance. By mobilising their own resources and the masses of the population and developing their collective self-reliance, the developing countries contribute to the establishment of new economic relations for the common good.

The non-aligned and other developing countries are investing considerable efforts in the establishment of mutual links, especially in those fields where co-operation could speed up development, through a number of areas of economic co-operation, as well as through various other forms of economic and technical co-operation which have been particularly supported by the Group of 77. However, the role of women as a factor of development has rarely been taken into consideration in the designing and practical implementation of the projects for economic and technical co-operation among developing countries. It is becoming increasingly clear that concept of integrated development and the sustained elaboration and integration of the role of women as a factor of development— through coordinated activity of the non-aligned and other developing countries supported by the United Nations and other international organizations—could contribute to a better adaptation of the economic and technical co-operation among the developing countries to the concrete conditions and actual needs of the people.

MAJOR ISSUES AND PROBLEMS

Any in-depth examination of the integration of women in development as well as of their position and role in different sectors and areas of activity undoubtedly depends on an appropriate conceptual framework. In addition, an insight is needed into the institutional mechanisms that promote or prevent changes and transformations in individual sectors or areas of social and economic life. In this Study the sectoral approach is used as an analytical device to illustrate the role and position of women in developing countries. It should, however, be kept in mind that the harmonisation of women's productive, reproductive and participatory roles cannot be achieved at the individual level. The interlinkages among sectors and areas are therefore crucial when general development concepts are operationalised through development planning, development of human resources, employment, technological and scientific change etc. The sectors and areas included here have been chosen because of their relevance for the advancement of women. Some relevant areas, such as employment, have been treated within all sectors.

The measures proposed in relation to specific sectoral issues influence other sectors and institutions, and thus have a synergetic development effect. This is especially so in the case of science and technology. The transfer of technology from developed to developing countries influences the organization of the production process in all economic sectors, and affects all other socio-economic spheres.

Rural Development and Agriculture

The current situation in developing countries in agriculture, food production and rural development derives from a historical pattern of development in which investment has been skewed in favour of industrialisation and urban areas with the result that in the majority of countries rural areas have lagged behind in their development. In Africa, Latin America, the Middle East and certain parts of Asia the development paradigms pursued so far have created food shortages and a structural cleavage in rural society.

The resultant rural transformation has led to a cleavage between commercial or large-scale agriculture, which has been rapidly modernized through application of scientific and technological innovations, higher capital investment with higher returns, and small scale subsistence agriculture with little or no capital investment and a low level of technology, requiring high labour inputs with low and even declining returns. Such developments in agriculture have sometimes been due to the need to earn foreign currency. Furthermore, this cleavage has taken the form of a gender differentiation in which men predominate in the decision making and management of commercial or large-scale agriculture, while women continue to predominate in the food and subsistence sector in which they expend large amounts of labour—as evidenced by the long hours of work with low levels of technology and low returns. Moreover, within commercial agriculture the gender division is also reflected by the high demand for female labour in those cycle of production requiring hoe and hand methods (e.g., weeding or paddy transplanting) with low remuneration.

This cleavage has meant that many developing countries have not been able to attain the goal self-reliance in the areas of food, agriculture and rural development. A substantial number of countries continue to experience a severe decline in food production, leading to food shortages and even outright hunger and famine. Moreover, even in countries which have been able to expand their food sectors, the system of distribution is inadequate and poverty, hunger and malnutrition still afflict large masses of the people.

According to the FAO, malnutrition and hunger increased by 15 per cent during the seventies, affecting 450 million people in Asia, Africa and Latin America. In developing market economies as a whole, daily per capita calorie consumption has remained at 2 per cent below the minimum requirement. The gap is largest in Africa, followed by South and South-East Asia. In Sub-Saharan Africa, the growth rate of agricultural production fell to 1.3 per cent annum while population growth remained at 27 per cent over the second development decade. (Acharya, 1984, pp. 1-2).

South and South-East Asia have witnessed a rise in the cost of food production, falling rural employment and landlessness, the latter being particularly marked among rural women. Structural changes in many Latin American countries have led to unemployment and lack of entitlement to food among large sections of the population, including the most vulnerable section, namely those involved in subsistence agriculture.

Women in developing countries are a major resource in agriculture, food production and rural development, as evidenced by their numerical proportions, their share of labour in agriculture and food production and the division of labour by sex in this sector. Their share of labour is particularly significant in view of the fact that in many cases they perform their agricultural work in addition to long and arduous work in child-care household maintenance, cooking and fuel wood collection, as well as food preparation and processing.

Despite women's crucial role in agriculture and food production their potential for accelerating rural development has not often been well understood or appreciated. Inherited biases in the agrarian development approaches have led to an inadequate perception of women's economic role, undercounting or devaluation of their work and thus to a perpetuation of the dependency of developing countries on external factors of production.

Revised FAO Estimates of Sex-Composition of Agricultural Labour Force in 82 Countries

Region	*Famale labour as percentage of agricultural labour force*
Sub-Saharan Africa	46%
North Africa/Near East	31%
Asia	45%
Caribbean	40%
Average	42%

Source: Acharya, p. 7.

The undercounting of women's work in rural economics results from:

(a) The use of industrialised countries definitions of work, employment, jobs, primary activity etc.

(b) the invisibility of many types of work in the subsistence mode of production and

(c) the association of women's non-work with the family's social status in Asian and Latin American Societies.

Since agricultural productivity in the developing countries for many years to come must depend on the quality of human labour, it is imperative to recognize that the farm that insufficient attention has been devoted to the improvement of the productivity of labour is a major constraint to agricultural development.

In practice, women have not benefitted from adequate policy support. First of all the accumulated evidence suggests that agrarian and land tenure policies have restricted women's access to land and other factors of agricultural production, such as technology, credit subsidy and inputs (e.g. fertilisers and seeds). Secondly, women have not had equal access to support services and incentive system for expanding agriculture, food production and rural development, for instance, extension and training services and information. Thirdly, lack of an integrated approach to development at the national level has consistently perpetuated a fragmentary approach to women's position in the society and their role in development, thereby perpetuating the promotion of women's programmes through social welfare, humanitarian and demographic approaches only, without provisions for long term integration.

In traditional societies women's role in agriculture and food production was recognized by customary rights of access to land, forests, and to support from family labour. Structural changes under colonialism and in the post-colonial phases have eroded many of these rights, but the responsibility of feeding the family still rests primarily with the women in many rural communities of Africa and in the economically least affluent sections of many Asian and Latin American societies. The privatisation of land and the introduction of cash crops for domestic and foreign markets, the need to feed expanding populations, and the depletion of forest resòurces for industrial and communications growth, which were initiated during colonialism and continued after independence, have steadly reduced women's access to basic resources. The withdrawal of male labour—for deployment in mining, roads and railway building, plantation of export crops and new industries—which was initiated by colonial regimes also increased women's burdens.

Despite international recognition of rural women's right to own land (World Conference on Agarian Reform and Rural Development-Rome, 1979), attempts to incorporate this principle in land tenure and land development policies have been marginal. Forest policy, including policies for reforestation has yet to recognize the role of women in forest development, even though in some areas women have initiated major protest movement against deforestation which have negatively affected their ability to feed their families and livestock. Case studies from Asia and Africa indicate that rural women are very dynamic and innovative in these fields when they are give the opportunity to participate collectively in such developmental activities. They also indicate a process of increasing self- confidence among women and an enhancement of their status within their families and the community. However, extension of such experiments to other areas will require uncorporation of women as a target group in policies and structures for agarian reform, and development of forests, agriculture, animal husbandry, silk pròduction, fish culture, land development (including waste lands) etc.

Unless the structural constraints and the existing 'invisibility' of women in rural development policies and agrarian reform are removed, it is difficult to envisages an equitable growth and expansion of agriculture, food and forest production. It is important to take specific short-run measures to make them sensitive to women's potentials and the promotion of research and communication programmes for rural women in these areas. However the solution to the problem lies in the establishment of long-term strategies and measures to implement them as a matter of national priority in the context of solutions to, for example chromic food problems deforestation and ecological imbalances, unemployment and poverty, and to enhance the process of corrective and individual self-reliance.

New initiatives are needed to reorient agricultural policies at the national level which would give priority to a balanced approach to agricultural communities and food production. Within this policy restructuring process, a number of specific issues arise. These include:

— creating a balance between export production for foreign exchange purposes and food production in such a way that women can directly benefit from their labour in food and commercial agriculture;
— achieving better treatment for materials exported to the world market and better marketing opportunities for them;
— changes in commodity pricing (specially of commercial crops) accompanied by subsidy arrangements to compensate farmers for crop failure and market fluctuations;
— creation of opportunities for equitable access to land for women;
— increasing investment in research on food crops, especially drought resistant cereals (in particular sorghum and millet) and legumes. Experiments in these areas should enlarge the knowledge base already amassed by food farmers and agricultural societies. In this way, research can permote and benefit from endorgenous bases of knowledge in food farming which in many cases has had the advantage of long and well-tested results. In the same way, science should enlarge the endogenous knowledge base on animal husbandry and agricultural production.

A food strategy might be designed to support rural development and agrarian reforms and other relevant measures for strengthening and food sector recommended, for example, by the World Conference on Agrarian Reform and Rural Development of 1979 or the Lagos Plan of Action for African Development of 1980. Since food strategies are relatively new initiatives, whose policy guidelines are still being drawn up, they could provide an important policy intervention to strengthen women's role in food production.

In view of the role of women in farming and the inadequacy of access to services for expanding production the following measures could be fruitful:

— savings and investment programmes should aim at providing credit, finance and subsidies for women through various channels:

(a) regular agricultural financing institutions and credit programmes could include the elaboration of specific mechanisms for assisting farm women; and

(b) revolving funds and credit subsidies extended to women through their associations net-works, and local level groups, as well as government offices at the local level, in conjunction with information campaigns to encourage women to use these services.

— current farmer training programmes, including the ECBC TCDC programmes, could be reviewed and modified to cater for women farmers. An important elements of adjustment here would be to provide agricultural training programmes which would increase women's technical knowledge and allow them to combine mothering and training opportunities;

— new organizational schemes, especially those at the community level should be extended through women's groups and associations:

— increasing women's competence to participate in rural institutions, decision making and designs for agricultural and food programmes.

The persistence of the subordinate position of women in society, as illustrated by the experience in the agriculture and food sector, is a negation of the goals of development, which affects ill members of society equally, regardless of sex or creed. Conversely, the elimination of sex-based inequality could constitute a legitimate basis for innovating approaches to the implementation of the objective of self-reliance and provide an opportunity to test integrative development in practice.

Development Through Technology

In view of the importance of industrialisation, the pattern of industrialisation adopted in developing countries is most relevant. Differences in the socio-economic environment of individual developing countries resulted in various industrialisation strategies. However, regardless of the different industrialisation policies and practices of the individual developing countries, they have a common desire to generate national product, promote employment and secure the most dynamic possible modernization, so as to secure a greater degree of technological and financial independence from the developed countries. The level and the features of the industrialisation of developing countries are usually determined by the individual country's resources, both material and human, and by its past experience of development.

The great dependence of the industrialisation processes in developing countries or developed countries, on technology transfer, capital investment, export markets, etc., has resulted in a high degree of exploitation and in unbalanced industrial structures which are highly sensitive to international economic fluctuations. Thus, the introduction of new industries and changes. In the industrial structure of a developing country may profoundly and rapidly influence the overall economic structure. Such influences may bring about unexpected or unplanned changes unplanned and social life.

Developing countries often find it difficult to fully control the structural changes in their industries and thus avoid industrial instability and exploitation of the workforce. This may to some extent be possible for those countries which have large internal markets, strong public sectors, or were able to control investments in industrial development through generation of sufficient internal funds.

The industrialisation processes in developing countries have also been affected by transnational corporation from the developed countries, which often see industrial development in developing countries as a means of transferring obsolete and unclean technologies, or as a means of increasing profits through redeployment of labour-intensive industries. This has particularly affected the position of women, since their employment in the industrial sector has greatly increased, without, however, securing legally recognized working conditions, protection, remuneration, etc.

The share of women in industrial employment in developing countries rose from 21 per cent in 1960 to 26.5 per cent in 1980. About two thirds of the net increase in the female industrial workforce (the number of women employed in industry in the world increased by 104 per cent in the last two decades) took place in developing countries mainly in Asia. In contrast to Africa and Latin America, Asia has a higher share of the female than of the male world industrial labour force (UNIDO, pp. 3-4).

However, for an appropriate assessment of the improvements in the field as analysts of the qualitative aspects of such employment is needed.

Women are usually engaged in labour-intensive industries with low productivity (e.g. processing industries—textile, food, leather, etc.). Their wages are influenced by their poor bargining position, and they have no influence at all on working conditions. Thus, for instance, although the working hours in manufacturing have generally tended to decline, in some developing countries working hours have tended to rise. The treatment of the female labour force is to a large extent a reflection of women's low status on the labour market (reserve labour army), lack of proper education and training low or non-existent organization, the lack of or non-implementation of protective legislation (particularly in export-oriented industries) and their generally unfavourable social position. The recent upward trend in women's employment in developing countries is not very significant in relation to the absolute size of the female population or workforce in these countries. Moreover, although this increase is in some of the most modern industries in the world, it does not appear to have made a substantial difference to women status, since it has done little to break the isolation and discrimination of women in the industrial workforce.

The extension of the practice of subcontracting of home workers for certain stages of industrial production processes may have considerable counter-productive consequences, for women's formal employment. Such organizational changes may sometimes lead to a circumvention of legal protective measures for labour, a deterioration of working conditions, lower wages within and outside industry, greater exploitation of women's and children's labour, diminishing union activity and, in the long run, also to increased formal unemployment of both men and women. While the short-term positive effects of income generation cannot be discounted, the negative effects of channeling or restricting women's employment to the informal sector make it considerably more difficult and could lead to a higher degree of isolation, exploitation and inequality of women, by excluding them from the mainstream of socio-economic activity.

It is unlikely that the position of women in the industries of developing countries can be changed without changes in the models of industrial development and organization of industrial production. Therefore, formulation and implementation of national industrialisation policies based on the needs and interests of all strata of the population, as well as on an evaluation of domestic potentials continue to be priority tasks confronting developing countries. The existing potentials of developing countries are certainly conducive to positive changes. Balanced development planning and policies which aim at maximum utilisation of national resources and at an expansion of domestic demand are also the proper framework for the advancement of the role of women in this sector of the economic and for promotion within overall development.

To improve women's position in industry, a number of measures would have to be incorporated in the industrial policies of developing countries:

— changes in education, which would enable women to improve their position in industrial employment, and to acquire transferable skills through various forms of vocational and informal training;

— legal arrangements covering all aspects of industrialisation, from investment codes to regulations, which would provide for better general treatment of labour in industry. In this connection, there should be regulatory measures in free exporting zones to ensure that social costs are also covered. However, it must be recognized that collective action by the developing countries is needed for the successful legislation and implementation of such measures;

— extention of employment opportunities in accordance with human resources development policies;

— adoption of technologies which ensure stability of employment and professional progress to women workers;

— establishment of overall social control and of schemes for genuine workers' participation in management and decision making;

— elaboration of criteria for determining the size of enterprises in various industrial branches and the ways of organizing them; promotion of small and medium-size enterprises in developing countries; establishment of industrial co-operatives;

— selection, development and transfer of technology and know-how as well as training of personnel;

— strengthening of self-reliance in industrial policy through industrial co-operation among developing countries, exchange of information and experience through ECDC/ TCDC programmes and projects.

This would improve the bargaining position of developing countries *vis-a-vis* developed ones, particularly in case of transfer of technology or foreign investment, in enforcement of national legal mechanisms for the protection of the industrial labour force, including women workers. All this calls for urgent action among developing countries in the field of industrialisation.

Technology Development

Developing countries have, relatively poor scientific and technological capacities at their disposal. The promotion of science and technology in these countries thus requires strong international communications and a pooling of the existing scientific knowledge and technological potential, in line with the developmental needs of developing countries.

The main issue connected with the utilisation of science and technology as a pool to speed up the development of the developing countries is, therefore, the transfer of technology and, in this respect, the choice of technology. Technology being a system consisting of hardware, software and orgware, the transfer of technology must be viewed as a complex process, involving a range of economic, financial, legal and sociological factors. In this connection, local inputs—primarily knowledge and information on technologies, trained cadres, legal and other regulations, etc.—are needed. The process of selection of technologies calls for an analysis and assessment not only of the economic impact, but also of the social impact. While must be kept in mind is that while technology itself is natural, the application of technology can have considerable social effects, since, through technology, a system of domination and exploitation, as well as a set of social norms and ethics may be transferred. A social impact analysis should be a constituent part of any transfer of technology arrangement. This analysis should specifically consider the impact of technology on women family and community life and other social and cultural values of the new environment to which the technology will be transferred.

Women are involved in science and technology through the structural transformations that occur with the transfer of technology and scientific and technological development, and as participants in research and technological activities; and experiencing the impact of the technologies on their everyday lives. In all cases, their involvement should be much stronger than it is at present. It is also very important that women understand scientific and technological innovations, because this enables them to influence the general social attitudes towards technological change through the existing non-formal education.

The radical changes in the organizational pattern and activities of the society, associated with rapid scientific and technological change in the overall organization, which are presently being experienced in the developed countries, may also dramatically affect all developing countries, and lead to either a more dynamic and humane development or to an ever higher degree of dependency and exploitation. The problem of the marginal position of some members of society, and of women specifically, cannot be solved unless the elements of these new technologies can be built into development strategies in accordance with the concept of integral development.

Furthermore, the latest so-called frontier and transdisciplinary technologies can be used in different ways and at different levels. Their use can serve to accontuate the productive role of women, because such technologies are applicable to a number of areas which are of relevance to the betters quality of life and to the integration of women in development, i.e. food production, clean water supply, improved housing conditions, use of alternative energy sources, in the services education etc. Such technologies also stimulate the growth of employment, as they offer a variety of employment combinations.

However, it should be kept in mind that it is economic and political considerations, rather than social and cultural ones, which determine the availability and terms and conditions for the access of developing countries to new technologies and which are important for national development. Women's access to technological development thus also depends on the global relations between the technology owners and users and those who try to secure access to new technology and to processes of industrialisation. This implies that major efforts should be made to maximise the utilisation of the existing knowledge in developing countries and to lessen the technological dependence on developed countries.

Women have traditionally gained knowledge and experience

(e.g., in agricultural production, energy utilisation, running the household, manufacturing objects for everyday use, home medicine etc.,) which have not been, exploited from the developmental point of view. The application of new scientific and technological devices and knowledge may lighten household drudgery in urban and rural areas, providing better water, energy and other community facilities. This would release energies which women might be encouraged to direct forwards active and useful participation in other economic and social areas, and in the overall technological transformation of the society.

A greater involvement of women in scientific and technological development would therefore require:

— popularisation of scientific and technological knowledge and skills in order to enable their further development, by mass media, through changes in school programmes, and through all participatory and community development activities (especially in agriculture but also in other areas, e.g., household activities, health, education, housing, etc.).

— an increase of the level of scientific and technological self reliance by developing national scientific and technological potentials, maximisation of the possibilities for technical proporation among developing countries and the introduction of selective transfer of technology systems.

— changes in the traditional attitudes towards women by enabling them to fully participate in scientific and technological development by stimulating their involvement in various forms of education and training.

— establishment of linkages between the existing traditional technologies and know-how and the new technologies. The involvement of women in the strengthening of these links could provide a firm basis for self-reliance and ensure a certain continuity in the development of authentic and original approaches, thus avoiding imitative modernization, and developing participatory research as well as relating scientific and technological development to the specific needs of the country.

— establishment and strengthening of co-operation among developing countries in the areas of information on scientific and technological knowledge and devices transfer of technology and exchange of experience on application of science and technology in development, joint research, etc.

Skills and Services

The term services or tertiary sector encompasses a wide range of activities. Therefore, the analysis of the role of women in the services sector covers the generally complex problem of services classification and data, the identification of the manpower problem in general, and women's hidden economic role in particular, and the relationship between the services sector and the overall economy of the country. Over the last decades this sector's contribution to GDP increased substantially, not only in developed market economies but also in developing countries, where this upward trend was evident even in the least developed countries. By 1980, the services sector accounted for the largest share of GDP in both developed market economies (56.9 per cent) as well as in developing countries (44.3 per cent). In developing countries the services sector expanded at a past faster rate than the GDP in the period 1973-80, implying that the general slowdown of their economies during these periods affected the services sector less severely than other major economic sectors.

However, the expansion of the services sector in developing countries, particularly in least developed countries, is probably due to quite different economic causes and could the attributed to the marginalisation of the labour force in agriculture and industry. The development of services is partly due to major changes in agriculture and industry, and partly to their heterogenous production and consumption characteristics.

The role of women in the tertiary sector is very difficult to determine. However, the distribution of the female labour force may serve as an indicator. In 1980, 66.3 per cent of the total female labour force in developing countries was employed in agriculture, 16.3 per cent in industry and 17.4 per cent in services. This is very different from the situation in developed countries, where the shares are 13.7 per cent for agriculture, 29.0 per cent for industry and 57.3 per cent for services.

In developing countries the share of females in the total labour force, by economic sectors, was highest in agriculture (36.4 per cent, even with universed figures) and much lower in the services sector (26.9 per cent) and industry (26.5 per cent).

There are considerable disparities between developing countries in the different regions—disparities between Latin America on the one hand and Asia and Africa on the other. In Asia the main feature is the relatively high share of women in the total labour force in industry (28.8 per cent) and the lower share in services (23.2 per cent). In Latin America the low share of women in the total agricultural labour force (9.3 per cent) is in sharp contrast to the situation in the other two regions. In this region female employment in the services sector is as high as 38.3 per cent. In Africa women account for 31.6 per cent of labour in services, while their share in industry is only 19.7 per cent. (UNIDO, 1984).

In relation to the integration of women in development some partial issues arising in the service sector have been studied. These include trade (women being active internal trade, mostly in the petty trade of the informal sector); transport (links between rural and urban areas, developed and underdeveloped regions, formal and informal sectors); banking (mainly in connection with the problems of access to credit); tourism (increased opportunities for productive employment, provision of lodging, catering, etc., could discourage some negative forms of tourism).

Many of the service activities in which women are employed do not require formal technical qualifications. Other activities such as health (especially nursing) and education (especially teaching) do require professional qualifications, but these are in many cases considered an extension of the essentially female role which has its origin in the household—the mother care offered to the family. Thus women's contribution in this sector has not really been adequately recognized.

Much of the productive activity of women in the services sector remains invisible because of its mainly traditional and informal nature in developing countries. Some thought should be devoted to the services which this sector could provide to meet the needs of households in this countries, that is, what the services sector should produce for the household and its members.

In view of the importance of the role of women in this sector and of the significance of the services sector for the improvement of the status of women in developing countries, it is suggested that:

— attention be paid to the analysis of the functioning, growth and development of the services sector (both public and private) in all developing countries, especially as regards the interlinkages among this and all other sectors;
— services classification and data collection should be made more transparent and accessible;
— the position of women in this sector should be viewed as developmental and integrative of other activities, which means that the new developmental trends observed in this sector must be closely linked to overall development and the advancement of women;
— women's hidden economic role in the services should be further studied and analysed;
— co-operation among developing countries in this sector, which is scattered over different areas and usually invisible being traditional and informal;
— could be pursued with a view to the development of self-reliant schemes. Co-operation among developing countries in this sector could contribute to exchange of experiences, to development of self-reliant schemes and linkages between micro and macro levels of implementation. This may be an avenue for the promotion of new approaches to the development of the services sector.

Creating Awareness

Education and Training

Education is a double-edged instrument: it can contribute to and be an ally of structural changes in society by training people in required skills—old, newly emerging and anticipated. It is also a value-generating process—influencing the behaviour, norms and cultural attitudes of people, particularly younger ones. From the beginning of the movement for the equality of women in recent history, great emphasis was placed on education as the major instrument for the elimination of gender inequality. Developing countries have viewed education as an instrument to stimulate development in all fields, and to reduce their dependence on external advisers. The basic problems were to promote a rapid expansion of development and cultural structures to meet the manpower requirements of development and cultural progress in general. Scarcity of resources and the shifting priorities of development have constrained the balanced pursuit of these aims. One of the objectives which had a low priority in the allocation of efforts and resources was the elimination of gender inequality.

Literacy Among Women Compared to Men, 1970-1980
(Literacy Men= 100)

	1970	*1980*
World Total	84	85
More Developed Countries	99	799
Developing Countries	65	71
Africa	35	47
Asia and Pacific	69	73
Latin America	91	94

Source: UN, 1982, p. 116.

Illiteracy still remains a major problem in most developing countries and women constitute a large proportion of the illiterates. About 60 per cent of the approximately .800 million adult illiterates in developing countries today are women. Although the proportion of illiterates in the total adult population has decreased, the results are still unsatisfactory. The absolute number of illiterates in these countries is still increasing. Gender differences persist among illiterates, especially because the lower enrolment ratios for girls at the elementary level increase the number of illiterate women.

The gender gap among illiterates is increasing in developing countries. In 1960 the share of women among illiterates was 57.9 per cent. This increased to 59.5 per cent in 1970. (UN, 1980, p. 81).

Trends in the process of equalising the access of men and women to different levels of the educational system, as measured through enrolment ratios, show some interesting results. Over two decades (1960-80) the gender gap in enrolment ratios for the age groups 6—11 and 12—17 has remained virtually constant in developing countries, although there is overall improvement in entrolment for both sexes. At the higher level of education, the gap is much narrower, in contrast to developed countries, where the gender gap exists mainly at the higher level. At this level the gender gap has shrunk in the developed countries during the last decade, and it has slightly widened in the group of developing countries. (Sicherl, 1984).

The persistence of these gaps prevents the equalisation of educational opportunities with consequent effects on employment, skill acquisition and participatory opportunities in all fields. The widening of the gap in higher education is a matter of serious concern, because this sector is the training ground for entry into many areas important development, *e.g.*, science and technology, communication industries utilising high level technology, professions such as law, medicine, etc. It is also the training ground for most managerial and decision-making occupations. The participation of women in decision-making positions, which is already limited, could shrink still further if this gap were to expand.

In addition to resource constraints, educational progress in developing countries has been impeded by many other problems. Lack of harmony with productive and other developmental activities, which is often a consequence of borrowed models of educational systems, imposed the need to reform and adapt educational systems and institutions, to turn increasingly to the informal aspects of education (vocational training, on the job-training, etc.), and to introduce mass media and other modern devices as useful means of spreading educational programmes and contents in an effort to reach as many social groups as possible. Developing countries have been experiencing great problems in education, reflected in poor material basis and functional difficulties, in sometimes alarming drop-out levels (especially in Sub-Saharan Africa and South Asia), in the fact that a substantial proportion of children are unable to read and write even after going to primary school for four or five years, etc.

Women are still mostly employed in traditional and informal sectors where there has been a lower level of technological and information support. This further compounds their educational handicaps. However, women with education have entered many new areas of occupation where their participation was virtually non-existent before. This process of occupational diversification through education has been accelerated during the Decade in many developing countries.

The enable women to participate actively in all spheres of economic and social life, vocational and professional training must be further developed. In this respect, the training of trainers is of primary importance, as is the introduction of management training for women. Apart from the conventional types of training (seminars, workshops, export group meetings training through doing, etc.), the non-conventional types are often also suitable. Of special relevance are also the new participatory types of training, which include learner-centered methods developed in the framework of non-formal education in which trainers are facilitators, to elicit productive response and interaction-and local social and cultural forms that can be built upon for effective training. These include-decision making patterns, social groupings and communications networks.

Culture

The major lacunae in educational development are in the areas of cultural change and promotion of social values which support and reflect the goals of development. Cultural transformations are taking place in developing countries, but in many cases through processes over which the people and even the governments have little control. New values and aspirations are often promoted, directly or indirectly, for profit maximisation-by forces inside or outside the country. Changes in consumption patterns and role models are stimulated by mass media, commercial interests and a process of borrowing or emulation of life styles from developed countries. In many countries such changes have contributed to a widening of the gap between the elites and the masses of the people between the rural and urban populations, between the rich and the poor. This presents a challenge to the educational system, which must correct the trend if it is to promote the goals of participatory development, and collective self-reliance, eliminate the dependency on external support and contribute to comprehensive integrated development.

While there is evidence that the process of unplanned cultural change helps to promote illusory images which are far removed from the social realities of developing countries, cultural reaction, which tries to counter these influences by looking only to the past, may also have a negative impact on development. In their efforts to preserve their cultural identities developing countries have sought to reaffirm their attachment to their cultural heritage. While pride in this heritage can contribute to the spirit and the value of self-reliance, this process may also lead to distortions-to a withdrawal from present-day problems and realities to a glamorisation of the past, to the imposition of the culture of dominant groups on other culturally diverse groups and to a strengthening of some of the forces and institutions that oppose the goals of comprehensive, participatory development of all peoples, classes and groups. Such trends have often inhibited the equality of women and attempts to enhance their role in development.

In view of the crucial importance of culture values in the dynamics of development, it will be essential to enhance the role of the women and to promote new cultural values that take into account existing social realities and support the efforts to build a different future. Integral development, which subsumes equal participation in development *i.e.*, in production and decision making will enhance the role of culture in the development context. Women will no longer be viewed as marginal producers (or providers of an auxiliary workforce), but rather as equal partners in the promotion of development.

Educational institutions will have to play an active role in the promotion of the development of such new cultural values. Hitherto, their contribution has been inadequate. Structurally pedagogically and philosophically, educational institutions will have to play a far more active role in the development of a new cultural context that can contribute to the realization of the goals of comprehensive development—human and material. This also requires that they internalise the concern for the equality of women and the enhancement of their role-in their curricula, pedagogic methods, organization and research agendas.

A strategic interrelationship between education and cultural and socio-economic development which integrates concern for the emancipation of women would have to be characterised by respect for the specific cultural features of a particular environment and clearly define the cultural and developmental function of education in social transformation and support the process of educational reform.

In this connection, the promotion of new knowledge about women and new perceptions of the role of women in development could be viewed as an instrument for educational and cultural development with a view to:

— strengthening and extension of training activities so as to embrace all relevant problems, such as: improvement of professional skills, education for family life and responsibilities, training for community organization and management, decision waking etc.;

— equal participation of the local population, and particularly of women, in devising, deciding upon and implementing development programmes; this can be achieved by clearly defining the developmental interests of all groups of the population;

— promotion of integral and interdisciplinary links among developing countries in the field of cultural transformation and education and especially in professional and vocational training as well as in all forms of non- conventional training, to ensure availability of cadres capable of handling the new technology.

— enhancement of the collective self-reliance of nonaligned and other developing countries in culture and education by intensifying their communication in these fields, especially as regards the methodologies for educational reform which incorporates the advancement of women as one of its concerns.

Mass Media

This section focuses on the possibilities which the media offer provided they are used judiciously to reflect the contribution which women are making to the nation's development efforts. Communication media have been a powerful social influence, both as instruments of change and for maintaining *status quo.* In the last decade, an impressive amount of literature on the portrayal of women in the media has been produced. These studies have expressed concern about the stereotyped and negative images of women which are being projected through the media without any cognizance of the new and expanded roles of women in society. Communication media are a powerful tool for the creation of an alternative and positive image of women and could promote new attitudes and strategies for action directed towards the achievement of the goal of equality for women. It is imperative to democratises the control over the communication media and to make them an instrument for the creation of an awareness of women's needs and problems.

Mass media, especially the audiovisual media, play an important role by influencing the consumption patterns and life-styles, and usually promote commercial interests (often of external producers), thus creating pressures to distort trade and industrial policies. They also contribute to the distortion of cultural development, promoting imported values which militate against comprehensive integrated development and the principle of collective self-reliance. There has been a recent trend among media professionals in developing countries towards greater realism in their portrayal of social problems. Realism, however, must be used to inspire people to struggle for change. A search for new options in human relationships, the reshaping of social institutions, political and economic structures and cultural values, would go a long way towards integrating women into the world of the media, and enable the media to play a more positive role in integrated development.

In the past, there has been a one-way flow of information from the developed to the developing countries, and from government to the people. The goals of self-reliance and participatory development, which are being actively pursued by the non-aligned countries, involve a shift from excessive reliance of the developing countries on foreign resources towards a mobilisation of their indigenous resources, which would make these countries less vulnerable to external pressures and develop their own potential for growth. The new information and communication technology, the micro-chip revolution, has considerably magnified the power of the media. Satellite communication has exposed millions of people to new information. The strengthening of the autonomous capacities of the individual countries and improvement of the organizational framework and media content will depend on the socio-political context of each country.

Women are today an important factor in the strategy of self-reliance and the media could do much to create public awareness of the role of women and their potentials. There are a number of steps which the media could take at various levels to strengthen the role of women as equal partners in development:

— a democratisation of the structures and control of the communication media could contribute to the representation and participation of women in the media at the decision—making levels;

— more women should be involved in media training programmes; communication and advertising policies involving participation by women could be developed;

— media content could be improved through coordinated efforts for increased interaction between non-governmental organizations in formulating guidelines for monitoring programmes;

— listeners and viewers from consumer groups or NGO action groups, etc., could be effectively utilised to create an awareness of women's issues and to evolve common strategies for the promotion of more positive approaches to women's issues;

— various international seminars, conferences and expert group meetings, which have already covered a wide range of issues connected with women and the communication media indicate the need for further in depth studies, research training for women in communication technology, the organizational framework, including the development of a code of ethics with regard to the presentation of women in media and using traditional folk media to encourage participation of women.

— horizontal communication and co-operation among developing countries in this field could be strengthened in order to create an awareness of issues of common concern, identifying solutions to common problems and areas of co-operation.

Issues of Crucial Development

The still largely unresolved problems of the interconnections between economic and social development and the increasing concern for the distributional and human dimensions of development indicate the need to pay more attention to all aspects of social development. The issues of health, social security, population trends and family planning, housing urbanisation and the environment, are linked with the general problem of the level of socio-economic development of a country its resource base and social policies.

Systems of Health Delivery

Millions of people in developing countries are trapped in poverty, malnutrition, hunger and disease, although there are regional variations in living conditions. It is estimated that acute forms of potential energy malnutrition affect *35* per cent school children in Africa, 16 per cent in Asia and 4 per cent in of Latin America. Similarly, it is estimated that two-thirds pregnant women in the developing world suffer from nutritional anaemia. High maternal and infant mortality rates are closely linked with inadequate maternal and child health care services, lack of proper sanitation and a safe drinking water supply. By the end of the last decade, only 42 per cent of households in developing countries had access to a potable water supply and over three quarters of the population lacked access to sanitary facilities.

A disaggregation of social indicators by regions reveals that not only is there a very great gap between the developed and developing countries but also that there is great diversity among the developing regions.

The average life expectancy in Sub-Saharan Africa is 47.4 years while it is 63.9 years in some Asian Countries. Similarly, infant mortality is highest in Sub-Saharan Africa (127.1 per thousand live births), while it is 56.2 in South East Asia. In the South Asian region the mortality differentials by sex indicate higher infant mortality among females and empirical data also show sex-based health and nutrition related behaviour. In the health care sub-systems, there are interesting variations: Latin America—with the highest per capita GDP— has 7.5 physicians and 11.7 nurses per 10,000 population, followed by some countries in South East Asia, where despite low GDP per capita the averages are 5.4 physicians and 5.2 nurses per 10,000 population.

Most developing countries are faced with the problem of a decline or slowing down of the growth rate of production, rising unemployment, growing deficits in balance of payments and inflation. All these adversely affect the availability of resources for social services, *i.e.,* health, education and social security.

Despite the methodological weaknesses of the existing social indicators and an absence of data on access to and distributional characteristics of the social development infrastructure, the trends indicate that results differ sharply also within regions and that social improvements definitely do not come automatically as a by-product of economic growth. In many cases health resources are disproportionately concentrated in big cities, at the expense of primary health care for the masses in rural areas. Problems requiring careful study include disparities in increase and living standards, and the care available to different social groups, inadequate planning and management of health development, problems of inter and intra-sectoral coordination, administrative decentralization and involvement of the people in the planning, programming and implementation of health care programmes.

Very few developing countries have systems of social security. Even where such systems exist, a large part of the population in the informal sector—a substantial proportion of which are women—is not covered by the existing systems of mater benefits, health insurance, old age benefits, etc. In some countries voluntary and philanthropic organizations supplement state action. However, their work is often uncoordinated and not adequate to deal with the increasing, demands of urbanisation and poverty. The development of social protection is linked to changes in the development strategies and orientation directed towards the satisfaction of basic minimum needs, the reduction and elimination of poverty, promotion of employment opportunities and improvement of the working conditions of labour.

The global strategy of *Health for All by 2000* adopted by the Thirty Fourth World Health Assembly in 1981, which emphasises basic health protection, the primary health care approach and organization of an effective health care and health information system, identified priorities for health co-operation and drew up an Action

Programme, stressing the need for a review of a number of policy orientations in the areas of primary health care, health information and monitoring system, community involvement in health programmes, prevention of infectious diseases, development of national services of health care and health education, production, distribution and consumption of drugs and protection of the human environment.

On the basis of the Medium-Term Programme for Technical Co-operation among Developing Countries for Health for All (1984-89) and in view of the calls for an acceleration of the development of national health care capabilities and the establishment of local points for TCDC in the area of health some priority activities may be identified:

- introduction of effective health surveillance systems at the national level, of health indicators for target setting and formulation of national priorities and plans of action, and of appropriate Systems for assessing strengths and weaknesses of national health programmes;
- linking of health policies and 'programmes with economic development and those facilities which can directly reduce women's drudgery and work burden and directly improve their health situation, *i.e.,* provision of adequate housing, water supply, sanitation, health regulations at the work-place, and health protection of women, particularly those working in the informal sector of the economy who are not covered by social protection policies;
- integration of maternal and child health care with family planning services and accelerated development of national capacities through development of health institutions and infrastructures and increase of the number of health experts and particularly health workers;
- involvement of women's organizations in primary health care activities and their representation on national and local health councils;
- promotion of health education and indigenous system of health care;

— involvement of woman's organizations in primary health care activities and their representation on national and local health councils;
— promotion of health education and indigenous systems of health care;
— introduction of ECDC/TCTC programmes for the promotion of industries which are important for the development of health care systems. The developing countries could evolve suitable mechanisms for co-operation in training and development of human resources, collaborative research, joint programming, exchange of information and references, and exploring the application of low-cost technologies for water supply and waste disposal.

Demographic Factors

It is becoming increasingly obvious that population policies should be implemented parallel with better health care and general socio-economic development as population issues touch on very fundamental human values.

As the Mexico Conference on Population in 1984 stressed, population strategies cannot be limited to the analysis of population trends, since there is a dynamic interrelationship between these and socio-economic transformations. Hence, what is required is a set of coordinated strategies and activities for the promotion of economic development of the quality of life, human rights and in particular the fundamental right to individual choice.

The status of women and the advancement of their role in development remains a critical element in the achievement of these objectives. The persisting inequalities between men and women—which are evident in the higher incidence of poverty, unemployment and illiteracy among women—the limited range of employment categories offered to women, and the uneven sharing of borne and family responsibilities make it difficult for women to participate actively in the socio-economic development of the country. Population policies should be viewed as an integral part of overall socio-economic development.

There is sufficient evidence to show that it is lower income groups with a low level of literacy, low and insecure income and low health and nutritional levels which have larger families. This is points to a need for planning policies which have a more integrated approach. Rapid population growth will affect the efforts of countries to achieve food security and to reduce pressure on the natural resources; also, its effects on urbanisation and on land and capital will exacerbate inequalities.

Many governments have launched subsidised family planning programmes. However, incentives are offered to encourage people to reduce family size. Experience has shown that a clinical approach which threatens social values, beliefs and customs does not succeed and is actually a disincentive. To breakthrough the vicious circle of poverty, high fertility and mortality calls for a more careful and humane public policy with a judicious balance between individual choice and dignity and promotion of a sense of responsibility among parents to ensure a better future for all children. This could be further stimulated and promoted through various forms of technical assistance at various levels as well as enriched through mutual exchange of information and experience among developing countries.

Coping with Over Population: Women in the Cities

The rapid growth of cities in developing countries has created serious problems, since a large proportion of urban migrant workers are living in temporary hutments and settlements without adequate basic amenities. The growth of cities and the steep rise in rural-urban migration is a manifestation of imbalances in the location and expansion of productive activity. Women are particularly affected, as many of their activities are connected with their homes and bad housing and hygiene conditions are detrimental to both their own and their families health. The growth of cities has also created ecological problems. The growing demands of expanding cities have put undue pressure on natural resources, destroying the harmony between human beings and nature, and has led to a degradation of productive resources like water, land and forests. With increasing pressure on the land, overgrasing and deforestation, severe environmental damage has followed.

The expansion of agriculture by clearing large tracts of forest has caused desertification due to severe soil erosion, a problem which is extremely serious in Sub-Saharan Africa (Sahel), north-western Asia and the Middle East. Forests are crucial to the ecological life of many developing countries and deforestation has created serious problems, as the consumption of forest resources has exceeded replacement possibilities through natural growth. This has affected millions of rural households and the role of women in these households, as well as the nutritional level of the families. The human costs of malnutrition, famine and disruption in the lives of people seeking employment are a matter of serious concern.

Environmental issues conceiving the environment in its broadest social context are most relevant for women. The increasing marginalisation of certain sections of the population, growing poverty and deprivation of the masses, decreasing food production, the energy crisis and human environmental degradation in many developing countries are all symptoms of a pattern of growth and resource utilisation which is geared to existing power structures and prevents a large section of the population from satisfying its basic needs. The multidimensional problems facing developing countries are interconnected, but often these connection are not understood by those who formulate sectoral policies. In the long run, social development policies will have to be closely integrated with economic development policies and a strong commitment to the improvement of the quality of life. The methods and instruments of analysis and planning of socio-economic development should therefore take adequate account of environmental constraint.

INSTITUTIONAL ISSUES

Both the conceptual and sectoral parts of this study have indicated the basic features and tendencies of the changing role and status of women in developing countries. This was primarily the result of an analysis of the overall impact of development on the position of women in the societies of the developing countries and of the role of women in the developmental process.

The effects of socio-economic development in individual sectors of the economy and public life have been identified and analysed. The endeavours at operationalisation of national development policies, including the integration of women in development raised the issue of instruments and institutions to implement these policies.

Issues addressed in this sections are: the role of government of public and private enterprises and of political participation and the role of women in decision-making processes as factors of development.

Institution Effort and Government

In principle, most governments have accepted the improvement of the social, political, economic and legal status of women, and the integration of women into development as desirable goals and planning objectives. The response of government, parliament and other political institutions at various levels to the need for the integration of women's issues into development plans is important for the effective implementation of appropriate strategies.

Country experiences indicate that during the UN Decade for Women many countries established governmental machinery, either as part of the existing administrative structures, as independent agencies (commissions, bureaux, ministries) for women's affairs, or in the form of National Councils which were extra-governmental organizations. Most of these mechanisms were created with the objectives of establishing responsibility and accountability within the government for planning, programming and implementing programmes for women and to act as a catalyst; providing the necessary infrastructure and resource support and training personnel: and reviewing, monitoring and evaluating policies and programmes and their impact on women.

The Mid-Decade review of the efficacy of these administrative and institutional mechanisms indicated that the constraints to action have ranged from conceptual of resource and organizational fractional factors. They do not have strong executive and resource support and have a limited mandate. The tendency has been to locate such units mainly within departments of social welfare and culture which are considered non-productive and are usually not in the mainstream of the development effort and also suffer most from budgetary constraints during economic recession. The experience of some developing countries also indicates that the existence of governmental or state mechanism of this kind tends to reduce the concern of other administrative organs and of society as a whole for the advancement of women and leads to a diminution of activity in this direction.

As already indicated, the problems with regard to the role of women are closely linked with the problems of overall development. However, most of the governments have perceived the role of women as a specific interest issue without making any attempt to integrate the problems involved into the mainstream of development planning. In many developing countries women—specific projects were designed to provide income—generating activities and basic needs to poor rural and urban women. These efforts basically addressed the immediate needs for survival faced by women in the poorer sections, without addressing the multi-dimensional and multisectoral processes and structures that marginalise these women. The governmental bodies deliberating on the crucial strategies of food production, industrialisation rural development, science and technology, and monetary reforms still face the problems connected with the integration of the role of women into their overall plans of action.

It is becoming increasingly evident that issues related to the position of women cannot meaningfully be dealt with only through specific projects, without effectively linking them to economic policies, plans and programmes, and making these projects an integral part of the long-term process of development. The typical women and development projects may, however, perpetuate the reformist stance by promoting marginal, often non-viable activities not linked to major sectors of development and sometimes lead to a considerable increase in women's burden without providing the necessary supportive institutions for their new role and expanded opportunities. They fail to deal with structural inequalities which lead to changes in policies and programmes and affect the allocative, distributive and participatory processes.

The access of women to productive resources is a necessary precondition for their advancement. Recent discussions in both international and national flora have stressed issues such as title to land, access to credit and banking facilities, to employment on equal terms and under equal conditions, and to information and knowledge, education and training. Any policy aimed at improving the lot of poorer households should involve substantial changes in resource control, e.g., land tenure, investment patterns, access to information regarding markets, technology, employment opportunities, availability of financial or other support, training etc., to increase women's control over their own labour and income. Answers to these issues will have to be found within the framework of nation states.

During the UN Decade for Women, besides the integrative approach, arguments for specific transitional strategies and policies by the government to deal with the historically disadvantaged position of women were put forward. The approach was based on the assumption that the understanding of the role of women could be strengthened within the complex framework of government by setting time-specific and measurable goals within each important sector, thus operationalising the concern for the position and role of women and translating it into programmes of action. Further, recognizing the close link between class and gender issues, it was expected that targetting for each group, in addition to the overall development target, would narrow the gender gaps in various sectors. To ensure a more meaningful intervention, a blending of the two approaches, i.e., integral development with specific action, is suggested. Minor transitional activities should be in line with the long-term perspectives, if they are not to be counter-productive. A survey conducted by the ILO in mid—1984, on the integration of the question of women in national development plans, reveals that only 12 of 44 developing countries has incorporated employment of women by sectors in their national development plans, 28 countries had set up governmental bodies dealing with the question of female workers, and only 19 of 44 countries had undertaken sectoral surveys to investigate the problems and prospects of female workers. Much ground remains to be covered before the legal guarantees and administrative measures can be put into practice. Attempts at removing legal obstacles and improving access to education and other social services have not prevented growing poverty and malnutrition, rising unemployment and underemployment coupled with an increasing work burden, and persistent marginalisation of women in the economy and in decision-making structures, although there have been varying results in the individual countries and regions.

However, governments have experienced considerable difficulties in their attempts to articulate these new approaches in policies and development action. These are due to a number of factors: the persistent invisibility of women as a critical and important factor within development structures; continued lack of awareness and understanding of the difficulties that women face even when they are participating on equal terms in development—both as beneficiaries and as agents; and delays in developing an adequate set of monitoring and evaluation measures and instruments to speed up effective implementation of adopted policies.

The most urgent task which now faces governments is more innovative blending of the role of women into the design of action programmes, policy instruments and evaluation criteria or monitoring procedures in all sectors of development. The issue of women's role in development cannot be a concern of women only. The value-creating mechanisms, i.e., the educational system, and the media, may be suitably modified to project values of sex equality. Governments could modify or eliminate legal provisions that still uphold the unequal status of women.

The strategies for action suggested in the sectoral chapters all call for operational instruments. Who is to initiate, implement and evaluate these measures at the national and at the regional and international levels? The emphasis should be on perceptional, organizational and infrastructural development. At the government level, executive and administrative measures need to be taken to ensure recognition of women's productive, reproductive and participatory roles and to provide supportive services such as child care and need social services, i.e., health care, education, catering, housing and drinking water, etc., to reduce their work burden and enable them to assume wider responsibilities.

What kind of policy instruments have been effective in incorporating the role of women into sectoral structures? A concerted effort is needed to bridge the gap between the highest levels of government and the intermediate and lower levels where plans are operationalised. A comparison of organizational and infrastructural models and approaches in different countries could provide an insight into the strengths and weaknesses of various arrangement.

The Mexico Conference had visualised the National Commission as watchdog bodies—to review and recommend measures necessary to enhance the equality and participation of women in development and decision making. Some countries have defined the functions of the national mechanisms in this manner and provided them with the requisite powers of resource support. At the same time the strength of the argument that women's affairs cannot be separated from the sectoral agencies responsible for planning and implementation of development in the fields of agriculture and rural development, industry, energy, science and technology, urban and rural development, education, health and other social services must be acknowledged. Since the objective is the integration of women in all these sectors of development, it could be useful to institutionalise this concern, or mandate—to continue the task of making the Sectoral agencies sensitive, concerned and accountable. Such sectoral mechanisms could also continue to increase the level of competence of women, advancing their role in development in various sectors.

In view of the stagnation of overall development, the modest resource support has kept efforts to promote the role of women at a marginal level in most developing countries. Thus in some developing countries such efforts have been primarily dependent on international aid. Apart from the fact that this may have precluded the integration of these efforts into major development sectors, this dependence has in some cases also diverted attention from the goals of collective and national self-reliance, and sometimes also distorted national priorities.

Research on women in development, which has evolved during the Decade as an important instrument for the advancement of the role of women has been useful, since it has been instrumental in the collection of empirical information which has, to date, provided most of the data to assess the impact of various development policies on women; it has sensitised the people involved in development planning and administration by posing issue resulting from their empirical investigations and promoted an ideological climate and public concern thus raising the level of consciousness among women and others.

So far, such studies have primarily been confined to research and have made little impact on the training and value transformation of younger generations. The promotion of such studies as an instrument for enhancing the role of women in development, through educational and training institutions agencies responsible for research and information has emerged as a critical need. Such an approach would be most appropriate within the areas of co-operation among the non-aligned countries in order to eliminate the dependence on external aid—with the possible risk of distortions. In view of the fact that the role of women in development has been acknowledged as an important component of the research and information system that is being promoted within the movement of the non-aligned countries, it is suggested that this component could be included through a combination of research, training and information dissemination.

The incorporation of the aspects of the role of women in development in existing teaching/training and research institutions may reduce investments in physical and administrative infrastructure—and improve the prospects for integrating/articulating women's problems, issues and concerns within all educational institution/disciplines, instead of allowing them to remain a separate, marginal activity, whose isolation makes it ineffective. National, regional and international networks of such institutions should be encouraged to share and expand share and expand their experiences, which would help to increase their competence, and strengthen the ties or intellectual and developmental co-operation among non-aligned nations. Such efforts would help to increase the extent and improve the quality of data needed by national governments. They would also make it possible to train an increasing number of cadres to take up the various functions identified as necessary for the advancement of women in development. Above all, the incorporation of studies of this kind within the educational systems and in training institutions would help promote the needed cultural transformation. Science and technology, which could be powerful instruments for the advancement of the role of women in development have so for usually by-passed women because their educational and other handicaps. Science and technology have also often been misused to marginalise women and reduce their status. It is therefore important not merely to facilitate the access of women to science and technology, but also to ensure that practitioners will be aware of the problems involved in the employment of women in his areas. It would be useful to introduce these concerns as early as the training stage.

In particular, developments in the fields of communication technology and communication sciences pose a critical challenge to the decisions of the non-aligned Countries to enhance the role of women in development. If these new developments are not harnessed in accordance with the policies for the advancement of women, they will continue to be used by social forces which oppose the equality of women and development, and help to strengthen and perpetuate values and behavioural norms that thrive on the subordination of women. The transfer of technology in some of these fields has already bad consequences which militate against the improvement of the status of women.

The improvement of the systems for data collection and development of quantitative and indicators for measuring women's development is another critical area. Despite repeated decisions at various international conferences, many national data collection agencies still do not have adequate data on women, nor do they provide sex break-downs or gender differentiation in different fields. They continue to be pervaded with a biased understanding of what is important information regarding the status of women and its impact on the conditions and equality of life of families, communities and development in general. Similarly, there has been little follow-up action at the national levels to the very useful international efforts and decision to develop and compile comparable socioeconomic indicators to measure the role of women in development, as initiated recently by INSTRAW and the UN Statistical Office.

A system of reporting by sex disaggregated data would help the flow of information from the bottom up, monitoring the actual implementation of programmes and benefits accuring to women, and through women to the entire community, and increase the accountability of government agencies. Simultaneously, such a process would initiate improvement of data systems, concepts and methods of statistics, and development of indicators.

Numerous studies from developing countries have demonstrated the importance of women's grass-root participatory organizations. When genuinely participatory they become dynamic instruments—not merely for the advancement of women, but for the improvement of the quality of the development process as a whole. But in many developing countries; such organizations have not yet been evolved. Where women's co-operatives, village level organizations and voluntary agencies to exist, they generally receive little support in the way of resources, information or recognition.

In acme cases, the efforts of non-governmental organization have provided some support to break the isolation of these grass-root groups. The NGOs have often played the role of an intermediary, providing the needed support to the grass-root groups helping to establish direct communications between them and development agencies, and also helping to develop networks of grass-root groups to enable them to learn from each other. An important strategy for governments to consider is recognition of some organization/institutions as intermediaries to increase the governments' reach, to obtain the needed feed-back from the grass roots and to raise the level of information and knowledge at both ends.

The concept of intermediaries provides a new channel for organization/institutions outside the government to play a role in advancing the status of women in development and help operationalise some of the strategies already accepted. The concept of an autonomous intermediary— supported by government resources and acting as a channel of communication between grass-root groups and government without the negative features of a patron-client relationship at either end—officers an operational instrument to implement some of the accepted strategies.

Strategies to further strengthen the role of women in the overall development efforts could be oriented towards:

- continuation and redoubling of efforts to make the role of women visible in various sectors of development, in various agencies and instruments for government action, such as the legislature, the judiciary, planning agencies. public enterprises, specialised agencies created by governments for particular aspects of economic and social development, financial institutions, etc.;
- provision of the necessary infrastructure, resource and cadre support for planning and execution of the governmental policies in this regard;
- reviewing, monitoring and evaluating policies and programmes and their impact on women in development and *vice versa* —from an integrated and coordinated point of view;
- promotion of value transformation, in view of the long-term objective of the advancement of the role of women in development;
- further research and training of all those involved and

concerned in promoting the status of women information gathering systems should be promoted in order to provide essential inputs for government policies and actions;

- enhancement of the opportunities for women to take part in decision making as fully informed citizens;
- access of women as well as of men, to information on the decisions taken by their governments, on available assistance and support and agencies and structures from which to obtain such support;
- raising of the literacy level and upgrading and dissemination of knowledge. This is where communication technology and traditional communication channels should be harnessed;
- exchange of information and experience, as well as consultative arrangements at venous levels, particularly at the regional and inter-government levels. In this matter a number of international, regional or interregional institutions might be requested to assist the identification of communication channels;
- elaboration of guidelines for all bilateral and multilateral technical co-operation programmes to ensure the incorporation of elevant aspects of the role of women in development. The UNDP Indicative Planning Figure should also incorporate these aspects for basic programmatic action;
- inclusion of the question of the role of women in development in the preparation of plans for negotiations at all stages of the project cycle at different levels of regional and international co-operation, so as to ensure that the result of these projects will not be in conflict with national objectives;
- incorporation of a social impact analysis into all projects to avoid negative results. Non-aligned countries' co-operation could help to develop the necessary methodology for such analyses;
- continuation of the work already initiated by national and international research institutions in refining and building up an adequate analysis (conceptual and methodological) and identification of indicators which can measure the work

done by women, especially in food production and agriculture. Data (time series data should reflect the real position of women within the context of overall long-term trends in development. Research should include gender-specific analysis to illustrate the types of inequality which still require measures to overcome them.

Development through Enterprise

One of the important factors in the development programmes and plans of developing countries is the growth and expansion of public enterprises and the public sector. Initially, public enterprises operated principally in the infrastructure and the public utilities, but their range of activity has now considerably expanded.

Being part of the broader stream of the public sector in developing countries, public enterprises are important instruments of national and collective self-reliance and are oriented towards increasing the countries autonomy in using and developing their natural and human resources in order to increase the well-being of the population as a whole.

One of the responsibilities of public enterprises is the promotion of the integration of women into the developmental process and of a conscious policy directed towards the advancement of women. The responsibilities of public enterprises in this regard, however, differ in accordance with their scope and nature, their mandate and function, their scope and coverage of national planning and the legislative framework. But, by and large, they cover a wide range of commercial and; or non-commercial functions of great importance in everyday life.

Practical experience in the operation of public interprises in developing countries has shown that they generate progressive social change in these countries, including positive moves towards involving women in the main streams of development. However, the public sector in general and the public enterprises in particular are still not strong enough to constitute a major or even a very important factor in involving women in the transformation of their socio-economic position and are thus not making a sufficient response to this complex task.

Within the framework of the national development programmes, the public enterprise in general, and each specific enterprise in particular should be provided with guidelines indicating the special steps expected from the enterprise for the promotion of the role of women in developing countries, which might include the following:

- More emphasis on clarity of aims and objectives, a regular review of the current status of women, including job profiles for the improvement of the position of women in training programmes, social welfare measures relating to child bearing and child rearing, provision of creches and the allocation of specific responsibilities to appropriate national institutions;
- preparation of concrete action plans which should include both short-term and long-term strategies in the area of manpower planning, recruitment systems promotional opportunities, incentives, training and women's representation at the management level. These strategies should also envisage a regular procedure and criteria for the evaluation of the performance of public enterprises in terms of the fulfilment of economic and social objectives;
- identification of areas of activity in which women are currently not represented but can be recruited. The human resources development plans should include a specific component on the employment of women;
- efforts should be made to involve more women in on going training courses, particularly management training, as well as to develop the curricula of these courses with an emphasis on the role and responsibilities of public enterprises in the advancement of women;
- in view of the need to involve more women at higher levels of management, special training programmes for the induction of women at these levels of enterprise management could be stimulated and developed as a short-term measure;

— Fuller involvement of women workers and men workers alike in decision-making processes as well as in forms of management at all levels of enterprise organization, which is seen as an essential means of their advancement, parallel with the improvement of public enterprises' management patterns and efficiency;

— public enterprises should exploit their opportunities of generating employment in down-stream activities with which they are related. This is of particular significance in the case of sub-contracting to public sector ancillaries. Some cases of sub-contracting to women's co-operatives and to regional development corporations which stimulate small business could also promote both employment and entrepreneurship among women. However steps must be taken to ensure that such practices are not deterimental to the position of women or to the overall regional development;

— an agreed system of performance evaluation arising from the predetermined corporate plans should identify the evaluation criteria for each social objective including the objective of advancing the status of women. Whenever possible, an attempt should be made to quantify the criteria;

— the existing or/and newly created mechanisms at the national level responsible for scrutinising the policies and practice of public enterprises and evaluating their operations and contributions towards the socio-economic objectives of development could advise governments on the formulation of policies through which public enterprises could act as model employers and real promoters of the status of women, and could also undertake regular evaluation and monitoring of these efforts of public enterprises.

In view of the need to implement the socio-economic objectives of development and the advancement of women, due consideration should be given to the role of private enterprises.

Governments should seek appropriate ways and means to ensure that public and private enterprises share the responsibilities for the improvement of the status of women. Some suggestions in this connections might be, for example:

(i) private enterprises are established in developing countries under various systems of public licensing which include certain provisions for the enforcement of laws and these could be used for regulating the working conditions of women;

(ii) similarly, credit/banking agencies which give loans to private enterprises for equity and working capital could give specific incentives for the promotion of the advancement of women;

(iii) it may expected that the linkages between the public and private enterprises could promote the realization of some of these ideas.

Role of Women in Decision Making Processes as Factors of Development and Political Participation

The political status of women in developing countries and the levels and quality of their political participation, are far from adequate, considering their share in the population structure, their part in social and economic reproduction, as well as their actual and potential role in the national development process. The unfavourable economic and social position of women in developing countries is directly reflected in the level of their participation in decision-making process at all levels.

In many developing countries a large portion of the women actively participated in the national liberation movements and in the creation of national political structures. However, they were often under-represented in the decision-making processes, in public and political life. Studies on women's participation have revealed that they are more active at the informal levels, which are closer to their problems than in formal political activity. This passivity of women in formal political activity is both a symptom and a cause of some major developmental problems.

The political participation of women has always been indicative of their position in general. Today, there are only very few developing countries where national law excludes women from formal political processes. However data on a global basis indicate an enormous disparity between women's formal political equality and their actual participation in decision-making processes.

Having understood this problem and recognized it as an important barrier to social and economic progress and development changes, most developing countries have been adopting and trying to implement policies and measures which would mitigate and remove it. Many of these efforts and measures have been promoted through the implementation of UN instruments, such as the Convention on Equal Political Rights of Women, the Convention on the Elimination of All Forms of Discrimination Against Women, etc.

There has been general recognition among those in authority in developing countries of the great importance of women's participation in the efforts towards social and human welfare. A general summary of the findings of numerous studies in this field shows that the number of women who actively realize their role in development and their rights in developing countries is continuously increasing, as is the importance of their participation in representative and legislative for at the national, regional and particularly at the local level. Women are especially active and are gaining increasing representation in local self-government bodies. The number of women in executive orans, in the judiciary, and in particular among high officials and in the political structures and public services is small and inadequate, but nevertheless growing. Their representation in the upper management echelons in the economic, scientific, cultural and social fields is unsatisfactory, but it cannot be said that the situation is not improving. In some regions political education and economic emancipation of women, as well as the creation of better family and household conditions have led to increased participation of women in political parties, trade unions, various movements, etc.

The need for effective and extensive popular participation, promotion of grass-root organizations and institutional mechanisms to facilitate such participation has already been recognized. There will have to be a commitment from governments to provide opportunities for greater participation of women in political and other fields of life and to eliminate all forms of discrimination. Examples of decentralized planning and decision-making, such as community development programmes, may be seen as positive moves towards the realization of such commitments.

In many developing countries genuine forms of popular participation have been established and are operating successfully, workers participation in management, industrial democracy, co-determination, self- management, etc. Most of these relate to the sphere of the economy, the public sector and public enterprises, but are often accompanied by various forms of citizens involvement in running the community's affairs at the local and regional levels. Workers and citizens involvement in the conduct of economic and community affairs also includes forms of direct sharing in the management of public and social services, co-operative, consumers associations, etc. All these forms, which have given women art opportunity to enlarge the scope of their participation in public and political life, have had a significant impact on the overall activisation of women in society in the mainstream of development processes. Such forms and experiences of workers, citizens and generally popular participation involving women equally, generate development and contribute to the realization of human rights. This is being recognized by many international and UN fora and documents and should be fully considered by the development countries in applying strategies for the advancement of women. Taking into account the overall context—constrained national economies, inequalities in societies and the high barriers to greater participation of women in political life—an organizational base is crucial for the promotion of a more dynamic role for women in the process of development. However, a supportive infrastructure (government, the academic system, education the media, etc.), is often also important.

Non-governmental organizations— ranging from international to national and grass-root level organizations—have a long history of fighting for political rights for women, campaigning for changes in laws and national policies and participating in democratic and civil rights movements peace movements and ecological movements. The UN Decade for Women witnessed a reactivisation of women's organizations and the emergence of new women's groups with an increasing emphasis on collective action for articulating women's concerns and increasing women's visibility to development planners and decision makers. There is a decisive shift now from social welfare work to involvement in income-generating projects, consumer rights and workers' right issues. The Decade also saw the emergence of radical action groups protesting against sex violence against women and curbs on women's liberties and rights. Self-help action groups have also emerged at the grass-root level to articulate women's employment needs and increase their access to credit, developmental inputs and services. The importance of the role of non-governmental organizations lies particularly in their function as mobilising mechanisms and organizing agencies of working women, protecting their interests, particularly in the informal sectors and providing necessary support services. Further they act as mediators between government and the people and between coordinating agencies for the provision developmental inputs and services, as well as pressure groups and catalysts for the development of cadres and local leadership potential and organizational skills.

Role of Women in Organized Action

The need for collective organizations of workers to safeguard their interests is acknowledged. In surplus labour economies and in economies in which women are largely employed in the informal sectors, it has proved extremely difficult to set up such organizations. In the organized sector, even where women are members of the trade unions they do not exercise authority within them because of their low position in the occupational hierarchy and they are by and large excluded from collective negotiation with employers. Female membership in trade unions is low, since there are no pressure on unions alter their priorities. In some countries, trade unions have created women's wings to specifically articulate the need of women workers. There are also examples of separate women's trade unions, workers organizations, particularly of women workers in the informal sectors of the economy who remain outside the purview of small producers is a must, but supportive structures are equally essential for survival of such organizations. There is a school of thought which maintains that separate women's organizations only divide the workers' movements. And in some cases such organizations neither succeeded in involving more women in public and political life nor did they gain social support. Nevertheless, separate women's organization, particularly organizations of the most disadvantaged groups of women workers, may play an effective role in protecting women's rights and thus contribute to the advancement of the status of women, also through joint trade union organizations.

Women in Co-operatives

The role of other mechanisms, such as co-operatives, in the promotion of collective ownership of means of production and in marketing is important. The limited data available on women's co-operatives indicate that one problem which has affected their functioning is the power relations within the organization and the need to democratise these organization so that women members feel that they own co-operative assets. This is particularly important in mixed co-operatives. Governments, banks and other donor agencies are more willing to support large-scale public and private enterprise than small co-operatives, and this has increased their isolation and vulnerability. Other examples indicate that rural women have problems in such areas as credit and marketing, because they do not understand market trends and the competitiveness of the market. Middlemen tend to exploit the distance between the producers and the buyers.

Select Bibliography

Andrea M. Singh and Alfred de Souza, *The Position of Women in Migrant Bastis in Delhi* (New Delhi, 1976), p. 55.

Andrea M. Singh, *Slum and Pavement Dwellers in the Major Cities of India* (New Delhi, 1976, mimeo.), p. 74.

Badruddin, Women Workers in Assam tea plantations, *Social Welfare,* VI, XXXVII, No. 2, May 1990, p. 29.

Beteille, Andre, *Position of Women in India Society*, Publication Division, Government of India, 1975, pp. 61-68.

Bhasin, Kamla, Girl child or fish among crocodiles. *Kurukshetra,* Vol. XXXVIII No. 12, September, 1990, p. 31.

D'Souza, Alfred, ed., *Women in Contemporary India: Traditional Images and Changing Roles,* New Delhi, Manohar Book Service, 1975.

Desai Neera Maithreyi, Krishnaraj, *Women and Society in India, op. cit.,* p. 94.

Desai Neera, Maithreyi, Krishnaraj, *Women an Society in India,* Ajanta Publication, New Delhi, 1987, p. 84.

Devendra, Kiran, *Status and Position of Women in India,* Vikas Publishing House Pvt. Ltd., 1985, pp. 31-p5.

Devi, Mahesweta and Ghos, Nirmal, *Bonded Labour in India* (In Hindi) Radhakrishna Publishers, New Delhi, 1981.

Esther Boserup, *Women's Role in Economic Development* (Chicago, 1970), pp. 139-140; 1976, xii.

Geetanjali Dash, *Status of Women Workers in Industrial Area in India,* (Unpublished M. Phi. thesis). Delhi University, p. 50.

Ghadially, Rechana (Ed.), *Women in Indian Society—A Reader,* Sage Publications, New Delhi, 1988, p. 203.

Gupta Ashoka, Let men change their attitude *Kurukshetra* Vol. XXXVIII, No. 12, September, 1990, p. 11.

Gupta, A.R., *Women in Hindu Society,* Jyotsana Prakashan, Delhi, 1982, pp. 153-248.

Gupta, Jyoti, 'Himalayan Polyandry: bondage among women in Jaunswer-Bawar' pp. 258-281 in Utsa Patnaik, and Manjari Dig-Waney (Ed.) *Chains of Servitude: Bondage and slavery in India,* Sangam Books India Pvt. Ltd., Madras, 1985.

Gupta, Vishwa Nath, Women work in tea plantations, *Social Welfare,* Vol. XXXVII, No. 2, May 1990, p. 3.

Jain, Devaki, (ed.), *Indian Women*, Publication Division, Govt. of India, 1975, pp. xi-xxii.

Jain, Mahaveer, *Metholi Revisited: An account of camp processes of Agricultural women workers,* National Labour Institute, New Delhi, November, 1985.

Joshi, Uma, 'Improving the Status of Rural Women,' *Social Welfare,* Vol. XXXVI. No. 3-4, June-July, 1989, p. 14.

K.P. Khanna and M. Mathew, *Women Workers in the Unorganized Sector of the Coir Industry in India,* ICSSR, 1979 (Unpublished thesis).

Kannon Jayam (Dr.) and Ilango P., Health Hazards of women working in Beedi Industries, *Social Welfare,* Vol. XXXVI, No. 12, March, 1990, p. 10.

Kaptan, S.S., The income, wages and working conditions of women in the inorganized sector, *Social Welfare,* May, 1989, p. 29.

Karanjia, T., "Women today what needs changing", *Flair*, Vol. 3, No. 1, January 1986, pp. 48.51.

M. Vanamala, "Employment Status of Women in Andhra Pradesh State Public Enterprises" in K. Morali Manohar (ed.), *Women's Status and Development in India*, p. 87.

Mathur, R.N., *Quality of Working Life of Women Construction workers.* Commonwealth Publishers, New Delhi, p. 45.

Mathur, R.N., Quality of working life of women construction workers, *op. cit.,* p. 35-36.

Mencher, Joan and K Saradamani, Muddy feet and dirty hands; rice production and female agricultural labourers, *Economic and Political Weekly,* December, 25, 1983.

Murali Manohar, K., Ed., *Women's Status and Development in India,* ed. by Gail Omvedt; *Draft Statement on Women's Liberation* Published by SOWSTUD and IIPA Local Branch, Warangal, pp. 222-244.

Nair, G. Ravindran, Women Workers—The lingering Paradoyes' *Social Welfare,* May, 1988, p. 5.

Patnaik, S.C and Debi, Sailabala, An assessment of Womens' Economic Contribution to the Farm Sector: A micro level study, *Journal of Rural Development,* National Institute of Rural Development, Rajendranagar, Hyderabad, Vol. 5, July, 1986.

Prasad, Sushama, Sahay, Economic and Physical Exploitation of tribal female labourers, p. 73, in Gupta J.L., *Challenges to the Fair Sex: Indian Women Problems, Plight and Progresses,* Delhi Giani Publ. House, 1988, XXIV p. 132.

Promila Kapur, *The Changing Status of the Working Women in India,* p. 69.

Pushpa Sunder, Characteristics of Female Employment—Implications of research and policy. *Economic and Political Weekly,* May, 1981.

Rajuladevi, A.K., Technological Choice and their Impact on Eomen. *Kurukshetra,* Vol. XXXVI, No. 2, Nov. 1987, p. 7.

Rojas, Isabela. "Factors in womens' labour force participation' quoted in "Women work Force. Trend and Pattern of Employment" by Atmanand, *op. cit.*

Roy Edmond, Development of Rural Women, *Orissa Review,* December, 1988, p. 32.

Sahool, B. (Dr.), Changing pattern of women employment in Orissa—Problems and prospects *Vision,* Vol VIII, No. 384, January-June, 1989, p. 38.

Saikia, Anuva, Seasonal variation of female participation in farm work, *Kurukshetra,* Vol. XXXI, No. 19, July 1-15, 1983 p. 17.

Saran, K.M. *Labour in Ancient India,* Vora and Co. Publishers Pvt. Ltd., Bombay 1957, pp. 64-65.

Shahnaz Ankesaria, "Slow Death is their lot", *The Statesman,* January 4, 1984.

Sharma, Narayan Prasad (Dr.) Wage differentials for women agricultural labourers, *Yojana,* July 1-15, 1989, 33(12), p. 8.

Shastri, Madhu, 'Status of the special protective provisions of penal and criminal codes under the constitution of India" In Sushila Agrawal (Ed.) *Status of Women.* Printwell Publishers, Jaipur, 198, pp. 23-24.

Sinha, Ajit Kumar, Improving the Lot of Rural Women. *Yojana,* Vol. 32, No. 9, May 16-31, 1988, p. 28.

Sundari, S. (Dr.) and Marunekhalai, N.—Women Workers in the paddy processing Industries, *Social Welfare,* Vol. XXXVI, No. 10-11, January-February, 1990, p. 14.

Sunita and others, Rural Women work: Differential treatment by land lord-elites, *Journal of Extension System,* 3(2) Dec., 1987, p. 80.

Tripathy, S.N. (Dr.), *Bonded Labour in India,* Discovery Publishing House, New Delhi, 1989, p. 17.

Urmila Patel, "Problems of Working Women in India" in T.M. Dak (ed.), *Women and Work in Indian Society*, p. 228.

Veena Das, "Indian Women: Work, Power and Status," in B.R. Nanda, (ed.), *Indian Women* (New Delhi, 1976), pp. 132-139.

Veena Das, *Indian Women's Work, Power and Status*, p. 193.

Index

❑❑❑